Solve Problems That Matter

Design, Build & Launch Your Social Enterprise Idea

Ben Pecotich

Dynamic4 | Certified B Corporation

dynamic4.com/sptm

Want some extra support on your social enterprise journey?

Some ways Ben Pecotich and Dynamic4 can help:

- Coaching and advice for individuals and teams
- Dynamic4 Jetpack incubator and coaching program for early-stage social enterprise ideas
- Workshops, masterclasses, and speaking
- Project-based experiential learning programs
- Discount pricing available on 10+ copies

To find out more or for media enquiries, please email hello@dynamic4.com or visit dynamic4.com.

First published in 2021 by Dynamic4
hello@dynamic4.com
Sydney, Australia

Copyright © 2022 by Ben Pecotich and Dynamic4
The moral rights of the author have been asserted
Cover and internal design by Ben Pecotich, Dynamic4
Solve Problems That Matter v1.06. Updated 9 November 2022

ISBN: 978-0-6452262-0-1 (Paperback)
ISBN: 978-0-6452262-1-8 (ePub)
ISBN: 978-0-6452262-2-5 (PDF)

Disclaimer
The material in this publication is of the nature of general comment only, and does not represent professional advice. It is not intended to provide specific guidance for particular circumstances and it should not be relied on as the basis for any decision to take action or not take action on any matter which it covers. Readers should obtain professional advice where appropriate, before making any such decision. To the maximum extent permitted by law, the author and publisher disclaim all responsibility and liability to any person, arising directly or indirectly from any person taking or not taking action based on the information in this publication.

Solve Problems That Matter

Design, Build & Launch
Your Social Enterprise Idea

The 90-day program helping you take a human-centred approach
to design, build, and launch your social enterprise idea –
and build momentum to solve problems that matter

Buy the book, download free worksheets,
and get other great resources at:
dynamic4.com/sptm

Written & Designed By
Ben Pecotich

My ambition is that as we work through this book together, you'll feel that I'm with you and working alongside you. Cheering you on, but also helping to challenge you, to test and refine your thinking, and iterate – to succeed sooner. Let's work together to solve problems that matter!

Ben Pecotich

Intro

Welcome to Solve Problems That Matter! What is it? Glad you asked...

You know when you have a social enterprise idea you think will help solve a problem that really matters, but you're busy, not sure how to make it happen, and it's easy to feel overwhelmed?

Well, Solve Problems That Matter is a 90-day program helping you take a human-centred approach to design, build, and launch your social enterprise idea – and build momentum to solve problems that matter.

In fact, this book is based on my experience coaching thousands of founders, leaders, designers, and university students over the years – especially social enterprise founders and NFP leaders on our Dynamic4 Jetpack program since 2014.

It also draws on the project-based experiential leadership, design, and innovation programs I've designed and delivered... and the many social enterprise startups I've co-founded.

Who's This Book For?

My aim with this book is to help more **social enterprise founders, NFP leaders, and changemakers** globally solve problems that matter.

I've coached thousands of founders, leaders, designers, and university students to design and innovate for positive impact over the years – so I'm focusing on these people and the key goals, questions, and challenges they face.

This book is for you if you are a:

- **Social enterprise founder** in the early stages of exploring your idea

- **Leader or changemaker** in an established social enterprise, NFP, or purpose-driven organisation creating a solution that delivers on your core purpose while generating sustainable earned income

- **Startup founder** wanting to embed purpose and impact in your business model

If you're just starting work on your idea, have been going for years but aren't making the progress you want, or designing and building a new solution within an established organisation – this book is for you. Innovation never stops.

Your Goals

Designing, building, and launching your social enterprise idea can be a very rewarding experience... but there are also plenty of challenges. This book will help you with these goals:

 Take a human-centred design approach to innovation to really understand my customers, what's important to them, and help solve problems that matter

Design a sustainable business model that has purpose and impact embedded in the way we do things while also being financially successful

Look after my own personal wellbeing while making a positive impact

Have a practical guide and method to follow so I can build momentum and get the support I need

Your Big Questions

Together we'll work through the big questions I consistently hear... how do I/we:

- Communicate our purpose, theory of change, and the social/environmental value we'll create?

- Identify our customers, understand what they really care about, and know if they'll buy and use our solution?

- Design, build, and launch our solution as an end-to-end experience, and test what our customers will pay for it?

- Calculate how much money we need, and when we'll break even?

- Build our team to make it happen?

- Plan our approach to get into a good rhythm to build momentum and get traction?

- Share our story to attract the support we need?

- Stay healthy and positive on this journey without getting overwhelmed and burnt out?

Why This Book?

Writing and publishing a book isn't a small investment of time and energy... so I've asked myself this question. A lot. There are a lot of books I love and that I think have done a great job covering startups, human-centred design/design thinking, innovation, mindset and positive psych, and agile ways of working... but there are very few I've seen that focus on these things specifically in a social enterprise context.

The majority of things I've read on social enterprise tend to be more like whitepapers with academics and policy makers as the intended audience – rather than practical guides for social enterprise founders, NFP leaders, and changemakers.

I spend a lot of my time helping build bridges between the commercially focused startup ecosystem and the social enterprise/impact-focused ecosystem. From my experience, these are generally separate bubbles – with value to share with each other.

I strongly believe – and the evidence shows – that when we take a human-centred design approach to innovation and embed impact into business models, it helps create the conditions for people to be happier and have increasing quality of life.

Good business needs to do great things for communities and our planet, while being financially successful... it's increasingly what talent, customers, and investors expect.

My Ambition

My aim with this book is to help more founders, leaders, and changemakers globally **solve problems that matter** in more empathic and innovative ways – and measure success in outcomes for people, our planet, and prosperity. Taking a human-centred approach to design and innovation is core to this approach. This book will help you with:

Focus

Time and headspace to work on the right things at the right time while staying healthy and positive on the journey – not overwhelmed and burnt out

Clarity

Guided path to design a sustainable business model that has purpose and impact embedded and is financially successful

Confidence

Build momentum and move forward with more certainty and less risk by testing and refining your idea and impact

Relationships

Support on the journey and ways to connect with collaborators and investors in the social enterprise ecosystem

My ambition is that as we work through this book together, you'll feel that I'm with you and working alongside you. Cheering you on, but also helping to challenge you, to test and refine your thinking, and iterate – to succeed sooner. Let's work together to solve problems that matter!

What's that mean? I'll get specific...

What This Book IS:

- Focused on helping you work through the big questions I listed

- Social enterprise framed as something you do rather than something you are. I outline key concepts and terms, and explain how I'll use them to provide clarity and a shared language

- A simple practical guide with worksheets structured around a 90-day (13-week) plan with a Sprint 0 and five execution sprints. You'll adapt the timeline to fit your personal situation as part of planning in Sprint 0

- Designed to be used in more than one way... depending on if you prefer to read something all the way through before starting, or work through each step before looking at the next. You can also use it as a reference book. The chapters are designed to be standalone, and referenced as needed

- Relevant for all types of solutions – physical, digital, products, services, and more

What This Book ISN'T:

- An academic deep dive into theory and frameworks – but I'll cover theory to a practical level needed for how we'll apply it, using a learning through doing approach

- About sharing inspiring stories and case studies – but I'll provide links to some places you can find great stories

- A duplication of other frameworks and methods – but I'll refer to other useful books and resources for more information on various models, tools, and research

- Marketing and fundraising oriented – but I'll focus on the big questions that will help your marketing and fundraising efforts be more effective

- Specific to tech/digital products or a UX/UI deep dive – but I'll cover the strategic design of the solution, and recommended ways to approach designing, building, and launching the early version of your solution, including the digital aspects

How To Use This Book

This book has been designed primarily as a practical guide to use – rather than just read.

I've designed this book knowing some people will want to read it all the way through before starting, and others will prefer to work through each step before looking at the next. Take the approach that feels the most natural for you.

You can also use it as a reference book. The chapters are designed to be standalone and referenced as needed... but the sequence is important. You'll get the most value by working through the book as a 90-day program. Here's a high-level outline of what you can expect.

I recommend jumping to the back of the book and reading Chapter 17 for a summary of the approach we'll take... and the journey you'll be reflecting back on in 90 days' time.

90-day Plan

This is a simple and practical guidebook with worksheets structured around a 90-day (13-week) plan – with a Sprint 0 and five execution sprints to build momentum through the double diamond.

You'll adapt the timeline to your personal situation where needed as part of planning in Sprint 0.

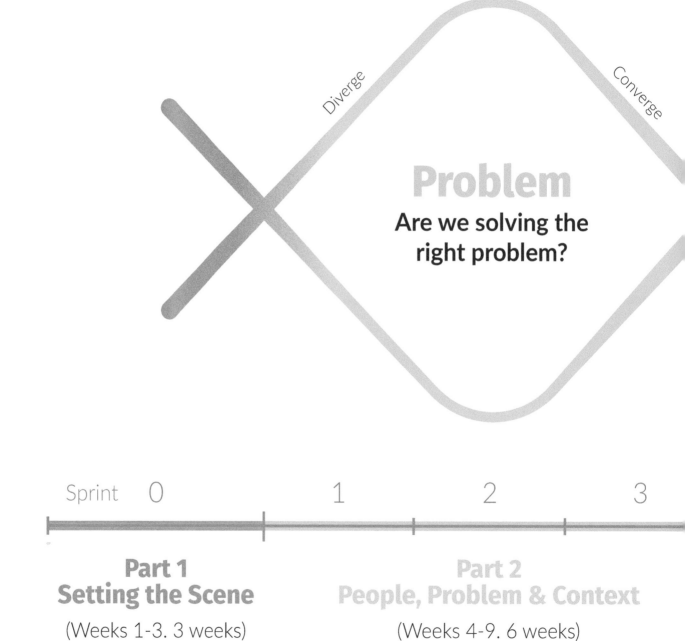

Diverge

Converge

Problem
Are we solving the right problem?

Sprint   0   1   2   3

**Part 1
Setting the Scene**

(Weeks 1-3. 3 weeks)

**Part 2
People, Problem & Context**

(Weeks 4-9. 6 weeks)

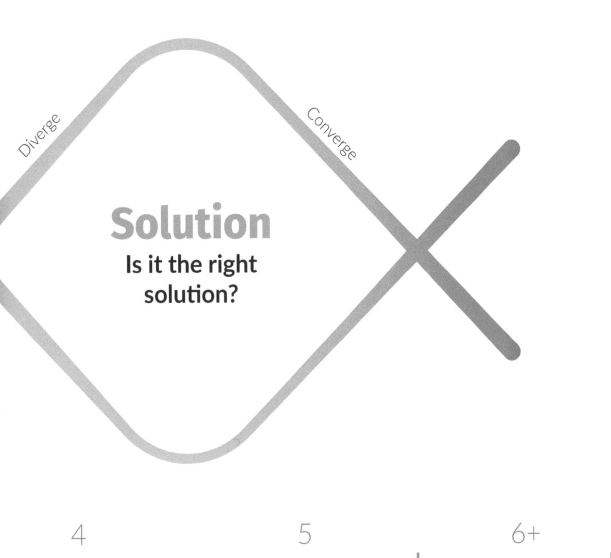

Solution

Is it the right solution?

Diverge

Converge

4

5

6+

Part 3
Solution & Business Model

(Weeks 10-13. 4 weeks)

Part 4
Momentum

(Week 14+. Ongoing)

Part 1: Setting the Scene

This phase is foundational. We cover the core theory with the concepts, terms, and ways of thinking and working that we'll continually refer to and build on. There's a strong focus on our mindset, personal sustainability, and happiness habits – to help us look after our own personal wellbeing while making a positive impact.

You'll articulate your current thinking on your vision, the problem you plan to work on… and your idea on what you'll specifically do to help create this change. This will iterate and refine as you progress through the book – based on evidence, insight, and empathy.

We also start setting up your workflow to get into a rhythm to build sustainable momentum.

The Big Questions

The big questions we focus on in Part 1 are, how do I/we:

- Communicate our purpose, theory of change, and the social/environmental value we'll create?
- Build our team to make it happen?
- Plan our approach to get into a good rhythm to build momentum and get traction?
- Share our story to attract the support we need?
- Stay healthy and positive on this journey without getting overwhelmed and burnt out?

Weeks 1-3. Sprint 0

The standard program allows three weeks for this phase. You'll adapt the timeline to fit your personal situation in Chapter 3: Make It Happen.

Part 2: People, Problem & Context

The focus during this phase is to really understand the current reality. What actually is – not how we might wish it to be. No matter how much experience we have of the problem we're focusing on, we need much more than just our own perspective.

This phase is about spending time with the people you hope will use and pay for your solution – to deeply understand how they experience the problem, test your risky assumptions, and refine your thinking. By the end of this phase, we want to have reached a point of sharp clarity on the real problem to solve – based on evidence, insight, and meaningful empathy.

The Big Questions

The big question we focus on in Part 2 are, how do I/we:

- Identify our customers, understand what they really care about, and know if they'll buy and use our solution?

Weeks 4-9. Sprints 1, 2 & 3

The standard program allows six weeks for this phase – three sprints. Depending on where you're at in your journey, you might be able to move through this phase quicker – or you might learn some things that mean you need to continue your research to really understand the people, the problems as they experience them, and the context they experience them in.

Important Note: Before starting on this phase, it's important to have clarity on your purpose and vision. If you feel you're not quite there yet, it might be worth spending a little more time on Chapter 4: Purpose, Vision & Theory of Change. The way you articulate it will evolve over time, but it's critical that you're clear on your "why".

I strongly recommend resisting the urge to skip the People, Problem & Context phase. It's very rare to design, build, and launch successful solutions without having deep insight – and empathy for the people we're designing with and for.

Part 3: Solution & Business Model

The focus during this phase is to build on the sharp clarity we've achieved during the People, Problem & Context phase – based on evidence, insight, and meaningful empathy.

We'll prototype and test possible solutions and your business model. The focus is on ways to design, build, and launch your social enterprise idea in a way that reduces the risk of overinvesting time, money, and energy in a solution no one will use or pay for. A way of rapidly learning and refining to create a solution that people want, that's financially sustainable, and that you can make happen.

The Big Questions

The big questions we focus on in Part 3 are, how do I/we:

- Communicate our purpose, theory of change, and the social/environmental value we'll create?

- Identify our customers, understand what they really care about, and know if they'll buy and use our solution?

- Design, build, and launch our solution as an end-to-end experience, and test what our customers will pay for it?

- Calculate how much money we need, and when we'll break even?

Weeks 10-13. Sprints 4 & 5

The standard program allows four weeks for this phase – two sprints. This is primarily focused on the strategic design of your solution and business model. This is the beginning, not the end.

Important Note: If you haven't spoken directly with at least 10 people who you believe you're solving a problem with and for – and hope will use and pay for your solution – you're not ready to be focusing on this phase yet. Please spend more time focusing on the People, Problem & Context phase before starting work on your solution and business model.

Part 4: Sustain Momentum

The focus here is to continue the sustainable rhythm and momentum you've been building to move forward with confidence past the 90 days of the standard program. You'll continue designing, building, and launching refinements to your solution based on insights from real use.

The Big Questions

The big questions we focus on in Part 4 are, how do I/we:

- Communicate our purpose, theory of change, and the social/environmental value we'll create?

- Identify our customers, understand what they really care about, and know if they'll buy and use our solution?

- Design, build, and launch our solution as an end-to-end experience, and test what our customers will pay for it?

- Build our team to make it happen?

- Plan our approach to get into a good rhythm to build momentum and get traction?

- Share our story to attract the support we need?

- Stay healthy and positive on this journey without getting overwhelmed and burnt out?

Week 14+. Sprint 6+

This is the ongoing part of making your social enterprise idea real. You'll design, build, and launch aspects of your idea during the Solution & Business Model phase, but you'll need to continue refining your idea as you continue to respond to what you're learning.

We focus on sustaining momentum and getting support.

From this point, you'll continue through cycles of doing more research to understand the People, Problem & Context – and experimenting with refinements to your Solution & Business Model. This is the continual nature of taking a human-centred approach to design, build, and launch your social enterprise idea – to solve problems that matter.

Always Evolving

I think of this book as a product rather than a traditional book.

Even though I've been doing this work for almost three decades, I'm learning every day. And I always will be. Very few things are static. Contexts change, trends and patterns emerge, new technologies come to market. Sometimes this happens slowly, other times suddenly and dramatically. The covid pandemic being a very real example.

Continual iteration is how I work and experience the world… this means I'm always learning, and my thinking evolves. This might be from a conversation, things I read, trends I observe, experiments I run, insights from the people and organisations I work with.

My initial thinking was to self-publish a digital-only version on Amazon, and possibly do a small print run depending on demand. From my early research, a key message I heard was most of my target readers buy this kind of book in a print format – and many buy both print and digital… but a print version was a clear expectation.

What does that mean for this book? A print book is a snapshot at a point in time, but I need to create space for the refinements – without the need to write a new book. The key way I've approached this is to make some resources freely available on dynamic4.com/sptm. This includes downloadable worksheets as well as links to websites, articles, books, and events.

The other thing I intend to do is refine the digital versions of the book (PDF and ebook) based on feedback, and as I learn new things. When you buy the book in these digital formats, you'll get the refined editions for free. I'm thinking of this first edition as v1.0 with more to come.

.

"A bend in the road is not the end of the road... unless you fail to make the turn."

Helen Keller

Ben Pecotich: A Bit About Me

Why me? To answer this, I need to nudge aside my impostor syndrome – though it never really goes away. I'm a designer, innovation coach, and social enterprise/startup founder. Since starting in financial services in 1993, I've focused on taking a human-centred approach to designing and leading strategic change in Australia, NZ, the UK, and Europe – combining strategy, design, technology, consulting, and program management. I co-founded my first startup in 1994, and have been working on startups and social enterprises ever since.

I'm also co-founder of the Sydney Design Thinking meetup (8,000+ members), a founding board member and treasurer of the Social Enterprise Council of NSW & ACT (SECNA), and a Social Entrepreneur-in-Residence at the Centre for Social Impact/UNSW Business School teaching masters students.

Dynamic4

I founded Dynamic4 in 2001. We're a social enterprise and certified B Corp focused on design and innovation for happier communities. We also run an incubator for early-stage social enterprise ideas called Dynamic4 Jetpack.

I spend my time coaching founders and leaders to solve problems that matter and deliver great outcomes for people and our planet while being financially successful. Over the years, I've had the privilege of coaching thousands of founders, leaders, designers, and university students to design and innovate for positive impact.

My Purpose & Vision

My vision is a world where organisations and leaders solve problems that matter in more empathic and innovative ways – and measure success in outcomes for people, our planet, and prosperity... so people and communities have increasing quality of life, are happier, and live on a planet that is cleaner and healthier.

All the work I do is aligned with my purpose and theory of change – focused on helping create the conditions for people and communities to be more empowered and inclusive, and live in more sustainable ways.

I don't pretend to know everything or have all the answers, but I do my best to be a trusted partner and guide to make things easier. I've been through this rollercoaster of a journey myself many times and coached others through it.

Through these experiences I've built the mindset, skillset, and know how to use the tools to help others work through and make sense of the ambiguity and complexity to find clarity. And I love it.

Acknowledgements

There are so many people I want to thank. I've been lucky to meet and work with so many awesome people since the early 1990s. I'll start with those most directly involved in this book and then work through a few more acknowledgements. I know it's long but think of this as the worked example of the Your Team action that you'll do in the first chapter.

My Book Team

A big thanks to my book team. Jaqui Lane is my book coach and has helped guide me through the process of being a first-time indie author. She's also my editor. Clare Wadsworth for proofreading and helping me keep things consistent. Rasika Um for taking my prototypes and helping me turn them into the final design. A virtual part of my book team has been Julie Broad from Book Launchers, whose Youtube content I've found extremely valuable.

I've been lucky to collaborate with and learn from some great friends over the years. A special thanks to Ben Crothers, Jess Williams, Hannah Miller, Luke Faccini, Jodie Moule, Kristy Dixon, Ben Nicholls, and Nat Musson. You've helped me on my journey of writing this book – nudging me along with words of encouragement, giving me honest feedback, sharing insights – and the odd beverage of course. I consider you part of my book team. And just awesome humans. Thanks!

Collaborators & Clients

The origin story of this book traces back to a little collective for positive impact called Design for Meaning that I started with great friends and collaborators Anthony Quinn, Yummii Nguyen, and Stephen Cox. This exploration led to Anthony and me designing the early versions of what is now Dynamic4 Jetpack in 2014. Our early blueprint included the book format of the program – and here it is.

Thanks to the thousands of founders, leaders, designers, and students I've had the pleasure of working with and coaching over the years. I always learn as much from you as I share.

I've co-founded so many startups and social enterprises since 1994, it's hard to keep count – but it's somewhere around 20. Most of these ideas didn't make it past the discovery and research stage, but some went for years, and some are still going. I count myself very lucky to be on the endless adventure that is startup life. A big thanks to the awesome co-founders I've started things with, and the founders I work with now.

A special thanks to my Dynamic4 team and collaborators from the past 20 years and the awesome clients we've been lucky to work with. Everything I talk about in this book is what we've put into practice together. The wins, the failures, what we've learnt, and the endless hunger to always be learning and getting better.

Academia

For the past few years, I've been lucky to be a social entrepreneur-in-residence at the Centre for Social Impact (CSI) at UNSW Business School – as a member of the multi-award-winning teaching team on the Social Entrepreneurship Practicum (COMM5030) – a capstone project for a Master of Commerce. This is a work integrated learning (WIL) course that helps the students learn through doing by working on a real project with a social enterprise client. I got to work with and learn from Lucas Olmos, Heather Bailey, Sandy Killick, and Sandeep Kirpalani in my first year before the team grew even bigger.

I also have the privilege of working with Paul Brown at UTS as part of the Bachelor of Creative Intelligence & Innovation (BCII) degree.

Thanks to Lucas and Paul for inviting me in and giving me the opportunity to do this work in an academic context. It's been an interesting experience. A big thanks to the teaching teams and students I'm grateful to work with.

Early Supporters

In addition to the people I mentioned as part of my book team, I've been lucky to have a group of early supporters who've cheered me on and provided feedback. Knowing you'd put your name down as a pre-order, and that you were waiting to read and use this book helped me keep going.

Communities

I talk a fair bit about finding your community – and to help bring it together if you can't find it. I'm lucky to be part of a few communities full of great people who I love sharing ideas, a few beverages, and a lot of laughs with. Come and join us!

Sydney Design Thinking (SydDT) meetup. We started the group in 2015, and we're now a community of over 8,000 members. A shout out to my co-organisers Lucas Mara, Zoe Rosen, Kate Linton – and Kingsley Jones and James Cooper from day one... as well as all of the great speakers we've had over the years, and most importantly, the community. People who are there every month like Arun Mistry and some others already mentioned, as well as those who visit occasionally. We're lucky to have a thriving human-centred design community in Sydney and Australia, and it's always great collaborating with the other groups like IxDA, EUX, CCX, UX Bookclub, Product Bookclub, UX Australia, etc.

Social Enterprise Council of NSW & ACT (SECNA). In 2019, we started SECNA – the member-led peak body for social enterprise in NSW and ACT. I'm excited by the momentum that is building in the social enterprise community across Australia, especially as we look forward to the Social Enterprise National Strategy (SENS), and Brisbane hosting the Social Enterprise World Forum in 2022. A big hug to my fellow SECNA board members (past and present), team, volunteers, members, and supporters... all of the other social enterprise peak bodies around Australia – and our ongoing collaboration as part of the Alliance of Social Enterprise Networks Australia (ASENA).

B Corp and B Local Sydney. It was great to officially join the B Corp family in 2016. A community full of interesting people focused on using business as a force for good. Plenty of great friendships and collaborations have come from this community – with even more interesting days ahead. I love helping spread the word about the value of B Corp certification – and the community is one of the most valuable aspects. Thanks for welcoming me in.

Catalyst 2030. This is a global community that I'm proud to have joined in March 2021. It's great to meet and collaborate with other social entrepreneurs and social innovators around the world to explore ways of taking a people-centric approach to attain the SDGs by 2030. We've got a lot of work to do – that we can only do together.

We have a thriving social enterprise and startup community in Sydney. Over the years, I've been lucky to collaborate with a lot of accelerators, co-working spaces, and conferences in the ecosystem. These include Spark Festival, Remarkable Disability Tech Accelerator, Founder Institute Sydney Accelerator, Catalysr Accelerator, Sydney Hardware Incubator, Good Hustle by StartSomeGood, Fishburners, Tank Stream Labs, Stone & Chalk, The Studio, SydStart/Startcon, and more.

My Work Family

There are too many people to name. In various reflection blog posts, I've called out some of the people who've helped me on my journey when I entered corporate life as a 17-year-old. I feel very lucky to have worked with so many awesome people over the years and have made lifelong friends. I'm stoked to still have so many of these people as close friends.

Acknowledgement of Country

I'm lucky to live, work, and play on Gadigal Country. The lands of the Gadigal people of the Eora Nation. I pay my respects to First Nations Elders past, present, and emerging across Australia – and recognise their ongoing connection to the land, sky, waters, and communities of this beautiful place.

I acknowledge the resilience, knowledge, and wisdom of the oldest living culture on our planet, and I'm committed to collaboration that furthers self-determination and creates a better future for us all.

Book Dedication

Finally, a huge thanks to my wife Marls and our two awesome kids Jasmine and Zara.

Jaz & Za, I dedicate this book to you. I feel very lucky and proud to be your dad, and your cuddles light up my world. I love sharing my endless curiosity with you. I'm often wrong, but I'm always experimenting and learning – and you teach me so much every day. I'm looking forward to a life full of fun adventures and exploring a world of possibilities together. Loveya loads. Dad

Contents

Part 1
Setting the Scene

Part 2
People, Problem & Context

Part 3
Solution & Business Model

Part 4
Sustain Momentum

Part 1

Setting the Scene

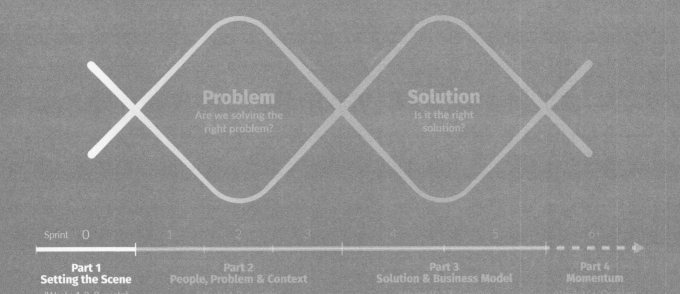

Sprint 0 1 2 3 4 5 6+

Part 1
Setting the Scene
(Weeks 1-3. 3 weeks)

Part 2
People, Problem & Context
(Weeks 4-9. 6 weeks)

Part 3
Solution & Business Model
(Weeks 10-13. 4 weeks)

Part 4
Momentum
(Weeks 14+. Ongoing)

Weeks 1-3. Sprint 0

The standard program allows three weeks for this phase.
You'll adapt the timeline to fit your personal situation in
Chapter 3: Make It Happen.

Part 1 Chapters

1. Mindset

2. Approach & Philosophy

3. Make It Happen

4. Purpose, Vision & Theory of Change

25

This phase is foundational. We cover the core theory with concepts, terms, and ways of thinking and working that we'll continually refer to and build on through the book. There's a strong focus on our mindset, personal sustainability, and happiness habits – to help look after our own personal wellbeing while making a positive impact.

You'll articulate your current thinking on your vision, the problem you plan to work on... and your idea on what you'll specifically do to help create this change. This will iterate and refine as you progress through the book – based on evidence, insight, and empathy.

We also start setting up your workflow to get into a rhythm to build sustainable momentum.

The Big Questions

The big questions we focus on in Part 1 are, how do I/we:

- Communicate our purpose, theory of change, and the social/environmental value we'll create?

- Build our team to make it happen?

- Plan our approach to get into a good rhythm to build momentum and get traction?

- Share our story to attract the support we need?

- Stay healthy and positive on this journey without getting overwhelmed and burnt out?

Chapter 1

Mindset

"When we are happy – when our mindset and mood are positive – we are smarter, more motivated, and thus more successful. Happiness is the center, and success revolves around it."

Shawn Achor
The Happiness Advantage

I want you to be happy.

My focus is design and innovation for happier communities. It's important to me that you enjoy this journey and stay healthy and well... ideally feeling even healthier as you do work that gives you meaning and fulfilment.

My ambition is that as we work through this book together, you'll feel that I'm with you and working alongside you. Cheering you on, but also helping to challenge you, to test your thinking, and iterate – to succeed sooner.

It might seem strange to start a book like this talking about mindset. So why am I? Research shows we're 30% more effective and productive when we're positive. I was lucky to learn the power of the mind and how we think very early in life. Over the years these lessons have been reinforced, and I've learnt a lot more about the neuroscience and psychology of how our brain and mind work.

You might be thinking, of course I want to be happy – everyone does but it's not that easy. I think of happiness as "being well and doing well", it takes action, and it's something we create for ourselves. This is consistent with Shawn Achor's happiness research, which led him to the conclusion that "happiness is not just a mood – it's a work ethic."

The great news is this means we can build some basic habits into our workflow to help create our own happiness. There are simple, practical things we can do to literally change our brain chemistry to increase our feeling of positivity – which leads to being more successful.

The purpose of this chapter is to set some foundations to help you look after your personal wellbeing while making a positive impact – so you stay healthy and positive on this journey without getting overwhelmed and burnt out.

Happiness Habits

Happy is a word we probably use several times a day without really thinking about it. The dictionary definition is "the state of pleasurable contentment of mind". Sounds nice.

I think about happiness a bit differently. Many years ago I stumbled across the fact that Aristotle talked about happiness – "being well and doing well" – as an activity rather than an emotion or state... a reframe I found to be so simple, but extremely powerful.

If you think of happiness as a state, it will always be fleeting and out of reach. If you can think about it as an activity, you can be where your feet are and immerse in the present.

> "**Happiness is not the belief that we don't need to change; it is the realization that we can.**"
>
> **Shawn Achor**

Success Will Make Us Happy. Right?

I'm a big fan of Shawn Achor's happiness research. A key finding is the belief most of us hold that we'll be happy when we achieve a particular goal and experience success. It's inherent in many of the things we're taught, and we often over-index for goals.

In his energetic, insightful, and hilarious TED talk, he says our brains actually work in the opposite order. "...if happiness is on the opposite side of success, your brain never gets there. We've pushed happiness over the cognitive horizon, as a society. And that's because we think we have to be successful, then we'll be happier". This was another powerful but profound reframe for me.

To quantify that... in a range of contexts, it was found that we are at least 30% more effective and productive when we are positive.

One of the things I love about Shawn Achor's work is his focus on the practical things we can do to create positive mindset habits... to increase our happiness. Happiness is something we need to create... and keep creating. It's a practice. A habit.

> "If you can raise somebody's level of positivity in the present, then their brain experiences what we now call a happiness advantage, which is your brain at positive performs significantly better than at negative, neutral or stressed. Your intelligence rises, your creativity rises, your energy levels rise. In fact, we've found that every single business outcome improves."

Shawn Achor

How Do I Create My Happiness?

From the research, there are simple actions we can take that literally change our brain chemistry and make us feel good – they also activate the learning centres in our brain, and make us more creative and open to new ideas.

For me, I find being mindful, meditation, and other happiness habits are key to helping me keep a sense of perspective. Part of this is regular reflection, including recognising and celebrating the wins – as they happen. There's always more to be done and it can be easy to fixate on the next thing. I keep working on my happiness habits, knowing that success follows happiness. It feels good and helps me sustain a healthy headspace.

Shawn Achor outlines some simple habits in his book *The Happiness Advantage*, which I recommend. Another great free resource is the Greater Good in Action website by the University of California, Berkeley (ggia. berkeley.edu). Have a look, and experiment with some of the practices.

I'll briefly share some practical, quick and easy things you can do to build happiness habits. If you already know and do things I cover here, great! Take a moment to reflect and see if there's something to refine.

Take a Breath

Breathing is one of the most basic things we do continuously every day, but many of us don't pay too much attention to what's going on. Breathing is life. It's key to our overall health, and how we breathe has a big impact on our brain and nervous system.

There's plenty of ancient and indigenous knowledge on using breathing for a positive impact on body and mind. Over the past decade or two, more and more studies have been done to understand how our breathing impacts our brains. A 2017 study showed several brain regions linked to emotion, attention, and body awareness are activated when we pay attention to our breath.

Focusing on and changing our breathing patterns is a simple but powerful tool to calm our brain – it literally changes our brain chemistry. These breathing exercises are called breathwork, and there are many different methods. The thing most have in common is they get you to bring your attention to your breath, taking slow, deep breaths – using your diaphragm, the large muscle located below your lungs.

What are the benefits of this practice? Deep breathing stimulates the parasympathetic nervous system – which helps us move from being stressed to relaxed. Studies have found a wide range of benefits, including reduced anxiety, a lower heart rate and blood pressure, better sleep, increased focus, and improved memory.

We're often juggling multiple competing priorities, and it can be a challenge to carve out the time and headspace to focus on the work we need to do. I find taking a moment to breathe is a good way to consciously change gears and turn off distractions at the start of a working session.

There are many breathing methods, and you might find they affect you differently – feel free to experiment. What's the best one to use? I'd say it's the one you'll use and stick with. Don't get distracted by trying to find the perfect method. Just start.

Simple Deep Breathing Exercise

Getting Started

I recommend starting your work sessions with a simple breathing exercise as a way to help get your brain into positive.

If you have a breathing technique you already use and already have a routine, continue with that.

If this is new to you or not something you're really into, all I ask is that you experiment with it for a week. If it's working for you, you'll want to continue – if it's not, don't push it.

This exercise is as simple as doing a couple of minutes of breathing.

It's best to choose a place where you feel comfortable and stable. An office chair is pretty good.

The Exercise

Breath in through your nose – and feel your belly fill with air.

Breathe out with your lips slightly apart – and feel your belly lower.

Focus on the breath coming in slowly… and going out slowly. You might want to close your eyes while you do this.

See if you can breathe out for the same amount of time that you breathe in – try counting to four or five to start. With practice, you'll be able to do it comfortably for a longer count.

That's it. There are endless techniques to experiment with, but if you haven't done any breathwork before – start simple, feel the benefits, and go from there.

Reflect on the Positive

A gratitude journal is an often recommended practice. Why's it worth trying? It's easy to lose perspective and focus on all the things that aren't going how we hoped or the endless list of things we need to get done.

This practice helps us to be on the lookout for the good things that are happening – and to celebrate them rather than taking them for granted. Research has shown this helps us be in a more positive mood, be more optimistic, and sleep better.

--- ACTION ---

Simple Gratitude Journal Exercise

It's really simple and only takes a couple of minutes.

All you do is write down three good things that happened in your day – with how it made you feel, who was involved, and why it made you feel good. Three new things each day.

Shawn Achor's research has shown that doing this for 21 days in a row causes the brain to retain a pattern of scanning for the positive.

I recommend you just write it down wherever you normally make notes. Don't get distracted by thinking you need to find a special notebook or app. It's important to write it down though, rather than just do it in your head.

There are more advanced versions of this practice, but start simple.

Bonus: Random Acts of Kindness

Now that you've identified good things that happened during your day and who was involved, an extra step is easy – a simple act of kindness that also makes us feel great and builds strong connections. Send a brief message to one of these people praising or thanking them.

Your Strengths & Assets

Let's build on these basic principles straight away. It's easy to take what we have for granted, including what we're really good at. There's a simple power in having your strengths and assets listed so you can refer to them easily. Using a strengths-based approach, it's powerful to recognise our own strengths – our skills, knowledge, connections, resources, and potential – and build on them. This isn't a time for modesty. Be generous with yourself.

If you're working in a team, I recommend repeating this exercise from a team perspective. What are the strengths and assets you have as a team?

If you're working within an established organisation, I also recommend repeating this exercise with an organisation perspective. What are the strengths and assets you have as an organisation?

What Are Your Strengths & Assets?

Being generous with yourself, create a list of what you're working with. Think beyond a work or professional context. Include your skills, experience, achievements, and relationships.

- What are you really good at?
- What do you love doing?
- What have you done or achieved that you're most proud of?
- What do you really care about?
- What do you get paid for doing?
- What resources do you have, including money and money you can get access to?

Your Team

Over the years, I've worked with a lot of founders – especially in the early stages, when it's common to be working solo. It can feel like a lonely journey with no one to turn to. It's really important for us to be proactive in identifying and building a team and support network.

Let's get started. This simple exercise helps us recognise that we're not alone.

Have a look at my acknowledgements in the intro for a real example.

Who's In Your Team Right Now?

Using a broad definition of "team", create a list of who's in your team right now, including your personal support network. This might include your formal team, volunteers, supporters, an advisory board, a coach, virtual mentors (books, video & podcast content, etc), and other stakeholders – as well as communities and networks that you're a part of. It can also include the close friends and family you go to for support.

When you have your list of people – make a note next to each person saying why they're part of your team, why you value them, and when you reach out to them for support.

Bonus: Random Acts of Kindness

Now you've identified your team and support network – a simple act of kindness that also makes you feel great and builds strong connections is to send a brief message to one of these people praising or thanking them.

Growth Mindset

Professor Carol Dweck at Stanford University studies human motivation – and how it relates to our success in life. She's famous for developing mindset theory, which she describes in a compelling and easy to understand way in her awesome book *Mindset*. Mindset is our beliefs and attitudes that influence the way we think, feel, and behave in any given situation.

Why am I sharing this? From Carol Dweck's work and other positive neuroscience research, it's clear that our mindset, including the way we view risk and failure, is critical to our happiness, creativity, and success. Her work shows us the power of our most basic beliefs – about the world, and especially about ourselves.

Before exploring the two mindsets, I think it's helpful to know a bit about the power of neuroplasticity.

Neuroplasticity

Until not that long ago, it was thought that the brain didn't really change after childhood – that it was pretty fixed by the time we became adults. Thankfully research over the past decade has shown that's not true.

Research shows that our brains adapt to new situations. When we learn or do something new, we create new connections and pathways in our brains – a dynamic process that's happening every day in response to our changing needs. This is called neuroplasticity. The power of these findings and the concept of neurogenesis make me very excited and optimistic.

Our established patterns of thinking, feeling, and behaving have become habits – building up connections and pathways in our brain over time to form our core beliefs and attitudes. Our mindset. A lot of this is very positive and makes up who we are and how we see the world. We all have some bad habits we'd like to change though. And we can.

When we think about something differently, we start building new pathways. If we choose to keep practicing this new way of thinking, it becomes a habit, and the new pathway will get stronger and easier – and the old pattern of thinking becomes weaker. When you've learnt something new, changed your mind about something, broken a bad habit – this is what happened. This is neuroplasticity in action. We experience it all the time.

Growth vs Fixed Mindset

With some basic understanding of the power of neuroplasticity, let's explore the two mindsets from Carol Dweck's work. Fixed and growth. Before outlining this, I think it's important to mention that this isn't talking about two types of people. Even though we might primarily show a fixed mindset, that's not who we are. We can decide to build and practice a growth mindset. That's the whole premise of mindset theory.

In reality, we all have a growth mindset about some things and situations, and certain triggers may cause us to fall into a fixed mindset. So, what do the two mindsets look like?

Growth Mindset

In a growth mindset, we have an underlying belief that our intelligence, skills and ability, creativity, talent, and more – all grow through effort over time. A belief that if we learn and practice, we can achieve what we want.

Common examples used for a growth mindset include:

- "Failure is an opportunity to grow"
- "I can learn to do anything I want"
- "Challenges help me grow"
- "Feedback is constructive"
- "I am inspired by the success of others"

- "My effort and attitude determine my abilities"
- "I like to try new things

With a growth mindset, we seek challenges and see failure as part of learning, we persevere when we face obstacles, see feedback as constructive, and are inspired by other people's success. We are reflective, curious, and open to change.

Fixed Mindset

Fixed mindset shows up as the belief that our qualities are fixed – these might be our intelligence, skills and ability, creativity, talent, or other things. You either have it or you don't. A fixed mindset is a belief that our intelligence and talent are limited. A belief that we're either good or bad at something because of the talent we were born with – and it can't really be changed.

Common examples used for a fixed mindset include:

- "Failure is the limit of my abilities"
- "I'm either good at it or I'm not"
- "I stick to what I know"
- "Feedback and criticism are personal"
- "I don't like to be challenged"
- "I'm jealous of other people's success"
- "When I'm frustrated, I give up"
- "That's just who I am. I can't change it"

With a fixed mindset, we avoid challenges, give up easily, and ignore feedback. When we're triggered into our fixed mindset, we also tend to demonstrate some negative behaviours.

Risk, Failure & The Power of Yet

Exploring a social enterprise idea means dealing with plenty of things that don't go quite as we might hope… and requires perseverance and resilience. It's worth the effort to develop more of a growth mindset and understand the basics of the neuroscience.

As Carol Dweck says in *Mindset* "in the growth mindset, failure can be a painful experience. But it doesn't define you. It's a problem to be faced, dealt with, and learned from".

She also talks about the power of "yet" in her great 2014 TED talk. She heard about a school where if they didn't pass a course, the grade they received was "Not Yet". This was a way to help students understand that they're "on a learning curve. It gives you a path into the future". Her research with students found those with a growth mindset performed better, and had a very different perception of their experiences.

"Not only weren't they discouraged by failure, they didn't even think they were failing. They thought they were learning."

Carol Dweck

Our ideas about risk and effort come from our mindset. When we're in a positive mindset, we realise the value of challenging ourselves, and we want to put in the effort to learn and grow.

Taking risks means having the courage to be vulnerable. To take on situations with "uncertainty, risk, and emotional exposure", as Brené Brown says. I love her quote:

> "No vulnerability, no creativity. No tolerance for failure, no innovation. It is that simple. If you're not willing to fail, you can't innovate."

Brené Brown

We need to build healthy ways to deal with the real and perceived threats that we'll face... in life, but especially on our journey of exploring social enterprise ideas.

Threats, Rewards & Triggers

We spend a lot of our time on autopilot, our minds following well-established patterns of thinking that we've built up over time, and also through how our brains have developed. Part of that autopilot is to respond to certain triggers in negative ways, which can also trigger our fixed mindset.

We'll talk about cognitive biases briefly in the next chapter, but neuroscientists have named one of these automatic habits of the brain "negativity bias". It's been found that our brains scan for threats every fifth of a second, below our conscious awareness. There are five times as many neural circuits that detect potential threats as there are that detect opportunities or rewards.

Another key finding is that our brains aren't very good at differentiating between physical threats and social threats. Research has found that just the words "let me give you some feedback" creates a threat response in our brain, especially in a culture with a fixed mindset.

The way we respond to potential threats – and opportunities – is emotional, and centred in the limbic system. Our brain uses the same instinctual response system in social situations as it does for physical survival.

From these insights, you can begin to see how easily we can be triggered into a negative headspace, resulting in behaviours that aren't good for us or those around us. This includes getting defensive, withdrawing, giving up, catastrophising, lashing out and blaming others, and complaining. I know it's not fun to feel like this, and I know I'm not fun to be around if I behave in these ways.

So, what can we do? One of the key things is to build awareness of our autopilot responses and identify the key triggers that cause us to feel threatened. Neuroscientists call this metacognition – thinking about thinking.

The SCARF Model by David Rock is a really simple way to think about the five key domains that influence our behaviour in social situations. SCARF stands for:

- **Status**: sense of personal worth, especially relative to other people
- **Certainty**: sense of feeling we can make accurate predictions about the future
- **Autonomy**: sense of feeling in control of our lives and events
- **Relatedness**: sense of feeling safe and connected to people
- **Fairness**: sense and perception of fair exchanges with people

I find this is a simple tool to think about ways I might feel threatened, and identify situations that might trigger my threat response. It's also useful when thinking about what other people are experiencing, building empathy, and consciously designing for psychological safety.

There's so much more research on this topic, but we've covered a bit on what's going on in our heads and nervous system... and some ways we can recognise our triggers and when we're likely to feel a threat response. What do we do with that information?

Reframing & Happiness Habits

Practising our happiness habits, including mindfulness, helps us build more awareness and the ability to slow down and observe our thoughts and feelings. We can get some distance and time to choose our response to these triggers, rather than an immediate emotional reaction. This engages different parts of our brain to when we're triggered into a fight, flight, or freeze response.

It doesn't change the fact that there will be things that don't go how we hope and occasionally we'll feel frustrated, hurt or upset. Sometimes we get stuck replaying these events on a loop in our head. They reinforce the negative stories we tell ourselves about who we are and how the world works. This is where reframing can be powerful.

In design, we often talk about reframing. Consciously looking at the problem from different perspectives to open up possibilities and generate innovative solutions. Reframing is about changing the story. There's a similar approach in positive neuroscience that applies to our mindset and the stories we tell ourselves. It's called cognitive reappraisal, or reframing.

If you want to learn more about the basics of this neuroscience and more reframing techniques, I recommend Anette Prehn's free *The Neuroscience of Reframing & How to Do It* course on Udemy.

Another great program is the *Brain Power Series* by Shelley Laslett from Vitae (vitae. coach).

--- ACTION ---

Reframing

Reframing helps us build on the awareness we've been developing. It uses techniques to reframe negative events, changing our perspective and how we perceive them. One technique is called Benefit Finding. This is a really simple exercise, and can be a natural extension to the Simple Gratitude Journal Exercise I hope you've started.

To get into a positive headspace, start with the Simple Gratitude Journal Exercise. Write down three things that make you feel good.

Thinking about the thing that didn't go how you hoped, write a few sentences to describe the situation. Focus on the situation rather than diving in to re-feel the whole experience.

Now, write down three positive things about the situation – flipping the focus from what didn't go well in the situation, to finding the things that did.

This is sometimes called looking on the bright side or finding the silver lining. It might sound way too simple, but research has shown it has a powerful effect. With practice, it helps to build new patterns of thinking and make the stories we tell ourselves more positive.

Personal Sustainability

In this book, we focus a lot on the importance of sustainable business models – models that can deliver value over the long term and be healthy. Our personal sustainability and wellbeing are even more important. Sometimes this is referred to as founder wellbeing. If we don't take proactive steps to look after ourselves, there's an increased risk of getting to a point of feeling overwhelmed and burnt out.

If you've been on this journey before, or have been at it for a while, you'll no doubt be very aware that it's often a bit of a rollercoaster. There will be days when things don't go as hoped and probably some days of crushing doubt. The good news is you're likely to experience extended times of extreme optimism and the feeling that you're doing exactly what you should be, with a deep sense of meaning and fulfilment.

Many start the entrepreneurial journey with the expectation of being their own boss and working fewer hours. That's probably not going to be the case – at least in the short term. Successful organisations care the most about their customers, which in practice means every customer is your boss.

"Do what you love and ~~never work a day in your life~~ work super f*ing hard all the time with no separation or any boundaries and also take everything extremely personally."

Adam Kurtz

Over the last few years, startups have become the romanticised garage bands of the 1970s... and by extension, social enterprise startups. Before diving into this together, I feel I need to say running your own social enterprise isn't the only way. There are plenty of existing social enterprises and NFPs who would benefit from your focus on purpose and impact, your skills, and your experience.

I'm not trying to talk you out of the social enterprise journey... I'm just making sure you know there's more than one way to do meaningful work and create a positive impact. It's also worth having some realistic expectations.

Personal sustainability is really important to me. Far too many founders get to a point of feeling overwhelmed and burnt out.

With social enterprise, there's an additional layer because we're working on meaningful social and environmental problems. It's common to see a social enterprise start delivering value that people need and are using... but for the founders it's not sustainable. The finances aren't working at both an organisational and personal level. The stress builds, taking a toll on their emotional, mental, and physical health. They feel close to being burnt out and know they can't go on, but also feel guilty about stopping. They can't let down all of these people who now rely on them. They feel stuck. This is a key problem I'm focused on helping with.

So, what do I mean by personal sustainability? Let's talk about personal wellbeing, including your personal finances. A quick note that I'm not a doctor or an accountant and it's not that kind of advice. This is general guidance, and doesn't replace advice and support you might get from experts who know your personal situation.

Personal Wellbeing

We need to look after our health and wellbeing. This is key to our quality of life. Our physical, mental, and emotional health are completely linked. The health of our mind affects our body, and the health of our body affects our mind. We need to look after both.

The focus of this chapter has been on our mindset, and the happiness habits we can develop – which play a key role in helping improve our emotional, mental, and physical wellbeing. These help us keep perspective and be resilient when facing adversity. They also help with our relationships and social connection. These are all critical elements of wellbeing.

In Chapter 4: Purpose, Vision & Theory of Change, we'll talk about your "personal why". This is a key part of meaning, which has been identified as another key element of our wellbeing.

Martin Seligman's PERMA theory is a simple model to help think about the different psychological areas. They are Positive emotions, Engagement, Relationships, Meaning, and Accomplishments. Directly or indirectly, we touch on all of these in this book.

I haven't talked about the physical side of wellbeing in any detail. There tends to be a high level of awareness of the importance of movement and being physically active. Some basic things that are often taken for granted though are the power of sleep and water. Get as much as you can of both.

Even though we're often working on very serious things, it doesn't mean we need to be very serious. At least not always. It's important to create and keep space for fun and things that bring us joy. We need unstructured time for play and to experiment. We need to live our lives in sustainable ways.

I recommend watching Laura Storm's 2017 TED talk. It's raw and powerful. And very relevant. I can't do it justice here, but she shares her story of recovering from a debilitating injury. Dealing with that, she went from "the whole concept of self-care was a luxury I had seen as something I didn't have time for. We have so many problems in the world to solve..." to "... a newfound peaceful way of being grounded in my own body. I felt stronger, and more content, satisfied. I felt happier than ever". Many of the things we've been talking about were key to her recovery, and she's been able to carry on doing great work. Her closing words:

"I'm excited to be... continuing my mission of building resilient and sustainable societies but with an equal focus on the importance of inner sustainability. Inner sustainability goes hand-in-hand with external sustainability. We can't have one without the other."

Laura Storm

Don't let your social enterprise journey become all-consuming. Keep your other interests active. This will help you keep a sense of perspective, which helps your personal sustainability.

This is something I've been working on for a while. I've spent so many years on this intense but mostly fun journey. For a long time, it consumed every waking moment – and many of my sleeping moments too. It's been how I pay the bills, my social life, and my hobby. I'm getting better at it, but I'm not there yet. My default state is to drift into thought about work... especially strategic planning. I still practice my happiness habits and work on finding my sustainable rhythm.

So, what are we going to do about all of this? I recommend setting up an action plan. There are two parts to this. The first is to be clear on the things you do that normally keep you feeling happy and healthy. These are the things to keep doing.

The second part is to set up lead indicators that identify when unhealthy patterns are developing with what we're going to do about it – before things get out of control.

"No valid plans for the future can be made by those who have no capacity for living now."

Alan Watts

Personal Wellbeing

What do you currently do that helps keep you feeling happy and healthy? It's worth referring to your earlier notes on Your Strengths & Assets and Your Team.

Here are some things to think about. These are the positive things to keep doing:

Physical Health
What positive things do you do for your physical health?

Mental & Emotional Health
What positive things do you do for your mental and emotional health?

Relationships
Who are the important people in your life? Especially people you have healthy relationships with?

Social Connection
What are the important groups of people or communities in your life?

Play
What do you love doing? What do you do for fun? What really brings you joy?

Backup Plan
Everyone's "normal" is different. It's natural to have days when we're feeling down or a bit overwhelmed. If this lingers for days or weeks, it might be part of an unhealthy pattern that's developing. I encourage you to think about the red flags or signs you've observed in yourself that indicate you're heading in an unhealthy direction. The goal here is to identify the pattern early and take the right action.

What are the patterns of thinking, feeling, or behaving that indicate you're heading in an unhealthy direction?

Over what time period?

What will you do, or stop doing, when you notice this pattern?

Who will you talk to for help?

How will you know you're back in a healthy place?

Personal Finances

Economic or financial wellbeing is also an important part of our personal sustainability. Our ability to meet our basic needs and feel secure. Exploring a social enterprise idea is going to cost you plenty of energy and time, and some money. There will also be opportunity cost.

It usually takes longer than we plan to break even on a monthly basis – the point where we have more money coming in every month than we're paying out. Most financial models I see also don't include the founders paying themselves – and even then, the numbers often don't stack up. Then there's the harsh reality that well over 90% of startups fail – this applies equally to social enterprise ideas.

On top of that, it's very common that of those who do survive, many never reach net breakeven. Net breakeven at an organisational level is when you've received at least as much money as you've spent – in total – from the time you started working on your idea. It should include paying yourself. We'll talk about this more in Chapter 12: Financials.

It's within this context that you need to think about your personal finances. It's common to talk about an organisation's runway – how long before they run out of money. It's less common to hear about personal runway.

Personal runway is an important calculation for every team member working on the idea who isn't being paid their usual rate. Often no one is getting paid in the early days but some might be being paid a small amount. Being honest about these personal runway calculations and what each person is investing or putting at risk is important for personal sustainability – and also for planning. We'll talk about having this as an open and fair conversation, and team legal agreements in Chapter 13: Legals.

Many people have a job to keep paying the bills in the early stages, and they work on their idea outside work hours or take some paid leave. In most cases, this is what I recommend as a way to manage the risk, and give you more time to learn. In some cases, people change to part-time work.

It's important that you know your personal financial numbers to be sustainable, and keep yourself and household in a healthy financial position. Financial stress is the cause of a lot of health and relationship issues.

Personal Budget & Investment

If you don't already have a budget for your personal finances, you need one. There are many free resources online to help with this. You need the information to answer these questions.

What's the minimum you need to earn each month to pay all your bills?

How much money do you have left over each month after paying all your financial commitments?

Do you have savings or access to funds as a safety net when something goes wrong?

You need to approach exploring your social enterprise idea like any investment. You should only invest what you can afford to lose, and you need to cap your downside risk.

How much money can you afford to invest in total? Over what time period?

How much time can you afford to invest each month? For how long?

Are you expecting the organisation will repay you for the time and money you've invested? (To treat this as a loan, a donation, or for a share of ownership?)

If you're expecting a return (loan or share of ownership), over what time period?

What would the impact be if that money is never repaid and/or you're never paid for the work you've done?

What will you do to manage this risk?

Your Risk Profile

We all have a different risk profile. What risks are we willing to take? What are the thresholds? How much capacity do we have to take those risks – or what risks can we afford?

Just as we all have "negativity bias" that we talked about earlier... we also have "optimism bias". It's a tendency to overestimate the likelihood that things will go well and underestimate the likelihood of experiencing negative outcomes. Research has found that entrepreneurs usually have relatively high levels of optimism bias.

I just mentioned that 90% of startups fail, and you're still here. What if I mention that 75% of new businesses don't last five years? If that doesn't put you off, that's probably your optimism bias in action.

I often joke that you need to be irrationally optimistic to be a founder... and a bit naïve. This combination helps us take the risks required to start something in the first place, and then keep persevering. If we really knew what we were in for, maybe we wouldn't start. I've been through that cycle many times despite the odds, and failed, and tried again. Maybe I'm not a very quick learner or have a high pain threshold.

This bias can go both ways. Daniel Kahneman, a winner of the Nobel Prize in Economic Sciences, and author of *Thinking Fast and Slow*, researched these biases and outlines some of the upside:

"Optimists are normally cheerful and happy, and therefore popular; they are resilient in adapting to failures and hardships, their chances of clinical depression are reduced, their immune system is stronger, they take better care of their health, they feel healthier than others and are in fact likely to live longer.

Optimistic individuals play a disproportionate role in shaping our lives. Their decisions make a difference; they are the inventors, the entrepreneurs, the political and military leaders – not average people. They got to where they are by seeking challenges and taking risks."

Daniel Kahneman

We need to be careful of the downside of the optimism bias though. It is sometimes known as "the illusion of invulnerability". The reality is the risks do apply to us. We need to identify and manage the risks. If we don't, this can lead to poor decision making and really negative consequences.

In the context of personal sustainability, the principle I strongly recommend is that you only risk what you can afford to lose.

Research has shown that people in general aren't very good at evaluating risks. When making decisions, there's absolute versus relative risk, different risk categories, and the often forgotten risk of doing nothing. Sometimes we don't do things or evaluate risks well because of fear.

Tim Ferriss says the most important exercise he still does to this day is Fear Setting. The purpose of the exercise is to identify our fears to help make good decisions. This is a good framework to help identify the risks – or the worst thing that could happen, what you'd do about it if it did happen, what the benefits might be... and it also looks at the cost or risk of inaction.

You can download the worksheet from tim.blog/ted or visit dynamic4.com/sptm for the link.

The whole approach we take in this book is about identifying risks and actively managing them. We'll be testing our riskiest thinking at every step, and doing safe to fail experiments. The idea is to reduce the likelihood of overinvesting in solutions that no one wants, will use, or will pay for.

The reality is that's still a very real risk. Even taking the best approach, the chance of failure is extremely high. If it is going to fail though, we want it to happen in the most graceful way possible with the least impact.

Perseverance & Giving Up

In 2020, I watched *Breathtaking K2: The World's Most Dangerous Mountain*, and I think this is a very accurate metaphor for the social enterprise journey. What is often a journey of many years working on a social enterprise idea compressed into a 46-minute film.

The film follows Adrian Ballinger and Carla Perez as they attempt to climb the world's second-highest mountain (8,611m) without supplemental oxygen. One in four people who reach the summit of K2 die.

On the expedition they experienced altitude sickness, adverse weather, the most snow in 30 years resulting in hazardous snow conditions, and an avalanche had already wiped out one team's camp. This was before they even really got started. From there they faced one setback after another.

Most of the climbers give up for the season and go home. Some die. Everyone says this isn't the season to do it. Adrian says he'll "go until the mountain tells me I can't go anymore". As they get to K2 basecamp he reflects that the trek took 50% longer than they planned, but he was "so stoked to be here". They then start the acclimatisation process, which he says "takes patience, persistence, and a lot of practice". He also says "I am so confident it's the right thing, but man it hurts".

Of course, they're supported by a team, and there's knowledge from people who've climbed the mountain before. There were team members who did some core preparation work that would enable getting to the summit, even though some wouldn't get there themselves.

"With their confidence shattered, and the obstacle in front of them seemingly too big to overcome, the team had a decision to make. They could pack up and leave with the rest of the climbers or they could stay and hope for a miracle".

Adrian says "I sort of came into the season knowing that it was gonna be hard and dangerous... all along I've kinda told myself that failure's okay and that we all fail, and that we just keep taking these small steps toward success and hopefully it comes and even when it doesn't the experiences are really, really powerful".

Trust and interaction between teammates are critical. "When I see them deal with stress and risk, their decision making is so on point and they're so focused, but at the same time, their attitude is just right. It's easy to be around, it keeps me feeling confident... they're just good humans. They care about the people around them. When they're asking you questions, you know they're listening and interested... and just having fun."

On the summit climb, you can see the emotional rollercoaster. "That was full on, scary, hard. We're gonna try to get to a safe spot around the corner and reassess". Followed not long after by "...we still have a long way to go. I'm totally emotional. I just can't believe it, we're at 8,400m. Perfect day. It's feeling awful good. Still a lot of work to go. A couple of hours to the summit, and then we gotta get down safe, but it's a special moment right now". And then the final reflection before they thankfully got back safely... "it's unbelievable that everything worked out with all of the setbacks".

There are so many examples of mindset, awareness of strengths and assets, the team, their approach to risk and failure, how they reframed situations, their optimism bias, and most importantly, their personal sustainability. They took the time to go slow where they needed to look after themselves, acclimatise, and be able to go again. These are all of the things we've been talking about in this chapter.

The key thing they did was persevere. Steve Jobs said "I'm convinced that about half of what separates the successful entrepreneurs from the non-successful ones is pure perseverance... Unless you have a lot of passion about this, you're not going to survive. You're going to give it up. So, you've got to have an idea, or a problem or a wrong that you want to right that you're passionate about; otherwise you're not going to have the perseverance to stick it through".

You definitely need to be resilient and persevere to be successful. Our mindset and happiness habits are what make that possible. That's why we've focused on this first.

It's also important to know when to go home. To give up. To stop. This is usually the hardest decision you'll make on your social enterprise journey. It's an emotional one and it has its own grieving process. From my experience this applies about as much for something in the very early stages as it does when you've been working on it for years.

When that happens – and statistically it will – you'll be hurting, but you don't want to have compromised your personal sustainability. You want to be able to reflect on what you've learnt, maybe take a breath... and try again.

Conflicting Advice

A brief note on conflicting advice. Expect it.

We all have our own perspectives based on our experiences. A lot of advice will be very relevant in some contexts, but less so in others. There's generally no shortage of people offering advice. It's up to us to receive it positively and learn what we can from it. A vital skill is to be able to receive it without getting defensive.

A key thing I often to talk to founders about is building the ability to filter advice and feedback for relevant patterns and insights that you can apply to your situation. This is one of the most valuable skills you can develop. When receiving advice, it's usually more important to understand the rationale rather than the prescriptive direction.

Customers will give us conflicting feedback too. We'll talk about that a bit more in Part 2: People, Problem & Context.

If you're interested in a robust way to filter advice and options, I recommend *Principles* by Ray Dalio. This includes his method for triangulating feedback and advice. He says there are really only two steps to making a decision: learning and then deciding. The biggest threat to good decision making is harmful emotions that prevent us from learning well. There's an impressive rigour to his believability-weighted decision making matrix.

"People interested in making the best possible decisions are rarely confident that they have the best answers."

Ray Dalio

The purpose of this chapter is to set some foundations to help you look after your personal wellbeing while making a positive impact – so you stay healthy and positive on this journey without getting overwhelmed and burnt out.

We've just covered a fair bit of ground and some pretty big concepts. More importantly, I hope we've put some practical things in motion to help you build your happiness habits. I encourage you to keep referring back to this chapter. If you're starting out for the first time, you might not have much context and understanding of the importance of these things. Over time though, I promise these are the concepts and practices that will help you to be healthy and positive on this journey.

"We cannot solve our problems with the same thinking we used when we created them."

Albert Einstein

Chapter 2

Approach & Philosophy

The purpose of this chapter is to cover the core concepts and terms that we'll continually refer to and build on through the book.

The approach we use in this book brings together thinking and practices from positive neuroscience, design thinking/human-centred design, lean startup, agile, and many more. We apply action learning principles, which are focused on collaboratively solving real problems with coaching. Everything we'll do is very practical, but also requires reflection and iteration. This means building our self-awareness and empathy.

I won't go into detail here, but I'm also heavily influenced by approaches like collective impact and collaborative change, collaborative consumption, regenerative practices, the circular economy, and frameworks like Kate Raworth's *Doughnut Economics*. Basically, I love approaches that bring people together to work on and solve their own social and environmental problems in collaborative ways.

Key Principles

There are some key principles that are foundational to the approach we'll take as we work through this program together.

I strongly believe – and the evidence shows – that when we take a human-centred design approach to innovation and embed impact into business models, it helps create the conditions for people to be happier and have an increasing quality of life.

Good business needs to do great things for communities and our planet while being financially successful... it's increasingly what talent, customers, and investors expect.

I frame social enterprise as something we do rather than something we are. I'll explain that as part of defining key terms in a moment.

This is not an academic deep dive into theory and frameworks – we'll cover some theory to a level needed for how we'll apply it using a learning through doing approach. This chapter covers the core theory and is a bit different to the rest of the book.

This isn't intended to be a duplication of other frameworks and methods – I refer to other great books and resources for more information on various models, tools, and research. The focus is on bringing different areas of thinking together into a cohesive approach to design, build, and launch your social enterprise idea.

Defining Terms

Here are some key terms that I think are worth defining upfront. These are terms I'll use a lot and they can mean different things to people in different contexts. For clarity, this is how I'll use them in this book. Most other terms that I think need more explanation will happen in context.

Social Enterprise

What is a social enterprise? The go-to question to kick off a robust debate by anyone in and around the sector – can we call it a sector? The answer is, there's no universally agreed definition. I'll primarily be framing it as something we do – a tool rather than something we are – an entity. A means to an end. A verb, rather than a noun. I hadn't heard it stated that way until a conversation a few years ago with Alex Hannant from the Yunus Centre Griffith University. I found it a powerful reframe that helps focus on what's important.

There are two well-established principles for social enterprise:

1. A clearly articulated social and/or environmental purpose – a lot of this is about demonstrable intent

2. The sale of a product or service is a significant source of revenue – doing business is how the purpose is realised

In the context of certification, membership of peak bodies, and in some jurisdictions – legal structures – there will be other requirements. Sometimes this will include how profit/surplus is treated.

Despite not being in the name, social enterprise is also very much about our environment and climate action.

A quick note: I don't believe social enterprise and market models are an appropriate tool to use for all social and environmental challenges. The evidence shows that the market doesn't always know best – social enterprise is often a response to address market failures. There are also contexts where the evidence shows a market model makes situations worse. An ethical debate for another time.

For the purposes of this book, we'll focus on social enterprise as a way to deliver on a clearly articulated social and/or environmental purpose by providing a solution with a paying customer. We'll be applying business model innovation as a way to achieve social innovation. I also strongly encourage models with embedded impact rather than redistributive models.

Design Thinking & Human-Centred Design (HCD)

I'm going to sidestep the esoteric debate on how and why design thinking and human-centred design (HCD) are the same or different because it's not productive. A web search will return hundreds of articles and posts with various people staking out their positions. The same goes for customer experience (CX), user experience (UX), service design, product design, and all the other variants that trend at different times. They can all mean very specific things in certain contexts at a practitioner level, but they're mostly a distraction for what we're focusing on here.

In this book, I'll mostly just use "design" or the term "design thinking" or "HCD", but in all cases, I'm talking about a human-centred design approach. That's the foundational concept. It's an approach based on building empathy for the people we're designing with. Design is a problem-solving activity, and my core philosophy is that means we need to build empathy with the people experiencing the problem and involve them in the creation of their own solutions.

It's also important to note that being human-centred includes playing our role as stewards of the natural world and the other animals in it. This is still human-centred because we can only see things through our human frame of reference and values.

Problem

Problem. This is a big one – and a keyword in the title of my book. A simple definition is that a problem is a situation that's harmful and needs to be dealt with and overcome. We have plenty of those in the world, and plenty that really matter.

With problems, comes opportunity. This can be a matter of mindset and reframing.

An important note I want to emphasise, **please never see people as problems to solve.** Deficit thinking is harmful to the people involved – and it doesn't address the real problem and its causes. We need to approach these problems with humility, empathy, and an understanding of the systems at play.

Solution

Your solution may take many different shapes. A solution is often the combination of the product, service, organisation, experience, process, and many other things – used to solve the problem you're focused on. The approach we're taking is relevant for all types of solutions – physical, digital, products, services, and more.

Customer

A customer is someone who pays you for your solution. Even if they're not the person who'll use your solution. In most cases in this book, when I say customers, I'm talking about your target audience. In some contexts where it matters, we'll differentiate between customers and users.

Organisation

An organisation is a group of people who come together for a particular purpose. While I'll primarily be referring to social enterprise as something we do, it is done by groups of people who come together as an organisation of some kind. This might be a business, a not-for-profit (NFP), or another type of organisation.

I work with a lot of NFP leaders who are exploring if they should design, build, and launch a social enterprise idea as a way of generating sustainable earned income. I also work with a lot of early-stage social enterprise startups who take a profit-for-purpose approach. Both of these and more are covered by the term "organisation".

Adaptive Challenges

We live and work in a dynamic and adaptive world – full of dynamic and adaptive systems and people. Things are always changing. Sometimes those changes are small and happen gradually. Other times there are big dramatic changes in what seems like an instant. 2020 gave us an example of what that can look like.

How do we design, build, and launch social enterprise ideas when there's so much uncertainty? So many possibilities and opportunities. So many risks to manage. A key thing we need to practice is recognising adaptive challenges and taking the right approach to meet them.

Recognising Adaptive Challenges

There are broadly two types of challenge: technical and adaptive. Usually our education and jobs have taught and rewarded us for focusing on and solving technical challenges. This means we often don't recognise when we're faced with an adaptive challenge, and even if we do recognise it, we approach it in the same way we do technical challenges. We look at the facts and try to use best practice and experts to solve them. This approach doesn't usually work well or for long with adaptive challenges.

> "The most common leadership failure stems from trying to apply technical solutions to adaptive challenges."
>
> **Alexander Grashow, Marty Linsky & Ronald Heifetz – The Practice of Adaptive Leadership**

The reality is pretty much all challenges have both technical and adaptive aspects to them. What are the characteristics of these two types of challenge?

Technical Challenges

There are technical aspects to challenges, and we need our technical skills to be able to take on those challenges to come up with solutions. With technical challenges, we tend to start with a clear problem.

With technical challenges, the focus is on facts and logic, and the context tends to be more predictable and consistent. This makes it easier to get to a very well-defined problem. The solution is pretty clear, and can be implemented by experts and people in authority – generally in quite short timeframes. People just need to be informed, and will often adopt the solution without much resistance.

Adaptive Challenges

Just as there are technical aspects to the challenge, there are adaptive aspects too – especially where there are people involved. The reality with social enterprise ideas is we spend a lot of time dealing with adaptive systems challenges. With adaptive challenges, we tend to start with a question.

With adaptive challenges, the problem and root cause are often hard to identify because we're looking at complex interconnected systems – and the context is uncertain and inconsistent.

A key difference to technical challenges is they can't just be solved by experts or people in authority. They require people to take action themselves as part of solving the problem – and this means changes in attitudes, beliefs, and behaviours. We all have a higher level of resistance to those kinds of changes, and it often takes some kind of transformative experience and learning – and often unlearning – for us to shift.

Working on adaptive challenges tends to happen over longer timeframes, often requires collaboration and co-design, and there's normally a lot more resistance to adopting the solution.

Two examples are often used to bring this to life. The first is someone goes to the doctor with a broken arm. There's a clearly defined problem. They can't fix it themself, but the doctor knows the problem, and with their expertise provides the solution. They leave with their arm in a cast, and once healed, the problem is gone. This is a technical solution to a technical challenge.

The other scenario is someone goes to the doctor with chest pain. There are many possible causes, and the doctor doesn't immediately know what the problem is. Several tests may be necessary to identify the cause. Long-term lifestyle changes may be required, and the doctor can't directly solve the problem. The patient needs to do the work. This is an adaptive challenge.

There are different types of challenges with different levels of complexity.

Cynefin Framework

I find the Cynefin Framework by Dave Snowden very useful as a complexity sense-making model. The framework shows five domains or decision making contexts: clear (previously known as simple or obvious), complicated, complex, chaos, and disorder.

By accurately sensing our situation, we can respond in a way that's relevant to the level of complexity we're faced with.

So with some awareness of these different types of challenges, how do we make sense of what we're experiencing and observing in this dynamic and adaptive world?

Integral Theory & Sense-Making

We've identified different types of challenges with varying levels of complexity. There are also many different perspectives, contexts, and ways of seeing the world. Because of that, as humans we've tried different ways to make sense of things and find meaning over a long time.

There's a lot of theory and fascinating research in this area – far too much to cover here. I'll briefly mention three things I find useful as background to making sense and meaning of the world, and what we're learning on this journey of exploring your social enterprise idea. We'll get into the applied aspects for your specific context in Chapter 8: Make Sense. A quick note: when I say sense-making, I'm including the meaning we attach to it.

Mental Models

A mental model is simply our internal explanation of how things work, especially how we interact with our external reality – the world around us. Mental models are key to how we make sense of the world, approach problems, and make decisions. They guide our perceptions and behaviour. I have mine, you have yours, and everyone else has their own version too.

Cognitive Bias

We all have cognitive biases. They shape what we believe, how we reason and make decisions, what we remember, how we form relationships, and ultimately how we behave. They affect every area of our life.

These biases can affect us and those around us in negative ways, but many of them can be beneficial, and necessary to how we function. The Cognitive Bias Codex visualises over 180 documented cognitive biases, grouped into four everyday scenarios: too much information, not enough meaning, need to act fast, and what should I remember?

Visit dynamic4.com/sptm for a link to the interactive version of the Codex, which links to Wikipedia pages to learn more about each of the biases.

The codex is shared here thanks to John Manoogian III under the Creative Commons Attribution-Share Alike license.

Building awareness of our mental models and how our set of cognitive biases are tuned helps us refine how we make sense of things, the conclusions we draw, and how we choose to behave. We also need to be mindful that, to varying degrees, other people experience things differently – which is why empathy is so important. We'll talk about empathy in a moment.

Cognitive Bias Codex

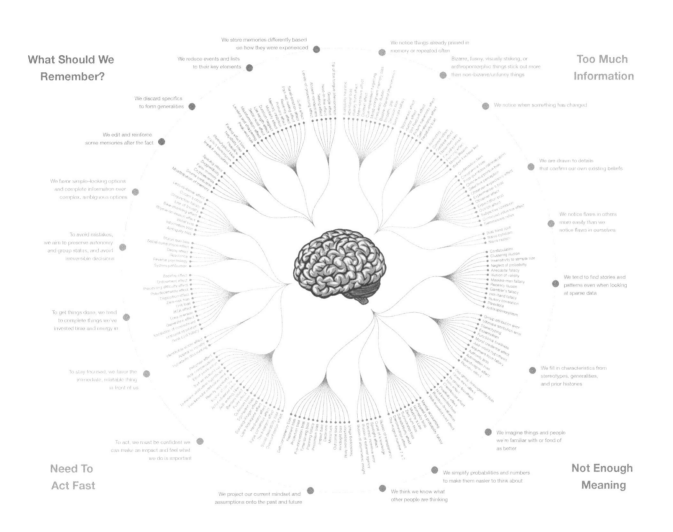

What Should We Remember?

Too Much Information

Need To Act Fast

Not Enough Meaning

We store memories differently based on how they were experienced

We reduce events and lists to their key elements

We discard specifics to form generalities

We edit and reinforce some memories after the fact

We favor simple-looking options and complete information over complex, ambiguous options

To avoid mistakes, we aim to preserve autonomy and group status, and avoid irreversible decisions

To get things done, we tend to complete things we've invested time and energy in

To stay focused, we favor the immediate, relatable thing in front of us

To act, we must be confident we can make an impact and feel what we do is important

We project our current mindset and assumptions onto the past and future

We notice things already primed in memory or repeated often

Bizarre, funny, visually striking, or anthropomorphic things stick out more than non-bizarre/unfunny things

We notice when something has changed

We are drawn to details that confirm our own existing beliefs

We notice flaws in others more easily than we notice flaws in ourselves

We tend to find stories and patterns even when looking at sparse data

We fill in characteristics from stereotypes, generalities, and prior histories

We imagine things and people we're familiar with or fond of as better

We simplify probabilities and numbers to make them easier to think about

We think we know what other people are thinking

> "There is a kink in my damned brain that prevents me from thinking as other people think."

CS Peirce

Abductive Reasoning & First Principles

The approach we take in this book is based on first principles thinking and reasoning – especially abductive reasoning, alongside deduction and induction. I think it's important to briefly mention first principles and abductive reasoning – this is more about knowing the underlying approach we're using to make sense of things, rather than needing to immerse in the theory.

First Principles

First principles are defined as "one of the fundamental assumptions on which a particular theory or procedure is thought to be based" by the *Collins Dictionary*. Descartes said "they must be so clear and evident that the human mind cannot doubt of their truth."

In simple terms, first principles are the most basic things we believe to be true – based on strong evidence.

First principles thinking is critical when working on complex problems. It involves breaking down the problem and its causes into its basic elements. We ask the question "what do we know to be true?"

We seek to remove assumptions to get to the set of things we can be confident are true. From this set of first principles, we then start building up what might be – testing our thinking and making sense as we progress.

Abductive Reasoning

In design research, synthesis is the stage where we make sense of what we've heard, and the information we've collected. This is an abductive sense-making process.

CS Peirce, the philosopher famous for defining the concept, said "abduction is the process of forming an explanatory hypothesis. It is the only logical operation which introduces any new idea... Abduction merely suggests that something may be."

In his excellent book *Exposing the Magic of Design*, Jon Kolko says "abduction allows for the creation of new knowledge and insight... The various constraints of the problem begin to act as logical premises, and the designer's work and life experiences, and her ease and flexibility with logical leaps based on inconclusive or incomplete data, begin to shape abduction. Abduction acts as intuition and is directly aided and assisted by experience of any design or cultural patterns... Design cannot prove the solutions to the mysteries because **solutions are only demonstrable and testable, not provable.**"

When working on solving problems that matter, we first need to really understand what is – the current reality. Get down to first principles rather than building on faulty assumptions. We use abductive reasoning to generate hypotheses about "something that may be". We then test our hypotheses and ideas using approaches consistent with the scientific method.

Integral Theory

Integral theory is huge, but also beautiful in its simplicity. I won't be directly referencing it in this book, but I find it a powerful framework to understand myself, others, organisations, leadership, systems, ecology, and pretty much everything else. It's primarily based on Ken Wilber's work as a meta-theory that seeks to unify all fields of human research, knowledge, and experience. It's also closely integrated with Clare Graves' work which became Spiral Dynamics.

For decades my focus has been on developing myself and building a more holistic world-centric perspective – increasingly taking a planet-centric and integrated systems view. Most of this was before I discovered Integral. The frameworks and language of Integral have brought much sharper clarity to my approach. So, what is it?

AQAL

One of the things I find very valuable is using Integral as a transdisciplinary approach to making sense and meaning – and working on complex problems. Integral is all about making space for multiple perspectives and integrating them into a coherent whole.

AQAL (or "all quadrants, all levels, all lines, all states, and all types") is the basic framework of Integral. There are so many aspects of this I'd love to share, but it would be theory for the sake of it. The Quadrants are the only part of the framework I'll outline briefly, because they directly inform our approach to solving problems in this book.

There are four different perspectives that apply to all human experience, and they're all interrelated. These are on the axis of individual and collective, internal and external. The quadrants are:

1. The **"I"** perspective. This is the individual internal quadrant – our first-person subjective experience. The "I" perspective includes our thoughts, emotions, memories, states of mind, perceptions, and immediate sensations

2. The **"We"** perspective. This is the collective internal quadrant – our social inter-subjective perspective, also called the second-person perspective. The "We" perspective includes shared values, meanings, language, relationships, and cultural background

3. The **"It"** perspective. This is the individual external quadrant – the objective third-person perspective. The "It" perspective includes our physical body (including our brain), and anything you can see and touch (or observe scientifically) in time and space

4. The **"Its"** perspective. This is the collective external quadrant – inter-objective systems and structure. The "Its" perspective includes systems, networks, technology, government, and the natural environment

While we're working on our social enterprise ideas, especially those focused on systemic change, we must understand these different perspectives and find ways to integrate them meaningfully.

Holacracy

We won't explicitly focus on leadership and organisation design, but everything we do is both of these things and an area I spend a lot of my time on.

Holacracy is a way of structuring and running your organisation where power is distributed – giving individuals and teams freedom while staying aligned to the organisation's purpose. Holacracy isn't directly part of Integral but was heavily influenced by its principles.

If you're keen to find out more, Brian Robertson is the author of *Holacracy*, a practical book worth reading. He also explains some of the key principles in his great 2012 TED talk *Why not ditch bosses and distribute power*.

This structure can fit very well with collective impact and collaborative change approaches.

Holacracy is often spoken about in the context of "teal organisations", and the stages of organisational development use red, amber, orange, green, and teal. This is a direct reference to some of the Integral development levels. I've spent a lot of my work life building the ways of thinking and practices that make green and teal possible.

Enspiral is a global community that started in New Zealand, and applies Holacracy principles. It's "a virtual and physical network of companies and professionals brought together by a set of shared values and a passion for positive social impact. It's sort of a "DIY" social enterprise support network. At its heart, it's a group of people who want to co-create an encouraging, diverse community of people trying to make a difference". *The Enspiral Handbook* (handbook.enspiral.com) is a great practical resource.

So, we've got some ways to help recognise different types of challenges, and some awareness of how we and others make sense of them and from that meaning. How do we approach solving them? That's where design thinking comes in.

Design Thinking

Design thinking is a human-centred approach to innovation and solving complex problems – it's as much about doing as thinking.

In many contexts, design thinking and human-centred design are treated as synonyms. Don't get distracted by the labels. What we're focusing on is solving problems by really understanding and building empathy for the people experiencing the problem – and designing solutions with those people.

This approach is very consistent with the values and ethics of social enterprise, community development, and collaborative change. Principles like "nothing about me, without me".

There are two iconic visualisations of mental models for this approach to design. The double diamond and the three lenses. They're a couple of my favourite shapes.

Double Diamond

The double diamond came from the Design Council in 2004 as a simple way to visualise the design and innovation process. It's been remixed by many since. The model was designed to be relevant in any field of problem-solving. At the time of its creation, this included business, science and technology, and social challenges. Yes, the social context has been there all along – not force-fit as an afterthought.

You'll have already seen this shape all over this book. It's the core approach I've applied to all of the programs I've designed over many years, including Dynamic4 Jetpack in 2014, and therefore this book.

I love how simple but powerful it is as a visualisation of the problem-solving process. The first diamond is focused on the problem and the second diamond on the solution. An easy reminder that we always need to really understand the problem before jumping to solutions.

The other core concept is we go through iterative cycles of diverging and converging. When we're diverging, we're exploring, gathering information, opening things up. Obviously we can't diverge forever because we run out of time, money, and stakeholders' patience – and nothing is resolved. So, we also need phases of converging. This is when we're making sense of what we've found, testing our thinking, and narrowing options. Even though you might have a preference for one or the other, it's critical that we practice both.

This simplicity makes it a powerful orientation device. There will be times when you feel a bit lost, uncertain of where you are and what to do next. I often use it as my homing beacon. I can do a quick and easy sense check. Are we primarily in the problem diamond? Or have we already got clarity on the people, problem, and context – and we're now exploring different ways we might solve for that? Are we going through a divergent phase and opening things up? Or are we trying to converge and narrow our focus?

You'll notice that I use this as an orientation device throughout the book. I'll keep referencing where we're at with the double diamond, and how this aligns with the sprints.

As much as I love the double diamond, it's a simplified visualisation and imperfect. The reality is there are endless smaller diamonds within both the problem and solution diamonds, where we're diverging to gather information and converging to make sense of it. It looks like a linear journey, whereas in reality it's circular and iterative. You may be on the solution diamond for some aspects of your idea, and the problem diamond for others – or diverging in one area and converging in another. I tend to think of it as an infinity symbol or Möbius strip, because it's never finished – we're always iterating and continually improving. Because things aren't static, this means continually revisiting the problem diamond to make sure we're solving the right problem – that matters.

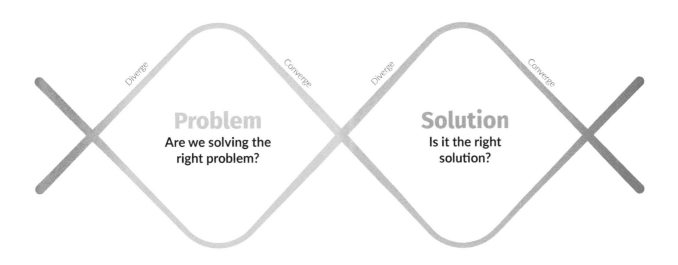

Problem Diamond

The focus of the problem diamond is to get clarity and build deep empathy for the people, problem, and context you're focusing on. This often starts with a question or a challenge. As we progress, we're constantly testing our thinking to see if we're focused on the right problem. Is it the real problem, or just another symptom? There's no point in having great solutions that don't solve problems that matter.

I often refer to the famous quote attributed to Albert Einstein at this point... "If I had an hour to solve a problem, I'd spend 55 minutes thinking about the problem and five minutes thinking about solutions". When we really understand the problem, solutions tend to come much faster and easier.

Part 2 of this book is focused on the problem diamond.

The first part of the problem diamond is a divergent discovery process – we're exploring, gathering information, opening things up. Who are the groups of people and individuals? How do they see the world? What problem are they experiencing? What context are they experiencing these problems in? How do they feel about it?

I hope it's obvious that you can't reliably get this information and build empathy without directly interacting with the people you want to help. Sadly, it's amazing how often people are building solutions for people they don't really know anything about, and haven't even had a conversation with.

We can't diverge forever, so we need to converge. This is where we make sense of what we've heard – identifying the patterns, themes, and getting down to the key insights and opportunities. This is a process of making things more concrete with fewer options.

The problem diamond is focused on collecting information, building empathy, and **understanding what is** – resisting the urge to jump to what might be.

The temptation will be to skip or shortcut the problem diamond. We tend to love our ideas, and we often conflate how other people value our ideas with our value as a person. Immersing in the problem space is often confronting and emotional. It's where we learn the problem isn't quite what we thought it was, and our thinking is challenged, requiring us to iterate. There's a lot more uncertainty and ambiguity in the problem space – and this is uncomfortable. These are some of the reasons people jump straight to solutions. The solution space tends to be a lot more comfortable for most people.

Jumping straight to solutions usually leads to not solving the real problem or the problem that actually matters. It results in focusing on symptoms rather than the root cause and often creates solutions that nobody wants or will use. Not a happy place to be.

Clarity

When we get to the point in the middle of the two diamonds, our ambition is clarity. Sharp clarity on the clearly defined problem to solve that's now informed by evidence, meaningful insight, and empathy.

It's common to phrase this problem as a "how might we..." (HMW) statement.

With our sharp clarity on the real problem to solve, it's now time to explore solutions.

Solution Diamond

The focus of the solution diamond is to get clarity on the solution concept, describe how it works, design the experience, and start building it. This means a lot of prototyping, testing, and iteration.

Part 3 of this book is focused on the solution diamond.

The first part of the solution diamond is a divergent process to explore many possible ideas to solve the clearly defined problem you've identified – that's now informed by evidence, meaningful insight, and empathy.

We often fall in love with our ideas very quickly, and the temptation is to just dive straight into the original solution idea – which you probably had on day one. I encourage you to resist that urge, and spend some time exploring multiple ways that you might solve for the problem.

In the solution diamond, the convergence process means rapidly prototyping, testing, and iterating. We're going to have a lot of assumptions about the solution concept, the business model, and how people will adopt our solution. We need to test our assumptions and learn as much as possible – as quickly and cheaply as we can.

This is the point where it is very common to overinvest time and money in something that no one will use or pay for. That's a path I want to help you avoid. I've been down that path too many times. And it hurts. There's nothing quite as demoralising as having a polished solution that you can't even get people to adopt for free.

The Three Lenses

One of the most common questions at this stage is "how do I know if it's the right solution?" This is where the three lenses model comes in – the other iconic design mental model visualisation I mentioned earlier. We need to assess our ideas through three perspectives: desirable, viable, feasible. The aim is to have the biggest possible overlap between all three. Of course, we use it to understand the current state and perspectives in the problem diamond too.

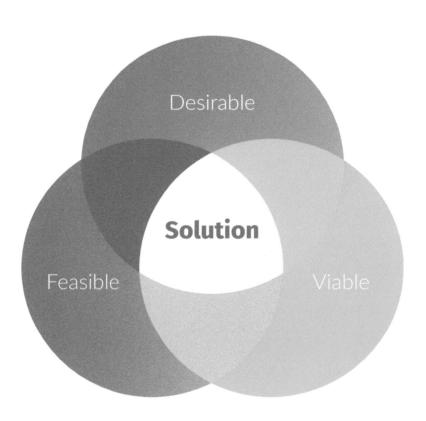

Desirable

Taking a HCD approach, we always start with the people. So, the first perspective to understand is what's desirable for the people you're focused on. Really immersing in this perspective is what we do in the problem diamond. We continue doing this in the solution diamond. What motivates them, and what do they find appealing? What do people actually think about our solution idea? How do people make decisions? Does it create meaningful social and/or environmental value? Are we solving a problem that matters?

Viable

From the organisation's perspective, what's viable? Can we afford to do it and be financially successful providing the solution, ideally in a self-sustaining way? What will it cost? How will we fund designing, building, launching, and running it? How much will people pay?

Feasible

From the organisation's perspective, what's feasible? Do we have or can we get the skills to design, build, launch, and run this solution? Can we realistically make it happen? Are we the right people to be doing it?

This is why we test our assumptions. If we get these assumptions wrong, it's easy to see how everything else in our solution and business model falls apart.

- If it's not desirable, we end up with a solution that no one wants
- If it's not viable, we can't afford to make it happen – and we'll run out of money
- If it's not feasible, we can't design, build, launch, and run the solution – which means we can't deliver the value even if people want it

The sweet spot of success is at the intersection of these three perspectives. The bigger the overlap, the more likely you're onto a good idea. An idea that people love, delivers real value, and solves problems that matter... you can afford to do it and be financially sustainable... and you have the skills to design, build, launch, and continue to run it. That's the happy place.

Empathy

Design thinking is built on empathy. It's the bedrock on which all good design happens. It's a word we use a lot, but it can mean different things to people.

It's a really interesting area of research. The Greater Good Science Center (GGSC) at the University of California, Berkeley, do a lot of research in this area, and they say "emotion researchers generally define empathy as the ability to sense other people's emotions, coupled with the ability to imagine what someone else might be thinking or feeling".

You might be wondering why it matters. The GGSC goes on to say "research suggests that empathic people tend to be more generous and concerned with others' welfare, and they also tend to have happier relationships and greater personal well-being. Empathy can also improve leadership ability and facilitate effective communication".

If you're wondering how empathic you are, they have a simple quiz on their website (ggsc. berkeley.edu).

When I ask people what empathy means to them, the most common response is "walking in someone else's shoes". I think this is a good start because we've at least switched places – or, as I joke, maybe stolen someone's shoes. To be more specific, the important thing is not just to be in someone else's shoes, but to also see and feel things as that person does. From their point of view and experience.

To be potentially controversial, I see empathy as the exact opposite of the Golden Rule "do unto others as you would have them do unto you" – which in some cultures, is held up as the pinnacle of human interaction. That view leads to the judgements that tend to follow the phrase "if I was them…" This is the antithesis of empathy. Taking the position that because I want something, I'm going to push that on to you is a very self-centred and selfish perspective. Instead, when we build empathy, we seek to understand and connect with the other person. How do they see the world? What's important to them? How do they want to be treated? Why?

Empathy is a big concept, and foundational for pretty much everything we do in this book, so I'll share one more layer of detail now.

Daniel Goleman, the psychologist and author of *Emotional Intelligence*, identified three types of empathy: cognitive, emotional, and compassionate. The neuroscience shows that each activates different parts of our brain. There's a spectrum of empathy, and the three types work together.

Cognitive Empathy

Cognitive empathy is what we're using when we "walk in someone else's shoes". It's sometimes called perspective-taking. We see things from the other person's perspective, but we don't really feel it. This is mostly an intellectual exercise, and keeps the other person at a distance. For the type of work we do, and to be a good leader, this is not enough. With this type of empathy, we can understand other people's mental models, and the language they use to describe their world. This is valuable to communicate effectively, but without emotional or compassionate empathy, it can just be used to manipulate people.

Emotional Empathy

Emotional empathy is when we "feel with" someone. Daniel Goleman says this is the type of empathy you need for any role where you relate to people. This is the empathy that creates a sense of rapport. It's about connection. Our mirror neurons fire when we experience this type of empathy, which is important for all kinds of social interactions.

This type of empathy is one of the key behaviours in great leaders and high-performing teams.

Compassionate Empathy

With compassionate empathy or empathic concern, we have the emotional empathy, and when we see someone in need, we're moved to take action and help however we can. This type of empathy can allow us to feel more empowered and positive, because we're helping someone else.

It's important to remember though, empathy is not about what we want – it's about what the other person wants and needs. When we're displaying compassionate empathy, **it's not about how we'd want to be treated if we were them... it's about how they want to be treated.** This is the key point about empathy that I really want to emphasise.

There's a strong link between empathy and our own personal sustainability that we talked about in Chapter 1.

We need to practice self-awareness and self-management to look after our own wellbeing. This is for a couple of reasons.

The first is it's very hard to practice empathy when we're not in a good place emotionally or are feeling threatened and defensive. Empathy comes from a place of being open and engaged.

The other reason is that when we're practising empathy in a social impact context, we can often be dealing with some very confronting realities. This can result in emotional exhaustion or compassion fatigue – which can lead directly to burnout.

A really important note is that building empathy doesn't necessarily mean we agree with the person we have empathy with or that we condone their actions – especially when working on certain social issues like domestic violence – but we need to build a level of empathy if we are to design solutions they're more likely to adopt.

It can often be easier to feel empathy with people who are more like us, but it takes more work to build empathy with people who are very different to us – and some people are naturally more empathic. Either way, the good news is we can learn and practice our empathy. In fact, this is a key life skill.

"Empathy has no script. There is no right way or wrong way to do it. It's simply listening, holding space, withholding judgment, emotionally connecting, and communicating that incredibly healing message of 'You're not alone.'"

Brené Brown

Action Learning

Action learning is an approach focused on learning through doing – by working on real problems… and a problem we feel compelled to solve. Not a case study. Not just theoretical. It's an approach that's perfect for working on complex and adaptive challenges.

The journey of working on our social enterprise ideas is all about real problems – that matter – and adaptive challenges that we care about. And of course, continual learning.

The whole approach we'll take together in this book is based on action learning principles. Action learning requires us to be humble and reflective. This fits very well with HCD and our focus on building empathy. I find some of the key principles both liberating and empowering:

1. Learning starts with not knowing

2. There are no experts in complex challenges

3. People who choose to take responsibility in a challenging situation have the best chance of positively impacting and resolving the challenge

Not knowing feels uncomfortable. We often measure our own worth by what others think of our ideas and our expertise. Our education and employment systems have primarily rewarded getting the right answer – to technical challenges. The combination of these things often leads us to jump to solutions, because it feels safer, more certain, and in many cases, what we've been rewarded for. Unfortunately, this means more often than not we end up focusing on things that aren't the real problem – and we end up with solutions that no one wants.

By taking an action learning approach, we can learn to embrace the ambiguity and uncertainty. We're on a learning journey and there are no experts. The great news is that because we're willing to take on the challenge, we've got the best chance to positively impact the situation.

What does this look like in practice? There are four phases of the action learning model: act, reflect, learn, and plan. This is adapted from RW Revans' *Action Learning: New Techniques for Management*.

Looking at this model, you might notice that you already do it to some degree. There's a lot of theory and methodology to action learning, but we'll stay focused on how to apply it. It will form the natural sprint rhythm we cover in the Agile Ways of Working section in a moment. It's an endless cycle of experimenting, reflecting, learning, and trying again. This reflective cycle is key to the way we'll work together.

Act

- Take an action
- Carry out plans

Reflect

- What happened?
- How do you feel?
- What went well?
- What didn't go well?

Plan

- What do we need to do now?
- How will we do that – what are the steps?

Learn

- Why did we have success?
- Why didn't it go so well?

Scientific Method

The scientific method is a way of learning. A way of solving problems. It's a way of testing ideas – identifying where the ideas are wrong and why, improving the idea, and testing again. When we apply the scientific method, we don't seek to validate our thinking – **we seek to learn and improve**. That's exactly what it means to successfully design, build, and launch your social enterprise idea. We're doing science. Not as a body of knowledge, but as a way of experimenting and learning.

It's a structured process of asking a question based on our observations, doing some research, constructing a hypothesis that we can test, testing our hypothesis with an experiment, analysing the results, and drawing conclusions. This often results in more hypotheses, experiments, and analysis. This is how we'll approach solving problems that matter.

A couple of really important concepts I want to emphasise.

Testing vs Validating

It's become common language in the startup world over the past few years to talk about "validating your idea". It's semantic, but I think this is dangerous language. Our confirmation bias is already very strong. We preference sources and pieces of information that confirm what we already believe. If we set out to validate our ideas, there's a good chance we'll find – or select – evidence that supports our belief.

Instead, I encourage you to think of it as **testing** your ideas. Test to see where your idea falls down. And why. Then use this information to improve it.

Strength of Evidence

In their book *Testing Business Ideas*, David Bland and Alex Osterwalder introduce a powerful concept of strength of evidence – and apply it in very practical ways. They describe the book as "a field guide for rapid experimentation". And it is. Each of the experiment methods in the book has an "evidence strength" rating. Just like opinions though, not all evidence is equal.

I strongly recommend getting a copy of *Testing Business Ideas*. This is one of a few books that I'll refer to when it comes to more thinking about detailed techniques to try, rather than duplicating great work that's already been done.

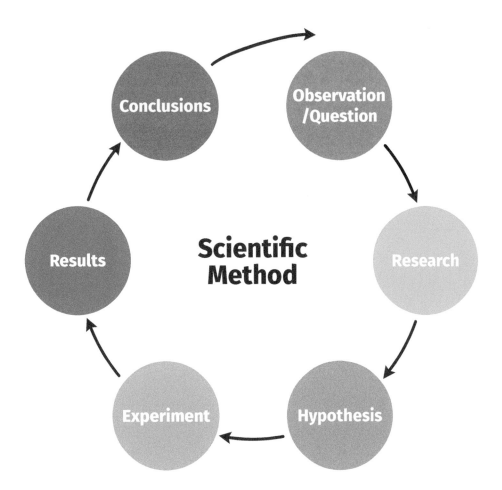

Scientific
Method

Observation
/Question

Research

Hypothesis

Experiment

Results

Conclusions

Lean Startup

During the 2010s, lean startup became the generally accepted way to do startups – or how an established organisation should launch a new solution. It takes a very scientific approach, and the cycle looks very similar with its build, measure, learn loop. You're probably noticing some recurring themes with the approaches I'm outlining.

Eric Ries' *The Lean Startup* from 2011 is one of the most famous books from this movement – and it builds on great work by Steve Blank.

Business Model Generation by Alexander Osterwalder & Co in 2010 gave us the Business Model Canvas – which had already been around for a couple of years. This is still my favourite business book. It's not necessarily part of the lean startup movement, but it's definitely widely used by it.

In 2010 Ash Maurya published the excellent *Running Lean* and adapted the Business Model Canvas to create the Lean Canvas – with more of a focus on early-stage startups or solutions. His *Love the Problem* blog (blog.leanstack.com) is always insightful and worth following.

A lot of principles from the lean startup movement can be traced back to lean manufacturing and lean software development. The original lean principles can be summed up as "...a way to do more and more with less and less – less human effort, less equipment, less time, and less space – while coming closer and closer to providing customers exactly what they want". You can probably see the attraction.

These are some of the books I recommend. They've been very valuable and the source of a lot of inspiration for me over the years. I still use these tools regularly, and I'll refer to them in this book.

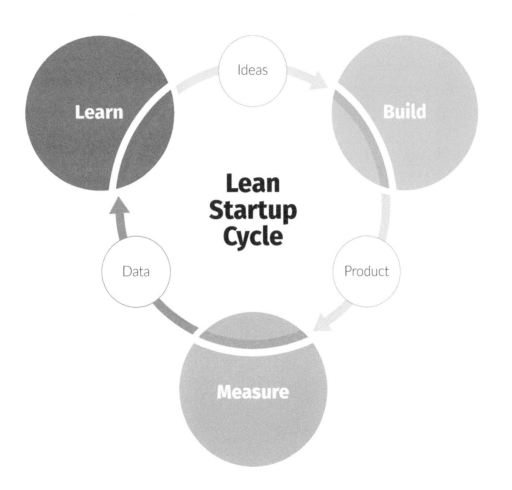

Agile Ways of Working

Agile originated in the world of software development, but over the years people have recognised the principles are also valuable in many other contexts. In this book we'll use some agile ways of working to help us plan, reflect, and build momentum.

The *Agile Manifesto* was published in 2001 as a response to challenges people developing software were facing in the 1990s – and still often face today. Some of the key issues were caused by the planning and documentation requirements of traditional methods like Waterfall.

When I say manifesto, you might picture a big methodology textbook, but the *Agile Manifesto* is actually a concise statement of four values and 12 principles, which only takes a couple of minutes to read (agilemanifesto.org). These values and principles apply just as much to any kind of innovation and solution, as they do to software.

If you read the manifesto you'll notice it's not a methodology with process, rituals, and tools. Over the years, frameworks have emerged layered on top of Agile principles – though sometimes dogmatically with rigid rules, ironically ignoring the very first principle of Agile: people over process. That's not how we'll approach it though.

How We'll Use It

Agile is a way of thinking and working that prioritises people – how they interact and collaborate – over process and tools. It's about responding to change and iterating, rather than holding yourself hostage to a static plan. It's about delivering value to the people who use your solution – early and often and refining your solution based on what you learn from them – not waiting until you think you have the perfect solution before getting it out into the world.

These principles are core to the approach we take in this book. We'll also use some practices that are common to agile ways of working, and help bring the principles to life. They work best when they become a positive habit, and a natural part of your workflow.

I've based this book around five sprints of two weeks each, plus a sprint zero of three weeks. That's a total of 13 weeks and about 90 days. I've found this is a good timeframe to keep focused and build meaningful momentum. You'll adapt this to your personal situation in Chapter 3: Make It Happen. Let's cover some of the key concepts now, so you know how.

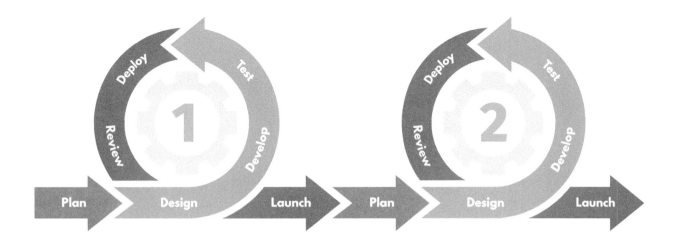

Sprints

A sprint in agile is simply a short repeating cycle that breaks projects or your workload into manageable pieces. They're usually the same length of time – two weeks is probably the most common – but applying people over process, you might find three or four weeks works better for you, or even one week. It will probably take some experimenting to get into your sustainable rhythm.

Over the years, I've found two-week sprints work best in most contexts – and I use this rhythm across all aspects of my life. It's a timeframe where I usually know the main things that will need my time and energy and how much capacity I'll have – same as the people I'm working with.

Within these known constraints, we can set realistic goals for the sprint, and plan the

work for it with a high degree of confidence. I also find it's a good timeframe for a rhythm of planning, doing and delivering the work, and reflecting on how things went.

I frequently use a sprint zero as a time to set the scene, mobilise, and plan the first real sprint. That's what you're doing right now. This chapter is part of Part 1: Setting the Scene – which is our Sprint 0. In certain circles the concept of sprint zero is a contentious one, but that's a distraction.

Part of the sprint rhythm is a session to finish the current sprint and get ready for the next one. The sequence of these sessions is normally a showcase to demonstrate what has been produced, a retro to reflect on how things are going, and then planning for the next sprint to have a clear plan to execute.

Showcase

The purpose of a showcase (also known as a sprint demo or review) is to demonstrate the work you've done at the end of the sprint. A key word here is "done". Being clear on what you plan to demo at the next showcase during your sprint planning will help you keep focused rather than leaving things open-ended.

The challenge here is to share a coherent story by the end of each sprint. This is about showing the product of your work – not a walkthrough of your task list. What a good showcase looks like will iterate as you progress.

I know you may be working solo – as a team of one right now. In Chapter 1, we used a broad definition of team to identify some important people in your support network. You might not do a showcase every sprint but it's worth doing one at major milestones, and one or more of these people could be a good audience for your showcase. At certain points you might want to present significant findings and insights to potential customers as your showcase. Treat showcases as a great opportunity to get feedback and fresh perspectives. This is an area where having a coach can be really valuable.

Retros

The purpose of a retrospective (retro for short) is to reflect on how things went over the past sprint and build a practice of continual improvement.

When doing this as a team, I recommend some personal reflection first.

Have a think about your mindset. When and how did you practice a growth mindset? When did you observe a fixed mindset in yourself? What were the triggers? What behaviours manifested? How did you move out of that state? What did you do well? What didn't you do so well (and why)? What did you learn? What will you personally do better or differently during the next sprint?

A team retro commonly focuses on those three key questions, and is something you discuss as a group. Some keys to a good retro are communicating openly and honestly, and keeping the focus on how to improve, rather than assigning blame.

1. What's working well?
2. What's not working so well?
3. What did we learn, and what improvements will you implement for the next sprint, and how?

The improvements you identify – and agree to prioritise – are then included in sprint planning, with how you'll implement them.

Sprint Planning

Some people will do no planning and call it agile, but agile is very much about planning – just in shorter cycles with iteration and learning embedded in the way of working. Sprint planning is focused on the sprint you're about to start. This is the short-term getting it done planning, but it also needs be in the context of the bigger piece of work or roadmap that you're working towards – which we'll start working on in the next chapter.

As part of the roadmap, it's generally good practice to give each sprint a theme or a focus. In this book, each sprint has a theme based on where we're at in the double diamond, and what our focus is. That's why I've mapped our sprints against the double diamond with the parts and chapters of the book. This will hopefully help you get into the sprint rhythm, even if you haven't used this approach before.

You'll need a more detailed level of planning specific to your situation to turn this into a plan to make it happen. This includes being explicit about the capacity you have for the sprint, the specific work to be done, how you'll know when it's done, and some rough estimates on how much work each activity is. It will take practice. But remember, learning and refining your planning is a natural part of this approach. I could write a another book just on this, but there are plenty of good

articles online, and it's definitely a case of learning through doing. This is an area where coaching can really help.

A principle from Kanban, a popular agile framework, that I think is really useful in our context to help with focus, is to limit work in progress. Rather than working on 50 things simultaneously, all partly done, try experimenting with working on just a few things at once, with a way of knowing when they're done – at least for now. When you reach that point, mark it as done (it feels good!) and add additional things you might improve in the future to your backlog.

By the end of the sprint planning session, everyone involved needs to be clear – and for it to be captured – on what you plan to do, by when, and how progress will be tracked and communicated – internally as a team, and with other key stakeholders. Or even just for yourself. I'm a fan of John Stepper's *Working Out Loud* principles – including "visible work", which I try to practice.

There are a lot of other terms related to sprint planning, like epics, user stories, backlog, backlog grooming, sizing or estimation, velocity, and many more. I'm sharing just enough core concepts here to get started and build our sprint rhythm. Visit dynamic4.com/sptm for links to some other useful resources when you're ready.

This chapter has focused on sharing some foundational concepts, terms, and ways of working that we'll continually refer to and build on through this book. It's now time to dive into you, your context, your idea… and how we'll build momentum to make it happen.

Chapter 3

Make It Happen

"Most people overestimate what they can do in one year and underestimate what they can do in ten years."

Bill Gates

Let's talk about making it happen. This means getting into your rhythm of prioritising, planning, reviewing, and building momentum so you can move forward with confidence.

The nature of this journey, and working with complex problems, is there are a lot of unknowns and uncertainty. While we need to embrace the ambiguity, we need enough certainty in the way we approach finding the answers to get clarity. This means having enough structure to guide us and sustain momentum without it being rigid and getting in the way of progress. I think of this as "freedom through structure".

Some key recommendations:

Don't let what you can't do stop you from doing what you can do. Something I regularly see working with people on leadership, design, and innovation programs is the tendency to pause or stop when there's a barrier – especially when something expected has been delayed. I observe this behaviour in myself too – including while writing this book. It's critical to keep moving with the things you can do rather than fixating on what you can't.

It's easy to get distracted hunting for the perfect planning tool. There are a lot of tools out there, and most of them do something well, but it's unlikely any of them will meet all of your needs. It can be very easy to trial one tool after another, trying to find the perfect one. I've done it plenty of times myself, and it's a massive distraction.

I recommend working with the simplest tool you have for now, even if that's just pen and paper, Word, or Docs. As things mature, you might want to look at more tools, but the primary focus is getting into a sustainable rhythm and way of working.

Momentum is extremely valuable, and a lot of what we'll cover now is about building and maintaining it. It can be hard to build and easy to lose, but when you keep it going, everything flows with much less effort.

I deliberated covering this topic early in the book because I know it can be a bit of a barrier, and many people don't enjoy planning... or enjoy it too much and use the perfect plan to avoid getting into the work. In the end though, I decided it's too important to delay.

The whole book is based on a 90-day plan which is broken into a Sprint 0 (we're in that now) and five execution sprints. In this chapter, you'll plan your 90 days and adapt where needed. You'll also refer to this chapter regularly until you've built your sustainable rhythm.

See Your Future

Something that really helps make your future feel real is to visualise the future you're working towards. Part of that is being honest with yourself about what you want – getting clear on your driving why – a purpose you really care about, and that will motivate you. Your clear and powerful driving why that gives you meaning will help you persevere and keep moving forward when you're facing obstacles and barriers. For this reason, it's critical to the process of making it happen.

We'll cover this in more detail in Chapter 4: Purpose, Vision & Theory of Change, but start with what you have now. This won't be the last time we look at this, and I'll nudge you back to this chapter as we progress to continue reflecting and refining.

Your 10-Year Vision

Visualising something 10 years from now can be challenging. It can feel like an abstract and distant future with too many unknowns. I find it helps to start by contextualising my vision with some things I know and some trends I anticipate. With systems change, we often talk about a seven-to-10-year time horizon for the social and environmental impacts that we're working towards to really manifest. Be bold and optimistic when visualising this future.

> "You don't need eyes to see, you need vision."

Reverence by Faithless (Maxi Jazz)

10-Year Vision

Let's start your 10-year vision. Start with what comes to you and loop back to iterate it as you think about it more.

Start by adding 10 to today's year. It's 20__.

What does your life look like?

- How old will you be?
- How old will members of your family and friends be?
- Where might you be living?
- What types of things might be going on?
- Add some layers of depth to it

What does the world look like?

- What are the trends you're seeing, and where do you anticipate it to be in 10 years?
- What are the effects of climate change?
- What are the social conditions? Think more broadly than the specific things you're focused on, and include the broader system trends

What does your social enterprise look like?

- How are you spending your time?
- How many people are in your team?
- What's the culture of your organisation like? What does it feel like to work there?
- What are the moving parts of your organisation?
- What social and environmental impacts are you contributing to? How do you know?
- What do your customers say about you?
- What do your financials look like?

Your 3-Year Picture

Now that you've got some detail and context for your 10-year vision, it will be easier to break that down and form a picture of where you want to be three years from now. This would be a major stepping stone to getting some key pieces in place on the journey to your 10-year vision. Working back from that 10-year vision, what would you need to have in place within three years?

Again, it can still feel like an abstract future with a lot of unknowns. Let's go through the same process to contextualise your three-year picture. If going from 10 to three years feels like too much of a jump, feel free to add a five-year picture too.

Your 3-Year Picture

Let's start your three-year picture. Start with what comes to you and loop back to iterate it as you think about it more.

Start by adding 3 to today's year. It's 20__.

What does your life look like?

- How old will you be?
- How old will members of your family and friends be?
- Where might you be living?
- What types of things might be going on?
- Add some layers of depth to it

What does the world look like?

- What are the trends you're seeing, and where do you anticipate it to be in three years?
- What are the effects of climate change?
- What are the social conditions? Think more broadly than the specific things you're focused on, and include the broader system trends

What does your social enterprise look like?

- How are you spending your time?
- How many people are in your team?
- What's the culture of your organisation like? What does it feel like to work there?
- What are the moving parts of your organisation?
- What social and environmental impacts are you contributing to? How do you know?
- What do your customers say about you?
- What do your financials look like?

Use Objectives & Key Results (OKRs)

Objectives and key results (OKR) is a goal-setting framework that helps you set and track measurable goals – or objectives. OKR was created by Andy Grove in the 1970s, but has become very popular over the past decade.

If you're not already familiar with OKRs, you might be more familiar with KPIs (key performance indicators). On the surface they might seem like the same thing, but I find OKRs simpler and much more powerful.

The main purpose of OKRs is to set clear goals for the organisation, and connect them directly to the teams and people in the organisation. They're focused on defining improvement areas and driving change rather than tracking business performance metrics. This helps with clarity on what we're working towards – even if we're still solo – and it improves collaboration and communication based on transparency and accountability. The intent is to connect these strategic goals with our daily work.

John Doerr, who learnt the OKR framework from Andy Grove at Intel, and is credited with popularising the method, distils OKRs to this simple sentence in his book *Measure What Matters*: "I will [objective] as measured by [key result]". Simple but powerful.

Let's cover the basics now, but you can visit dynamic4.com/sptm for links to other great resources on OKRs.

What Time Period?

The first thing to think about when setting OKRs is the time period you're setting them for. We'll talk about setting one-year and 90-day OKRs in a moment. Generally, you start with the longer time period, set the OKRs, and then set shorter-term OKRs that contribute to the longer-term OKRs.

Be Ambitious

OKRs are intended to be used as a stretch goal. They need to be ambitious and slightly out of reach. This might feel a bit uncomfortable. We'll talk about that in a moment, but when grading OKRs to see how we've progressed and performed, the sweet spot is getting to 60-70% achieved.

Set Your Objectives

The first part of OKRs is the objective. This is a simple, clear sentence stating the outcome or goal that you want to achieve. They provide direction. It is qualitative and states what you want to improve. You don't want any ambiguity with what the objective is. Objectives answer the question "what are we doing?"

An example: "Increase the use of solution X".

It's generally recommended that you have up to five objectives for the time period you're setting the OKRs for.

I strongly recommend that at least one of these five be specifically focused on impact. With an embedded impact model, all of the OKRs will be actively contributing to your impact. These are important lead indicators that let you know if you're on the right track and making progress towards delivering on the social and environmental impact you've described in your theory of change – which we'll look at more in the next chapter – and your triple bottom line.

Set Your Key Results

The second part of OKRs is the key results. They're quantitative and help you know how you've progressed toward achieving the objective. Key results answer the question "how do we know when we've achieved our objective?"

An example: "100 new active users". This would make the full example OKR statement "I will increase the use of solution X as measured by 100 new active users".

It's generally recommended that each objective has up to four key results. Each key result is very specific and measurable. The purpose is to be able to measure how much progress you've made and if you've achieved the key result and the objective. Key results aren't tasks or initiatives.

Map Your Initiatives

Initiatives are an important part of the OKR framework, and are often overlooked or conflated with key results. Initiatives are the specific work you'll do to make progress towards achieving a key result. This is how you map your daily work to reach your objectives. Initiatives answer the question "what will I do to achieve our key results?"

An initiative for our example OKR statement might be a marketing campaign to increase awareness and onboard new users.

Initiatives are your action plan. Each OKR needs to be mapped to at least one initiative. This might be a task, a set of activities, or even a project.

Grade Your OKRs

Reviewing progress against our OKRs and grading them is a key part of the framework. This is one of the reasons I find OKRs much more useful than other goal-setting frameworks. OKRs help us move beyond a binary pass or fail mentality.

OKR grading is simple. The original is a scale from 0.0 to 1.0. Rather than dealing in fractions, I find it easier to think of it as a percentage, which is how I'll talk about it here. So 1.0 equals 100% achieved.

Remember, our OKRs are ambitious stretch goals. If you're regularly hitting 100%, you probably need to be a bit more ambitious with your key results. A grade of 70% is actually a really good score. A common use of the range is:

- 0-39%: we didn't make any meaningful progress on this key result

- 40-69%: we made real progress but didn't quite get there

- 70-100%: we achieved our key result

Grading our example OKR statement is simple. Let's say we managed to get 60 new active users. Our ambitious target was 100 – so we got 60 of the 100 users we were aiming for. That gives us a grade of 60%. We made real progress, but didn't quite get there. It's not a failure though – we got 60 new active users, and that's something to celebrate!

To get the overall grade for the objective, you can average the key results. This generally works, but sometimes one key result is more important than the others and deserves a higher weighting. This is when I'll adjust the overall grade for the objective, so it makes sense.

I recommend approaching the grading with the "power of yet" thinking. The important thing is to reflect regularly on how you're progressing. Celebrate the wins as they happen. Anything in the 40-100% range means you've definitely got something to celebrate. Where things haven't progressed as you'd planned, understand why. Sometimes this is for a good reason, like a shift in priorities.

OKRs aren't intended to be static. Don't hold yourself hostage to them. Refine them as you learn, and as priorities change. Don't beat yourself up when you don't make the progress you planned. Understand the reasons and adjust.

From this description, I hope you can see how these pieces flow and fit together. Our purpose, vision, and theory of change drive our objectives. We measure progress toward our objectives with key results. The OKRs we've set determine the work we'll do (initiatives) to make it a reality. Our OKRs drive the prioritisation of the work we'll do… and the momentum we'll build.

Let's start putting this into action now.

Build Momentum

A core focus of this book is to help you build momentum to make it happen. We've just been talking about seeing the future over the next three and 10 years with OKRs as a tool to start making the big picture more tangible. Let's start getting down to a clear action plan to build momentum over the next year, and then we'll zoom in on the next 90 days.

We're going to use OKRs as the goal-setting framework for the one-year time horizon as well as 90 days. Generally, OKRs are used for 90-day periods with other frameworks for longer periods. To avoid that complexity, we'll use OKRs for both. The key is that OKRs are reviewed and graded regularly – and necessary refinements made. Over time you might want to experiment with other frameworks for longer-term planning.

1-Year Plan with OKRs

You spent some time visualising the future you're working towards with your 10-Year Vision and 3-Year Picture. This bigger picture is critical to have a vision state to be working towards. To achieve that desired future, what do you need to do over the next year?

The one-year time period is mostly arbitrary, and you might find it makes sense to anchor it to a date like the calendar year, the end of the financial year, or another date that means something to you. These temporal landmarks – or key events – are actually psychologically powerful.

Your 1-Year Plan

Let's start your one-year plan. Start with what comes to you and come back to iterate it as you think about it more. Don't expect that you'll be able to put together a complete plan in one session. Depending on where you're at in your journey, you won't know the answer to some of these questions yet – and that's ok.

What's the end date of this plan? Be specific.

What does your social enterprise look like?

- How are you spending your time?
- How many people are in your team, and what are their roles?
- What's the culture of your organisation like? What does it feel like to work there?
- What social and environmental value are you creating, and how do you know?

- What do your customers say about you?
- How many people are using your solution?
- How many paying customers do you have?
- How much revenue are you making each month?
- How much does it cost to operate the organisation each month?
- What's the financial surplus or deficit of the organisation each month?
- What's the total financial surplus or deficit of the organisation for the year?

This list isn't exhaustive, but it will help you think about your goals – even when you don't know the answer yet. Getting the answer might be one of your goals. Add other questions that are on your mind.

Your 1-Year OKRs

What are your goals for the next year? We're going to use OKRs to capture your thinking. Repeat this format for each of your OKRs – no more than five objectives.

Objective 1: Clear, simple, and compelling objective statement

> **Key Result 1:** What is the quantifiable measure that will help you know how you've progressed toward achieving the objective? Add up to four key results for each objective.
>
>> **Initiative:** What is the initiative that will progress this key result? Each key result might have multiple initiatives, and each initiative might contribute to multiple key results.
>
> **Key Result 2**
>> **Initiative**

Objective 2
> **Key Result (1-4)**
>> **Initiative**

I'll share more about reviewing and planning your one-year cycle in Part 4: Sustain Momentum.

Your 90-Day Plan

Up to this point, we've been setting the scene and easing in. We've covered important points on mindset, and hopefully you've started practising some happiness habits. We did a fly-through of the chapter on approach and philosophy, which covered the foundational concepts and terms that we'll now start building on.

You've also started the process of thinking about the vision you're working towards. Depending on where you're at in your journey, the one-year plan we just started might've been quite challenging to think through and might be pretty empty right now – especially the OKRs. That's ok. It will iterate and refine.

It's now game time! We're going to start changing gears and get really focused on your idea with an actionable plan over the next 90 days.

As you know, I've designed this book and program based on a 90-day plan. This is a starting point, and it might work with the realities of your schedule. It might not. Some people will need more time, and others will want to move through quicker. Both are ok. The important thing is to be clear on the overall approach and have a plan.

I still recommend focusing on the next 90 days for your plan. Refer back to the How to Use This Book chapter for the overview of what we'll focus on in each part of the book.

In a project-based experiential learning environment – with some preparation and guidance from an experienced coach – you can move through the whole program in 10 weeks.

Timeline Considerations

I'll briefly share some of my runsheet calculations and rationale to help with your planning. There's a lot here, but there's even more I'd love to share. We're getting down to the very specific detail needed for your actionable plan now. This is probably going to feel like a lot, but in the next section we'll work through it one step at a time, and you can refer back to this.

Part 1: Setting the Scene

We're into the second half of Sprint 0 which is three weeks long. I allowed just under two weeks to get to this point. It's been about two hours of reading – definitely the most text-heavy part of the book – and some actions. Probably a lot of thinking. Hopefully some interesting conversations.

I've allowed just over a week to put together your 90-day plan, briefly talk about your riskiest assumptions and sharing your story – and frame up your purpose, vision, and theory of change in Chapter 4. From this point in the book, it's much less reading and much more doing.

This is an inward-looking phase to sharpen self-awareness and start articulating your and your organisation's "I" and "We" perspectives – and what you really care about. This is the start of the problem diamond. The first people we need to start with are ourselves.

Part 2: People, Problem & Context

Part 2: People, Problem & Context is focused on the problem diamond. This is about really understanding the current reality, which means spending time with the people you are designing with and for – to deeply understand how they experience the problem, test your risky assumptions, and refine your thinking.

By the end of this phase, we want to have reached a point of sharp clarity on the real problem to solve – based on evidence, insight, and meaningful empathy.

Why three sprints/six weeks? Three key reasons for this:

- **Learning curve.** For most people, there are at least a few new things in this phase. One is customer research and synthesis, especially taking a design research approach rather than being marketing focused. Another big one is system mapping

- **Logistics.** Preparing for and setting up customer interviews often takes time. It's best to get this started early during this phase

- **Thinking time.** This phase is usually pretty intense and confronting – which means it can be uncomfortable. Expect your thinking and worldview to be challenged. This usually takes some time to think and feel through. It will be tempting to move through it quickly, but it's really important to immerse in the problem space

There are three areas primarily focused on divergent exploration of the current state:

- **Current state.** This is focused on where you're at right now and crystalising your current thinking. You'll also zoom out to briefly map the system(s) you're working in, and how your organisation fits in this context
- **Customer research.** This is preparing for and having conversations with the people you are designing with and for. You can't build meaningful empathy without this, and you need to take the time to build these connections
- **Market research.** This is understanding the market dynamics. Who's already in the market? How do they approach the problem? Are they successful? What's their business model, and how do they price things? What's the market size and opportunity? Most of this is secondary or desk research, but you probably want to include some of it in your customer research – to understand your potential customers' perspectives on the market.

What they see as their options, how they currently solve their problem, and how they make those decisions

The final piece here is to make sense of your research findings. Synthesising these different perspectives and integrating them into your thinking – which means your thinking will evolve. This is a convergent process to narrow your focus and get clarity on the real problem to solve.

There's a fair bit here, and it's not a linear process. It can be quite an emotional process. If you're not feeling challenged by what you're learning in your research and it's all confirming what you already thought… I encourage you to dig deeper. And be very aware of your confirmation bias. I've never been through this phase without it resulting in a massive shift in my thinking, and a realisation that I was making some very invalid assumptions. At the very least, it should result in a refined understanding of your customers' mental models, and the language they use to describe their experience.

In terms of sequencing, your current state snapshot should be very fast, and is worth doing first – it's designed to flow on from Chapter 4. Mapping the system will probably take a bit more time and thought, and can continue in parallel to your customer research. You'll want to test some of your understanding of the system in these conversations though.

I recommend starting on Chapter 6: Customer Research within the first couple of days of Sprint 1. As I mentioned, the combination of the learning curve and time to set up the logistics puts this on the critical path. There will probably be more than one round of customer research required – an exploratory phase, and another to test key assumptions to make sure you really understand the current reality.

Chapter 7: Market Research can be done throughout this phase. Make customer research the priority though. Your understanding of how the market is even defined will likely evolve as you build empathy and gain insight from talking with your customers.

Chapter 8: Make Sense. In reality, you'll be making sense and synthesising the information you're gathering throughout this whole phase. This is the series of smaller diverge/converge diamonds I mentioned in the Double Diamond section. I recommend allowing at least a week, probably two, to bring all of your research findings together to find the patterns, themes, and insights. This will include synthesising and integrating your original thinking and internal perspective with your increased understanding of the systems involved, the empathy and insights from your customers, and a clearer picture of the market.

By the end point of this phase, you want sharp clarity on the real problem to solve – based on evidence, insight, and meaningful empathy. You'll have mapped the current experience, have a list of key insights, and a draft value proposition that you'll take into the next phase to test and explore possible solutions for.

Part 3: Solution & Business Model

Part 3: Solution & Business Model is focused on the solution diamond exploring possible ways to solve the real problem you've identified. This means prototyping, testing, and refining the solution and your business model.

Why only two sprints/four weeks? A couple of reasons for this:

- The focus of this phase is primarily on the strategic design of your solution and business model. We'll be approaching this in a way that reduces the risk of overinvesting time, money, and energy in a solution no one will use or pay for. The priority is to test demand quickly and cheaply before building your full solution

- This is the beginning, not the end. You'll continue this process in Part 4: Sustain Momentum as part of continuing to refine your idea and respond to what you're learning

In terms of sequencing, Chapter 9 starts with exploring possible solutions – this flows on directly from Chapter 8, and is the start of the solution diamond. It's important not to skip the step of testing your draft value proposition, generating multiple ideas of how to solve the problem, and prototyping your business model.

I recommend setting up the logistics for some customer interview sessions a week or two before you plan to start this phase, which might include people you spoke with during your customer research. These interviews are to test your draft value proposition. You might even start co-designing some solution concepts with your customers.

We talk about specific things in Chapters 9, 10, 11, and 12, but in reality, they all go together and are part of a rapid and iterative process to test solutions concepts, business models, and pricing – with what that means for your financial model.

Chapter 12: Financials. This will iterate at a high level as you explore possible solutions and the business model. As you get more confident – based on evidence – that there's demand for your solution and the price people will pay, you'll develop a more robust financial model.

Chapter 13: Legals. Thinking about the legal requirements and implications needs to happen throughout the whole journey. You should probably read this chapter now. Definitely read this chapter before making decisions on your organisation's legal structure and team – if you haven't already. There are also some important considerations when it comes to potential requirements to be able to legally operate in certain industries and locations.

Part 4: Sustain Momentum

Part 4: Sustain Momentum is focused on continuing the sustainable rhythm and momentum you've been building to move forward with confidence past the 90 days of the standard program. You'll continue designing, building, and launching refinements to your solution based on insights from real use.

You probably want to include this in your next 90-day cycle of planning.

Now that you've got more context and rationale on how the overall program and timeline hang together, it's time for you to create your own 90-day plan with OKRs. This is a very experiential journey, and while it's important to have a plan and timebox the activities, it's even more important to respond to what you're learning.

Some of this won't make a lot of sense until you're actually doing it. Reflecting on what you're learning and refining your plan is baked into the rhythm. Coaching can really help guide you through this process.

90-Day Plan & OKRs

I'm conscious that the last section is probably a bit like drinking from a firehose, and it might be a bit overwhelming. You'll work through it one step at a time now though.

Before getting into your plan, let's consciously switch gears. Time to take a breath. Literally. It's also time to review the actions you've completed because they're part of this planning.

Review Your Strategy

Simple Deep Breathing Exercise

Hopefully, you've been doing your two minutes of breathing regularly. If you haven't and need a refresher, have a look at the Happiness Habits section of Chapter 1: Mindset. Do a couple of minutes of the deep breathing exercise now to calm things down and change your brain chemistry to a more positive state.

Your Strengths & Assets

Take a moment to review your strengths and assets that you have identified. Acknowledge and really value what you're bringing to this.

Your Team

Review the list of people you identified who make up your team and broader support network. Remember why they're part of your team and why you value them. How will you get them involved or at least keep them in the loop over the next 90 days?

10-Year Vision

Pause and really visualise that optimistic future you're working towards. Imagine how it will feel when it's a reality. You might want to try your deep breathing exercise while visualising this. See if you can immerse in it.

3-Year Picture

Continue visualising your 10-year view and bring it closer to your three-year picture.

1-Year Plan with OKRs

Review your one-year plan and the OKRs you drafted.

We've started with the big picture vision you're working towards and why. You know the value you're bringing to work on this. We've connected that vision to action over the next year, the stepping stones to get there. Now, it's time to zoom in on the next 90 days – the overarching approach and the sustainable rhythm you'll build and repeat on a two-week cycle.

Your 90-Day OKRs

Your OKRs for the next 90 days need to align with and help you progress towards the one-year plan and OKRs you set.

For now, I suggest the key theme of the next 90 days is to complete the approach outlined in Part 2: People, Problem & Context and Part 3: Solution & Business Model of this book. A key part of this is building your sustainable rhythm so you can continue moving forward with confidence.

Your 90-Day OKRs

Let's start your 90-day OKRs. This set of OKRs needs to align with and help you progress toward your annual OKRs. Start with what comes to you and loop back to iterate it as you think about it more. Don't expect that you'll be able to put together a complete plan in one session.

What's the end date of this plan? Be specific. Add this date after you've done the next action on your 90-day approach.

What are your goals for the 90 days? What questions do you want to answer?

Repeat this format for each of your OKRs – no more than five objectives.

Objective 1: Clear, simple, and compelling objective statement

> **Key Result 1:** What is the quantifiable measure that will help you know how you've progressed toward achieving the objective? Add up to four key results for each objective.
>
> > **Initiative:** What is the initiative that will progress this key result? Each key result might have multiple initiatives, and each initiative might contribute to multiple key results.
>
> **Key Result 2**
> > **Initiative**

Objective 2
> **Key Result (1-4)**
> > **Initiative**

I'll share more about reviewing and planning your 90-day cycle in Part 4: Sustain Momentum.

Your 90-Day Approach

A lot of the people I work with don't have much experience in planning this kind of work. I'm including some extra guidance, but if you're experienced in planning, use the process and tools that work for you.

This first planning action is high-level, and the purpose is to set the key dates and the sprint rhythm you'll follow. Each sprint will also have a focus or theme.

Choose the day of the week for your sprint to finish – and the next sprint will start on the following day. Every two weeks, you'll have a session on the last day of the sprint to showcase what you've just done, reflect, and plan for the next two weeks. This will probably take one to two hours, and it's best to keep a regular rhythm rather than changing days.

I recommend using a Kanban board tool and creating a card for each sprint as a starting point. You can do this on a wall with sticky notes, or Trello, Asana, and Clickup are some great tools for this, and have free plans. You can use the simple three-column setup to get started: "To Do", "Doing", and "Done". If you already have your own workflow, continue with what works for you.

Visit dynamic4.com/sptm for an example plan as a Kanban board.

Your 90-Day Approach Planning

Let's start with the base plan and time allocation. Adjust these to fit your schedule and capacity where you need to. It's preferable for each sprint to have a theme or focus.

Choose the day of the week for your sprint to finish. The next sprint will start on the following day.

Sprint 0

Focus: Purpose, Vision & Theory of Change

There's about one week left of Sprint 0. Make the end date about a week from now on the day of the week you'll have your regular sprint planning session.

Sprint 0 start date:

Sprint 0 end date:

Sprint 1

Focus: Current state snapshot. System mapping. Customer research prep and interviews

Sprint 1 start date:

Sprint 1 end date:

Sprint 2

Focus: Customer research interviews. Market research

Sprint 2 start date:

Sprint 2 end date:

Sprint 3

Focus: Making sense. Draft value proposition

Sprint 3 start date:

Sprint 3 end date:

Sprint 4

Focus: Explore possible solutions. Prototype, test, and learn. Pricing. Draft financials

Sprint 4 start date:

Sprint 4 end date:

Sprint 5

Focus: Prototype, test, and learn. Pricing. Refine financials

Sprint 5 start date:

Sprint 5 end date:

Your Sprint 0 Plan

Now you have your high-level plan with each of the sprints and dates. And you know what you plan to be focused on in each of these sprints. Let's do the more detailed plan for the remaining week of Sprint 0.

---- ACTION ----

Your Sprint 0 Plan

Focus: Purpose, Vision & Theory of Change

Sprint end date: You know your sprint end date from your 90-day Approach Planning

At the top of the "To Do" column of your Kanban board, create cards for each of the things we'll focus on to finish Sprint 0. Have a quick look at Chapter 4 to see what's involved for each of these actions.

- Your Personal Why
- Your Organisation's Purpose & Vision
  - Start With Who
  - Your Golden Circle
  - Your Purpose Statement
- Your Theory of Change
  - Your Theory of Change Logic Model
  - Test Your Theory of Change

- Measure Outcomes & Impact
  - Your Impact Measures
  - Your SDGs
  - Your Outcome Measures
  - Your Output Measures

This gives you a clear view of the work to be done. When you start work on a card, move it from the "To Do" column to "Doing". Most of the time, it's best to only have one or two cards that you're actively working on in the "Doing" list.

When you've completed the work on the card, move it from "Doing" to "Done". It's very satisfying seeing the number of cards in the "Done" column increase, and it helps you keep track of how much you've progressed.

Your Sprint Rhythm

The last few actions are the start of getting into your sprint rhythm with quarterly (90-day) reflections. As I've mentioned, it will take some practice and experimentation to find your sustainable sprint rhythm and get into a smooth workflow.

While we use the term "sprint", don't take this to literally mean that you're always running as fast as you possibly can. Think of it as two-week cycles of sustained focus. At the end of each cycle, you pause, take a breath, reflect on how it went, and plan for the next cycle.

There are different ways to do this, but I find it normally works best to have a single Sprint Review & Plan session to do a showcase, retro, and sprint planning. We covered some of the basics on each of these as part of Agile Ways of Working in Chapter 2: Approach & Philosophy. This is also an important part of our reflective practice that we talked about as part of Action Leaning in the same chapter. Please refer back to that chapter for more explanation if you need it.

Note: You'll probably do the showcase as a separate session when you include other stakeholders or customers. I still recommend including the showcase as part of your regular session as a good practice run.

Each Sprint Review & Plan session has three key elements. I strongly encourage you to consistently do this at the end of each sprint.

ACTION

Your Sprint Rhythm: Showcase

The purpose of a showcase is to demonstrate the work you've done at the end of the sprint.

Start the meeting by having everyone share their best piece of news – this might be work-related or personal. Sharing and celebrating these wins starts the meeting on a positive note, and helps set the right tone and energy for the session.

Show the product of your work from the sprint. Showing is a lot more compelling than telling. The aim is to share this as a coherent story.

This is also a good opportunity to practice and refine your story.

---- ACTION ----

Your Sprint Rhythm: Retro

The purpose of the retro is to reflect on how things went over the past sprint and build a practice of continual improvement. When doing this as a team, I recommend doing some personal reflection first.

Three key questions to reflect on and discuss:

1. What's working well?
2. What's not working so well?

3. What did we learn, and what improvements will we implement for the next sprint, and how?

The retro is also an important part of the reflect and conclude steps in your action learning loop. This is a good opportunity to review your key insights and assumptions.

---- ACTION ----

Your Sprint Rhythm: Sprint Planning

The purpose of sprint planning is to have a more detailed plan for the sprint you're about to start. Be realistic about the capacity you have, and prioritise the work to be done. You'll also need to define when each piece of work is done, and have some rough estimates of how much work each activity is.

This follows the same process and builds on the Your Sprint 0 Plan action you did.

By the end of the sprint planning session, everyone involved needs to be clear on what you plan to do, by when, and how progress will be tracked and communicated – internally as a team and with other key stakeholders, or even just for yourself. The plan needs to be captured and actionable, preferably on your Kanban board.

Create Space

You might be wondering how you create space to be able to focus on the things you've prioritised. The first step is to have an inventory to see where you're spending your time and if it's effective.

As part of my Sprint Review & Plan and 90-Day Planning sessions, I review where I'm spending my time and how that aligns with my strategy and goals. I use three categories to sharpen my focus and identify specific actions to transition to this state:

- **Prioritise**. Activities that'll get me closer to my goals

- **Optimise**. Important activities, and they're often enablers of the activities to prioritise

- **Minimise**. Distractions or activities that won't directly help me get closer to my goals. Sometimes things move to this category temporarily to create space for what needs to be prioritised and optimised

Example: This is a real example from December 2020 when I needed to create space to write this book. Most of the things in the minimise category are there temporarily and will later move back to prioritise or optimise. I also listed specific actions to make the transition and set expectations.

One of the specific actions I took to manage expectations was to set an email autoreply.

The autoreply let people know my replies to email would be slower than usual because I was focusing on writing my book and batching email replies. I also gave an alternate way to contact me if it was time-sensitive.

Prioritise
- Coaching social enterprise founders and leaders
- Designing and running programs (high value and impact)
- Writing Solve Problems That Matter
- Running Jetpack sessions and coaching/office hours
- Designing and testing our products and offers

Optimise
- Strategy and high-level planning
- Marketing and comms plan. Social posts and blogs
- Sprint review and planning
- Time/finance reconciliation and reporting

Minimise
- Strategic design on client projects
- Digital/tech solution architecture and build direction
- UX/UI design direction
- Meetings/giving free advice where it's not strategically aligned
- Business development, sales, and proposal writing

Your Time Inventory & Creating Space

The first step is to create your time inventory by listing all of the things you spend your time on. This doesn't need to be limited to work-related things. Getting a full picture, including your personal responsibilities, is powerful.

How do you currently spend your time?

In the context of your 90-day plan and OKRs, review your inventory list and decide if each point is something you need to prioritise, optimise, or minimise. You can also do this for the next sprint.

Prioritise

What are the activities that will get you closer to your goals?

Optimise

What are the important activities you need to optimise and do as efficiently as possible? They're often enablers of the activities that you're prioritising.

Minimise

What activities are a distraction and won't directly help you get closer to your goals? Which activities are you minimising temporarily?

Actions

You don't want to drop things and let people down, so you need to proactively set expectations and make the transition. What actions will you take?

Manage the Noise

Creating the inventory of what you spend your time on has probably highlighted some interesting things. At times I get caught in a reactive cycle, and I know I'm not spending my time and headspace on the things that will get me closer to my goals. This is a very frustrating feeling – and for me it's driven in part by commitments I've made, and also allowing other people's expectations and priorities to dominate my own.

How do I deal with it? With one of the least popular pieces of advice I give. I track my time. I've found knowing how much time I'm investing in different areas of my organisation and various social enterprise ventures gives me the data and patterns in the data to make more informed decisions. I also believe every founder needs to know this to be able to calculate the true cost of their social enterprise idea and factor it into net breakeven calculations – which we'll cover in Chapter 12: Financials.

Example: I track my time using a simple mental model I created years ago. I use the same across multiple ventures.

1. **Think**. Strategy, high-level planning
2. **Run**. Operations, people, partners, finances, admin
3. **Grow**. Business development, marketing, sales
4. **Build (or Deliver)**. Research, design, and build solutions

As part of this process, I set personal goals for the number of hours I work each month. I also set targets for the number of hours I spend on categories that directly generate revenue compared to those that don't. This fits with my personal sustainability plan that we talked about in Chapter 1.

In summary, I strongly recommend you track your time. There are plenty of great tools for this, including many free ones. Start simple, even if that means a spreadsheet, and you'll work out what level of time tracking is useful for you.

Get in the Flow

When we build momentum and get in the flow, things move forward with a lot less effort. The way we approach each day can play a big part in this. You've probably heard people talk about decision fatigue. Research shows that we make an average of 35,000 decisions each day, and these decisions deplete our energy a little. Our self-control and willpower generally deteriorate during the day.

The common advice is to do the critical work and make important decisions in the morning. Happiness habits can play a key role here too. By being mindful and having some awareness of your chronotype, you'll notice some patterns about your energy. Working with this, and prioritising types of work based on how your energy ebbs and flows, can be powerful. I find things flow best for me late morning, and then after a lull, my energy normally builds into the evening, and I often do my best work late at night. Some people are the opposite. What's your normal pattern?

Something I've found useful is from Michael McQueen's book *Momentum*. He calls it the Productivity Blueprint. It involves thinking about "your day as a series of blocks of time". Rather than just diving straight into the most important work, which is often the most complex, he recommends approaching it in the sequence of simple, then the more complex work, and finishing with more routine tasks.

The rationale for this is it's easier to build momentum with the simple tasks and feel like you're making progress – and then build on that momentum to work on the more complex tasks. This prioritises what is often the more important work rather than constantly finding that you've run out of the time and energy to focus on it.

You might find this approach helpful when juggling your social enterprise idea with all of your other responsibilities. Working with your energy to get in the flow will help you build momentum.

Your Riskiest Assumptions

Assumptions are important. We're always working with incomplete, inaccurate, and inconsistent information. We need to make assumptions to function. As I mentioned in the Making Sense section of Chapter 2, we all have our own set of cognitive biases – and our own set of assumptions.

We know we're making assumptions all of the time. But not all assumptions are equal – some are riskier than others. We need to be aware when we're making assumptions and work out what we'll do about them.

What we do with these assumptions is what matters, especially the risky ones. The riskiest ones are those that if we don't test them and find out what the reality is now, they'll catch us out sooner or later. Especially when we rely on them to be true, and base key decisions on that false reality. This is where first principles thinking is so critical.

For clarity, we're starting with assumptions here. An assumption is something we believe without strong evidence. Or, as the *Oxford Learner's Dictionary* says, "a thing that is accepted as true or as certain to happen, without proof".

An assumption can be investigated without the need to construct a testable hypothesis and experiment. An assumption is a foundational belief, and can usually be tested with some simple research to find out what is true.

A hypothesis generally puts forward an argument and is more predictive. A good hypothesis can also be tested by an experiment, and is falsifiable. In Chapter 10: Prototype, Test & Learn, you'll turn some key assumptions into a hypothesis to test with an experiment – but let's keep it simple to start.

There are different ways to rate and prioritise the assumptions you'll test, but my simplest recommendation is to test the highest risk ones first – and don't make any key decisions based on that assumption until you've tested it.

A basic risk matrix is a useful way to give your assumption a risk rating. If there's a low likelihood the assumption is false, and the impact of it being false is also low, the overall rating is Low. If there's a high likelihood of it being false, and the impact is high, the overall rating is High.

It can also be useful to categorise your assumptions. I like the method used in *Testing Business Ideas* because it's simple and brings in the three lenses we introduced in the Design Thinking section of Chapter 2. Is the assumption about desirability, viability, or feasibility?

In the Your Sprint Rhythm section, I recommended you review your assumptions as part of your retro in each Sprint Review & Plan session. It needs to be a regular part of your workflow, not done once and never looked at again. Testing your riskiest assumptions needs to be part of every sprint.

A spreadsheet is a simple way to track your assumptions. Visit dynamic4.com/sptm for more explanation with examples, and a sample spreadsheet.

Your Assumptions Log

I strongly recommend keeping track of your assumptions. Not just the assumptions you're making, but what you've done or are doing to test them.

The first step is to identify the assumptions. How do you spot your assumptions? If you hear yourself say or think the words "it should", "I think", "I hope", or other similar phrases, these are little flags that you've probably just made an assumption.

Remember, an assumption is something we believe without strong evidence.

List. Start by making a list of your assumptions in the first column of your spreadsheet – each assumption in its own row.

Rate. In the second column, give each assumption a risk rating of High, Medium, or Low.

Categorise. In the next column, categorise the type of assumption. Is the assumption about desirability, viability, or feasibility?

Method. In the next column, how will you test that assumption?

Share Your Story

Sharing your story is an important part of the journey. A good story will resonate with your audience, engage their curiosity, and generate conversation. There's a lot of focus on "pitching" in the startup world, and a couple of the tools we're about to talk about have "pitch" in the name. I find it more helpful to think of it as sharing your story.

The goal of sharing your story in this context is generally to start a real conversation. The people you're talking with or to – preferably not talking at – need just enough information to understand what you're talking about, and not so much that they get overloaded and switch off.

This can be a tricky balance to find. There are normally so many points that we feel are really important to share, but if we share them all at once, we can lose the opportunity to continue the conversation. I know I often get this wrong. Experimentation and practice are the keys to getting better at it.

Craft Your Story

So how do we craft an engaging and compelling story? Let's cover some of the basics.

Start With Who

What we're talking about here is communication design. Good design and good communication always start with the people. The who. Who are we talking with? What do we know about them? What do they care about? How do they see the world? What's on their mind right now? The more we know about our audience and the more empathy we can build, the better our chances of crafting a message that matters to our audience.

The reality is, we often need to share our story without knowing the specific people we're sharing with. This is often the case with websites, talking to a roomful of people, or even meeting someone for the first time and not knowing anything about them.

This means you probably have a few versions of your story. You can tailor your message and be more specific with some people, and you might communicate in more general terms with others. We need to meet our audience where they are.

A golden rule of design is when you try to design for everyone, you design for no one. This applies to your story too. Wherever possible, it's better to prepare your story for a specific audience, to be shared at specific times, through specific channels, and being mindful of the feedback loop and how the conversation can continue.

Your Message

What's your message? This is where many people start, and it's their primary focus when thinking about their story. What's important to us though, might not be important to our audience. There needs to be a connection between what we want to share and what our audience is interested in and ready for. This is why we started with who, our audience.

In the context of who we're sharing with, we also need clarity on what we want to communicate and why. What would you like them to think, feel, or do based on what you share? What do they need to know to achieve this? The answer to this is your core message.

It will take experimentation and practice to see what messages resonate with different audiences. It's a process of constant iteration and refinement. You'll also find that your audience may respond differently based on the timing of what you share and the channel you use. The when and how.

When & How?

Our timing can be everything. We can share the same message at different times and get a completely different response from the same person. We can't always control the timing, but it's something to consider when sharing our story and adapting based on what we learn.

How will you share your story? What are the different channels (or mediums or methods)? We'll focus a lot on conversations, but also think about how you share your story in a digital context like websites and social media, in print, video, audio, and giving presentations to groups of people.

Marshall McLuhan famously said "the medium is the message". How and when we share our story has a profound effect on how our message is perceived. When we're crafting our story, it's important that we design for the whole experience, not just the content or message.

Continue the Conversation

What's our audience's response to our story, and how do we continue the conversation with them? What do we want to happen next? What does the person we're sharing with want to happen next?

When we share our story, there's something we want people to know or do as a result. We need to provide a clear and compelling call to action – with a simple way to continue the conversation if they're interested.

Your Gaddie Pitch

Now that we've covered some of the basics to consider when crafting our story, let's put it into action. The Gaddie Pitch is a simple three-part story created by Antony Gaddie. It's an elevator pitch that you want to be able to deliver in a conversational way in under one minute.

I use this format in our programs as a way to share a brief and simple story, but what I've found even more valuable is it really helps you get clarity on the key points to share.

The format is simple and conversational. At least it will be with practice. There are four sentences:

1. You know how...?

Briefly outline the compelling problem you're focused on with who experiences that problem. Ideally, the person you're talking with engages at an emotional level and can relate to the problem because they personally experience it, or they at least know what you're talking about and can understand why it's a problem.

2. Well, what we do is...

Briefly outline what you do about this problem, with a focus on the benefit you help create for the people involved. Try not to get too detailed or technical here. The purpose of sharing this is to engage their curiosity and start a conversation. Resist the temptation to get all the points in at once.

3. In fact...

This is a compelling proof point that provides credibility. This will evolve as you progress. A key customer insight is often very powerful here.

4. Call to action...

This isn't officially part of the Gaddie Pitch, but it's worth having a simple and compelling ask or call to action, and include it when you feel it's appropriate. People will often ask how they can help. This might be something as simple as helping you spread the word or asking for an introduction.

Example:

You might've noticed I opened this book with a Gaddie Pitch. I use a shorter version when speaking, but here it is as an example:

"You know when you have a social enterprise idea you think will help solve a problem that really matters, but you're busy, not sure how to make it happen, and it's easy to feel overwhelmed?

Well, Solve Problems That Matter is a 90-day program helping you take a human-centred approach to design, build, and launch your social enterprise idea – and build momentum to solve problems that matter.

In fact, this book is based on my experience coaching thousands of founders, leaders, designers, and university students over the years – especially social enterprise founders and NFP leaders on our Dynamic4 Jetpack program since 2014.

It also draws on the project-based experiential leadership, design, and innovation programs I've designed and delivered… and the many social enterprise startups I've co-founded."

ACTION

Your Gaddie Pitch

Now it's your turn. Write your Gaddie Pitch using these four sentences:

1. You know how…?
2. Well what we do is…
3. In fact…
4. Call to action…

The next step is to practice it and refine it, based on the feedback and reaction you get from people. This is your first Gaddie Pitch, and it will evolve over time. I recommend focusing it on your current story and where you're at today. It needs to be authentic and believable.

In the Your Sprint Rhythm section, I recommended that you practice and refine your story as part of your showcase in each Sprint Review & Plan session. Keep testing and refining your Gaddie Pitch, and you'll find a version that feels natural and resonates with your audience.

Your Pitch Deck

A pitch deck is a brief presentation that provides a concise overview of your social enterprise idea. They're a common way to share your story, but I find a lot of people place too much emphasis on pitch decks and often overinvest in them. The reason I'm introducing it now is as a tool to help you get clarity on the key points to share.

Some recommendations:

- Think about it as a way to share your story. That means thinking about how you craft your story to be relevant and compelling for your target audience. The slides are better if they support your story rather than dominate the focus

- Keep your slides simple with plenty of white space. Guy Kawasaki's golden rule of "a pitch should have ten slides, last no more than twenty minutes, and contain no font smaller than thirty points" is a good guide. The simple template I use has some additional slides I've found necessary

There's a very standard format for startup pitch decks with a few minor variations. There are also some additional things I look for when hearing the story for a social enterprise idea. The slides:

Cover

Keep your cover simple and visually engaging.

Problem/Opportunity

What's the compelling problem you're focused on, and who experiences that problem? A key customer insight here can really boost your credibility.

Value Proposition

What's the value that you create? This is often communicated as the pain you take away or the benefit you provide.

Purpose/Theory of Change

What's your driving why for the organisation? What's the positive future you're working towards? How will this idea contribute to those social and environmental outcomes and impacts? This isn't included in traditional startup pitch decks, but these are key things I want to know about social enterprise ideas.

Solution/How it Works

How do you plan to solve the problem? Ideally, this can be communicated visually and without much technical detail.

Market Opportunity

How big is the problem? Are there enough people willing to pay to do something about this problem? Who will pay? This indicates if the market is big enough for the idea to be financially viable.

Competition

What are the alternative solutions for the problem you're focused on? How do people solve the problem right now? One of the worst things you can say is that you don't have any competitors.

Business Model

How do you plan to make money? How do you deliver social and environmental value? The focus of this slide is traditionally focused on making money, but I recommend focusing on the different types of value you create – your triple bottom line.

Team

Who are the people involved, and what roles do they play? Why is this a great team to make the idea happen?

Status & Traction

Where are you currently at on your journey? What progress have you made? What are your key achievements so far?

Financial Projections & Key Metrics

What's your financial forecast over the next three years? What are your forecasted social and environmental outcomes? What are your other key metrics and targets?

The Ask & Use of Funds

This is an optional slide but relevant if you're fundraising. How much money are you asking for? Anything else you're asking for? How will you use the funds?

Contact Details / How to Get Involved

How does someone contact you?

Visit dynamic4.com/sptm to download a simple pitch deck template.

Your Pitch Deck

Let's start your draft pitch deck. Start with what you have and iterate it as you get more answers. Depending on where you're at in your journey, you won't know the answer to some or most of these questions yet – and that's ok.

The slides:

- Cover
- Problem/Opportunity
- Value Proposition
- Purpose/Theory of Change
- Solution/How it Works
- Market Opportunity
- Competition
- Business Model
- Team
- Status & Traction
- Financial Projections & Key Metrics
- The Ask & Use of Funds (optional slide if fundraising)
- Contact Details/How to Get Involved

Your first draft will probably be very empty or have some placeholder content. I recommend having a short version with your current story, and know that it will evolve over time.

In the Your Sprint Rhythm section, I recommended that you refine your story as part of your showcase in each Sprint Review & Plan session. As we work through the program together, you'll be able to iterate your pitch deck with new insights at key points. Think of this as a way of crystalising your thinking and refining your story rather than trying to create the perfect pitch deck.

This chapter has focused on making your social enterprise idea happen by getting into your rhythm of prioritising, planning, reviewing, and building momentum so you can move forward with confidence.

We started drilling down into much more detail. I know some of this can be a bit overwhelming. Please don't let what you can't do or what you don't know **yet**, stop you from doing what you can do. It's critical to keep moving with the things you can do rather than fixating on what you can't.

Momentum is extremely valuable, and a lot of what we've covered is about building and maintaining it. It can be hard to build and easy to lose, but when you keep it going, everything flows with much less effort. This is a chapter you'll be referring to on a regular basis.

You now have a plan to complete Sprint 0, and we're going to build on the work you've done to zoom out a bit and get more clarity on your purpose, vision, and theory of change. This is the final chapter before starting Sprint 1.

Chapter 4

Purpose, Vision & Theory of Change

"Hope for a generation,
just beyond my reach.
Not beyond my sight."

Hope by Fat Freddy's Drop

Clarity of purpose helps us make effective decisions.

The big questions we focus on in this chapter are, how do I/we:

- Communicate our purpose, theory of change, and the social/environmental value we'll create?

- Share our story to attract the support we need?

- Stay healthy and positive on this journey without getting overwhelmed and burnt out?

Purpose

Everyone seems to be talking about purpose – especially as it relates to finding your purpose and what it means for business. But what is it? It's a simple word that just means intention, or the reason something is done.

In the purpose-driven community, we generally think of it as being focused on creating positive social and environmental change.

Let's explore this at a personal and organisational level.

Your Personal Why

Most of us are looking for happiness and meaning. Purpose is key to this. As Emily Esfahani Smith outlines in her great TED talk, she concluded from her positive psychology, neuroscience, and philosophy research there are four pillars to meaning: belonging, **purpose**, transcendence, and storytelling – especially the stories we tell ourselves.

We want to do work that is meaningful and matters. It's fascinating seeing the trend of expectation toward meaningful work. Research shows 90% of employees are willing to trade a percentage of their lifetime earnings for greater meaning at work. How much? The average was 23%! Though I disagree with the premise that we should earn less when doing purposeful work that creates multiple types of value (financial, social, and environmental). That's a failure in our market system.

There's a lot of talk about finding your purpose – often with language that implies our one true purpose will be revealed to us and we'll know what to do in life. I disagree. So does the research. As Kira Newman writes in her article *How Purpose Changes Across Your Lifetime*, where she reviews some of the research over the past 30 years:

"In fact, purpose isn't something we find at all. It's something we can cultivate through deliberate action and reflection, and it will naturally wax and wane throughout our lives."

Kira Newman

It's worth the time to reflect on what motivates us, what we get energy from, our driving why – but don't expect it to be absolute and unchanging. And if this isn't something you've already been working on for a while, don't expect to have it resolved after a half-hour session.

I find Ikigai a useful and simple way to articulate a lot of this – I've used it for myself and in coaching conversations with others. It's a four circle Venn where the intersection of the four circles is said to be "your reason for being". When you did Your Strengths & Assets action in Chapter 1: Mindset, you actually did a version of Ikigai – probably without knowing.

Here are the four Ikigai circles with the question I asked:

What you love	What do you love doing?
What you are good at	What are you really good at?
What the world needs	What do you really care about?
What you can be paid for	What do you get paid for doing?

Ikigai doesn't magically give you the answer to your personal why, but it helps you think through and reflect on some of the key ingredients. If you can bring these four pieces together with your social enterprise idea, it increases the chances that you'll do meaningful work that brings you fulfilment, creates social and environmental value, and is financially successful.

Your Organisation's Purpose & Vision

Organisations often spend a lot of time and money crafting mission statements, vision statements, cultural values, and maybe even principles. Traditionally these are inward facing and centred on the organisation. Over the past decade or so there's been a trend to try to focus these statements on the customer.

Customers or people who will buy and use our solution are very important and something we'll do a lot of work on, but in our context our primary purpose is even bigger. We'll focus on one real question – why does our organisation exist?

Clarity of purpose makes decisions easier. It gives us a clear filter to assess and prioritise options. When we have a meaningful driving why, it helps us keep going through all of the challenges we face. It will help us persevere. A compelling purpose and vision are also what our supporters will engage with.

Purpose is our reason for doing it. Vision is the better future we're working towards. Vision gives us hope and a clear direction to move in. Think about the 10-year vision you described in Chapter 3: Make It Happen.

Depending on what stage you're at with your idea, you might not be ready to complete all of these activities right now. Whatever stage you're at, we'll be reviewing and refining this regularly as we progress. These three actions build on each other.

If you're a team within a larger organisation, you might want to do this at a team level too. It should align with the overall organisation purpose. I recommend doing each action as an individual first, and then discussing it as a team to see where things are common and where there are differences. Understand why, and take the opportunity to align.

Note: It's beyond the scope of this book, but I strongly recommend articulating a set of values for your organisation. The important step is to turn this into practical guiding principles and be explicit about what these values look like as behaviours. The behaviours you expect of yourself and each other – and the behaviours that you won't accept.

This activity also works within established organisations with existing value statements. Too often, organisational values are a generic set of words that don't mean much in practice – and mean different things to different people. When done well as a collaborative process, they're a powerful guide for decisions and behaviours.

Start With Who

Simon Sinek famously says start with "why", and we'll do an action on that soon. First, we'll start with who.

Example:

I want to help all people have increasing quality of life and be happier – in communities that are more empowered and inclusive, and live in sustainable ways. I obviously can't do that myself directly.

I'm focused on helping **social enterprise founders, NFP leaders, and changemakers globally** – because if we can solve problems that matter together, we can realise these great outcomes for all people.

ACTION

Starting With Who

Who experiences the problem you've identified? Take 5 minutes to list the people and groups of people you are focused on helping.

Now that you've clearly identified the people and groups of people you want to help, think about your why. We'll use Simon Sinek's famous Golden Circle for this.

Your Golden Circle

Simon Sinek gave one of the most popular TED talks of all time in 2009, and he's the author of *Start With Why*. He's created a lot of great content on leadership and purpose, with a strong focus on empathy.

Simon Sinek simply and powerfully explains how compelling it is to be able to clearly articulate your Why. It engages and inspires others to action. There are specific biological reasons for this. Visit dynamic4.com/sptm for a link to his talk, it's best to hear it directly from him.

There are three circles to Simon Sinek's Golden Circle: Why? How? What? Here's a simple description so you can get started:

- **Why?** "What's your purpose? What's your cause? What's your belief? Why does your organization exist? Why do you get out of bed in the morning? And why should anyone care?" Those are Simon Sinek's own words

- **How?** What makes you special or unique? What's your "differentiated value proposition or your proprietary process or your USP"? How are you "different or better"?

- **What?** What's your product or service? What does your organisation do?

The process can feel a little uncomfortable. It's often hard to get to the Why because we tend to spend so much time focused on trying to work out the What. Clarity on our Why helps us make better decisions and filter options for the What.

Draw on the work you've done on your 10-year vision and Gaddie Pitch. All of these pieces fit together and complement each other.

Example:

Why: A world where people have increasing quality of life and are happier – and live in communities that are more empowered, inclusive, and sustainable.

How: We support people with social enterprise ideas to focus, get clarity, build relationships, and move forward with confidence.

What: My book Solve Problems That Matter, supported by our coaching and programs.

ACTION

Your Golden Circle

Now it's time to draft your Golden Circle. Spend about 3 minutes on each of these three parts. Don't worry about perfect wording, just do your best to capture the core concepts and important words.

Why?
What's your Why? Build on the work you've already done on the why that is driving you. The vision you're working towards.

How?
What makes you, your idea, and your organisation special? What's your value proposition?

What?
What's your solution? What's your idea? What does your organisation do?

Your Purpose Statement

We now have the ingredients to craft a simple purpose statement. Don't worry about perfecting the words, but see if you can bring these three parts into a paragraph – following the same order: Why? How? What?

Example:

We help create happier communities that are more empowered, inclusive, and sustainable – **by** supporting people with social enterprise ideas to focus, get clarity, build relationships, and move forward with confidence – **with** the Solve Problems That Matter book, supported by our coaching and programs.

Your wording, and even some of the core concepts, will refine over time, but looking at your purpose statement now, you'll hopefully get the feeling that you can link what you actually do, or what your idea is, to your driving why or purpose.

Your Purpose Statement

Your turn to draft your purpose statement, and bring together the elements of your Golden Circle. Take 5 minutes and follow the same order: Why? How? What? Use whatever words best help to join the three sections. I used "we help", "by", and "with" in my example.

Read it through. Do the three pieces flow logically?

The real test is to share your purpose statement with other people. See what parts resonate and where they have questions, or it isn't clear to them. Refine and test again. And again.

Your Theory of Change

A theory of change describes the vision, impact, and outcomes we're working toward, but takes them a step further. It also outlines our theory of how we'll create that change. The specific actions we'll take. The connection between the actions we'll take and the vision we're working towards needs to make logical sense and be believable.

Note: Theory of change and logic models are technically different things, but in common practice they're often used interchangeably. A true theory of change is a very system level and strategic view. We'll zoom out to map the system in Chapter 5. A logic model is more zoomed in on your specific solution as a way to articulate the change process. For our purposes, we'll use the terms interchangeably.

There's a lot of theory to this, and it's easy for it to become an academic exercise. I promised that I wouldn't be deep diving into theory, so let's keep it practical. The reasons I find it very valuable and worth doing are:

- The thinking and conversations on this help make the ideas in your head explicit
- Surfaces some key assumptions to test – including our understanding of the system we're operating in, which we'll talk about in Chapter 5: Current State
- Connects your idea to the outcomes and impact you want to contribute to
- Provides a framework to identify key lead indicators to measure where things are working and where things need to change

We'll use a variation of the Logic Model by the WK Kellogg Foundation. It has five steps: resources/inputs, activities, outputs, outcomes, and impacts. Each of the steps builds on the one before and flows to the next with simple "if… then" statements.

Visit dynamic4.com/sptm for links to some other useful resources including more detailed guides. Visit dynamic4.com/impact to see Dynamic4's theory of change as an example.

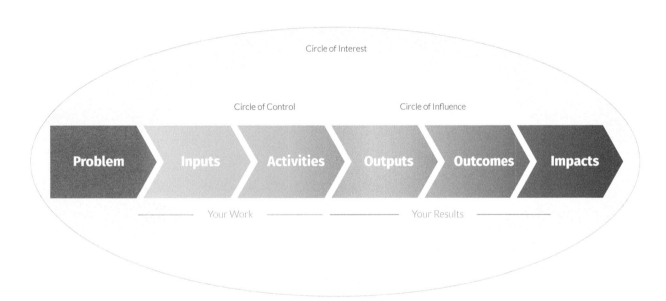

Circle of Interest

Circle of Control

Circle of Influence

| Problem | Inputs | Activities | Outputs | Outcomes | Impacts |

————— Your Work ————— ————— Your Results —————

Start Your Theory of Change Logic Model

The way we generally approach drafting a logic model is to start with the two ends – the impacts we're working to contribute to, and the problem we're focused on.

Impacts

Draw on the work you've done on Your 10-Year Vision. The impacts we contribute to are generally thought of in the seven-to-10-year timeframe.

- What's the vision you're working toward?
- What's the change you want to see in the world?
- What does it look like when it's been achieved (or been improved)?

The Problem/Root Cause

Your understanding of the problem, root cause, and the system will refine as you're working through Part 2: People, Problem & Context. Capture your current thinking on this now and continue refining.

- What's the problem you want to work on to help create the positive change?

- Who experiences this problem?
- In what context?
- What do you know about the systemic causes of this problem?
- Why does it matter to you?

Your Resources/Inputs

You can draw on the work you did on Your Strengths & Assets to list your resources or inputs – even before you start working on a specific solution.

- What are you really good at?
- What have you done or achieved that you're most proud of?
- What do you get paid to do?
- What resources do you have, including money and money you can get access to?

Your Planned Activities, Outputs & Outcomes

If you aren't already working on a specific solution, come back to activities, outputs, and outcomes as you're working through Part 3: Solution & Business Model. Capture your current thinking on this now, and continue refining.

Your Activities

- How do you use your resources/inputs to create and deliver value?

Your Outputs

- Who will you reach with the output of your solution?

- What are the direct and immediate results created by your activities?

- What do your customers receive as the output of your solution?

Your Outcomes

- What benefits are created over time?

- Who experiences these benefits?

- What are the short-term outcomes? One-to-three-year timeframe

- What are the longer-term outcomes? Four-to-six-year timeframe

Test Your Theory of Change

Review your theory of change to see if each step builds on the one before to create a logical sequence. Test the logic with other stakeholders to see if it makes sense to them.

Continue refining your theory of change as you explore your solution and business model.

- Does the connection between the actions we'll take and the vision we're working towards still make sense and is it believable?

- What are your riskiest assumptions?

- How will you test your riskiest assumptions?

Measure Outcomes & Impact

Social enterprise ideas are driven by a purpose to create social and environmental value – or impact. But how do we know if we're actually contributing to creating positive impact, especially when we're normally talking about timeframes of seven-to-10-years – or more? This is where impact measurement comes in.

While it's normally referred to as impact measurement, the focus is generally on outcome measurement – and in the immediate term, it's on measuring the quality of the outputs we create. You've probably noticed that we're using the same terms as we did for our theory of change.

Monitoring and evaluation can quickly become theoretical and complex. The principles are clear, but even mature organisations with significant resources often struggle to implement meaningful measurement. Despite it being a challenge, it's important that we think about measurement now and factor it into the way we design solutions.

Circles of Influence

The concept of circles of influence is important here. A version of this was popularised by Stephen Covey his *The 7 Habits of Highly Effective People*.

Circle of Control

Our circle of control includes the things we can have a direct impact on. In life, our circle of control is relatively small – at least relative to all of the things we're interested in. Our circle of control includes our mindset, thoughts, decisions, behaviours, and how we spend our time and energy.

In a theory of change context, we have direct control of our resources/inputs and our activities. We don't have direct control of outcomes and impacts.

Circle of Influence

Our circle of influence contains all of the things that we can directly influence, but that we can't directly control. This includes the perceptions, feelings, and behaviours of other people, and the systems we operate within.

This is why I talk about doing things that help "create the conditions" for people to be happier. It's why we "design for" great experiences and positive behaviour change. We can't actually make someone else have the experience we want or design someone else's behaviour. We can control these things for ourselves, and we can definitely choose to positively influence others though.

In the context of our theory of change, the quality of our outputs is within our circle of control, but how our outputs are perceived by others is within our circle of influence. This is an important feedback loop to understand where our solution resonates with others, and where we need to refine things. Over time, we can expand our circle of influence. We often have more influence than we realise.

The outcomes we aim to create are within our circle of influence. The longer the timeframe though, the more likely this becomes an indirect influence. Outcome Mapping is a related methodology, and has the concept of "boundary partners". These are the people, groups, and organisations you interact with directly and hope to influence in a positive way as champions of the change. Boundary partners help take the change beyond our current circle of influence.

Circle of Interest

Our circle of interest (or concern) is a wide range of things that we definitely can't control and can only influence indirectly – or not at all. They're part of our reality, and how we choose to respond is part of our circle of control. This includes the weather, traffic, natural disasters, world events, etc. Unfortunately, it can be easy to fixate on these things, and they're a common cause of stress and anxiety. That's why it's important to focus on our circles of control and influence – it helps us move into a more proactive space.

In the context of our theory of change, we can indirectly influence the longer-term outcomes, and the impacts we want to contribute to. Longer-term impacts are likely to be in our circle of interest, but not within our direct circle of influence.

Using circles of influence as important framing, let's start looking at measurement and what it means for your theory of change.

Impact Measurement

Impact measurement generally refers to system level change that happens over a long timeframe. We talk about "contributing" to positive impact because systems are dynamic, and there are also many other people contributing.

Impacts are mostly within our circle of interest – not direct control or influence, and it's unlikely we could claim sole attribution. Collaboration is critical to achieve system level change, and this is where boundary partners are key.

ACTION

Your Impact Measures

You might have already identified some ways to measure the social and environmental impacts you will contribute to as part of Your 10-Year Vision when I asked the questions "What social and environmental impacts are you contributing to? How do you know?"

If you have, that's great. Make a note of the impact measures you've identified under impacts on your theory of change.

UN Sustainable Development Goals (SDGs)

The UN Sustainable Development Goals (SDGs) are a great framework to align with. The current set of 17 SDGs were adopted by the UN in 2015 as a universal call to action to end poverty, protect the planet, and ensure all people enjoy peace and prosperity by 2030. They are a "blueprint to achieve a better and more sustainable future for all". You can read about each goal, the specific target and indicators, and see the progress at sdgs.un.org/goals.

The SDGs are a great place to start when thinking about measurement. They cover a broad range of focus areas but very importantly, they're integrated. This is something that's often overlooked. Actions in one SDG area will affect outcomes in other SDGs.

Part of what I like about the SDGs is all 193 Member States of the UN have signed up to achieve them by 2030. It has gone beyond that though, with other organisations and corporates also actively working to contribute to one or more of the goals.

Awareness of the SDGs has increased rapidly over the past few years, and they're providing a shared language, which is powerful. There's recognition and traction across a diverse stakeholder group. This is hard to achieve and is a key reason I'm an advocate.

It's not a perfect framework though, and it has its critics. You might also find that there isn't an SDG that directly matches what you're focused on – or that the targets aren't things you can directly contribute to. I recommend using the SDGs where they're helpful and focus on where they bring value.

The B Corp SDG Action Manager (bcorporation.net/welcome-sdg-action-manager) is a free online tool that will help you set goals and track progress on your SDGs.

SUSTAINABLE DEVELOPMENT G⊙ALS

Your SDGs

Review the SDGs (sdgs.un.org/goals) and identify one or more of the goals aligned with the positive impact you are contributing to.

Make a note of the SDGs your social enterprise idea is aligned with under impacts on your theory of change.

Review the targets and indicators of the SDGs you've identified. Make a note of the specific targets and indicators your social enterprise idea contributes to under impacts on your theory of change.

SDG 17 is Partnerships for the Goals. This is explicit recognition that to achieve the goals we need strong partnerships and collaboration.

I'm proud to be a member of Catalyst 2030, "a global movement of social entrepreneurs and social innovators from all sectors who share the common goal of creating innovative, people-centric approaches to attain the Sustainable Development Goals by 2030". The focus is on working with communities, governments, businesses, and others to change "systems at all levels through collective action and bold, new strategies". Visit catalyst2030.net to find out more and join the movement.

151

Outcome Measurement

Outcome measurement is where we focus in terms of measuring the results of our work. Specifically, we need to identify the positive outcomes we want to create as a direct and causal result of our solution. Remember that outcomes are part of our circle of influence, and we can't directly control them.

We need to identify enough measures and lead indicators to provide a feedback loop. This information will show us if we're on the right path, and our solution is having the positive effect we believe it will.

The reality is this measurement might show that we aren't creating the positive change we hoped – that our solution is either not doing anything meaningful, or that it's actually creating a negative outcome – an unintended consequence. This is important information so we can iterate our solution or in some cases stop.

Your Outcome Measures

Thinking about the outcomes you identified in your draft theory of change:

- Who experiences these outcomes?

- Who is the intended audience for your outcome measurement and what are they interested in? They are normally people within your organisation, especially leadership, but might also include other supporters, funders, and partners

For your longer-term outcomes (the four-to-six-year timeframe):

- What can you start measuring as lead indicators that will give you feedback to know if you're on the right path?

- What can you measure that will show the outcome is being or has been achieved?

- How will you measure them?

- How will you combine numerical data with the story behind the data?

For your short-term outcomes (the one-to-three-year timeframe):

- What can you start measuring as lead indicators that will give you feedback to know if you're on the right path?

- What can you measure that will show the outcome is being or has been achieved?

- How will you measure them?

- How will you combine numerical data with the story behind the data?

Make a note of these points under outcomes on your theory of change. Continue to iterate and refine as your solution and business model evolve.

Output Measurement

Output measurement is where a lot of impact reporting starts. Outputs are the direct and immediate results created by your activities. They are much more tangible and generally easier to quantify than outcomes. Outputs are normally described as the solutions you deliver, who you reach with your solution, and how many people you reach or how much of your solution is delivered.

You probably have some OKRs that relate to your outputs. What your output is and how it's measured depend on your solution, but common measurement examples include the number of customers, number of units sold, or number of participants. Our theory of change articulates the outcomes we expect when we deliver the intended amount of output to our customers.

Your Output Measures

- What's the amount of output you expect to deliver to create the desired outcomes?

- How many people in each of your customer groups have you reached?

- How much of your output have you delivered?

- What can you measure that will show you're creating and delivering the output required?

- How will you measure the outputs?

- How will you combine numerical data with the story behind the data?

Make a note of these points under outputs on your theory of change. Continue to iterate and refine as your solution and business model evolve.

I know the process of measuring outcomes and impact can seem very daunting. Don't expect it to all make sense straightaway. It's also challenging to set up measurement while your solution is iterating rapidly, and you're testing different ideas. It's important to include this thinking during your solution design though. You'll refer to this section during Part 3: Solution & Business Model.

Visit dynamic4.com/sptm for links to some other useful resources including the Centre for Social Impact's *Roadmap to Social Impact*, which is a free step-by-step guide to planning, measuring, and communicating social impact.

155

Well done! We've reached the end of Part 1: Setting the Scene.

I know we've covered a lot. The rest of the book is much more focused on the actions to make rapid progress through the double diamond. This assumes some basic understanding of the foundational theory, concepts, and terms – and we apply these ways of thinking and working. I regularly refer to Part 1 as a reminder of key concepts where needed.

We started with a strong focus on mindset, personal sustainability, and happiness habits – to help you look after your personal wellbeing while making a positive impact. The actions included your:

- Happiness Habits
- Strengths & Assets
- Team
- Personal Wellbeing Plan
- Personal Budget & Investment

You've started the process of articulating your current thinking on your vision and the problem you plan to work on – and we've started setting up your workflow to get into a rhythm to build sustainable momentum. The actions included your:

- 10-Year Vision
- 3-Year Picture
- 1-Year Plan with OKRs
- 90-Day Plan with OKRs
- Time Inventory & Prioritisation
- Assumptions Log
- Gaddie Pitch
- Pitch Deck
- Golden Circle & Purpose Statement
- Theory of Change Logic Model
- SDGs, Output, Outcome & Impact Measures

There's a lot to celebrate here. I encourage you to pause, take a breath, and reflect. It's a natural time to do a retro and apply your action learning self-coaching. When reflecting on what went well, and what hasn't gone so well... don't forget to ask yourself the important question. Why.

Together, we now start Phase 2: People, Problem & Context.

People, Problem & Context

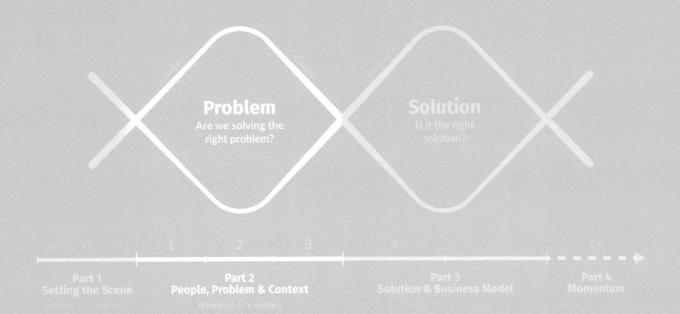

Problem
Are we solving the
right problem?

Solution
Is it the right
solution?

Part 1
Setting the Scene

Part 2
People, Problem & Context
(Weeks 4-9, 6 weeks)

Part 3
Solution & Business Model

Part 4
Momentum

Weeks 4-9. Sprints 1, 2 & 3

The standard program allows six weeks for this phase – three sprints.
Depending on where you're at in your journey, you might be able to move
through this phase quicker – or you might learn some things that mean you
need to continue your research to really understand the people, the problems
as they experience them, and the context they experience them in.

Part 2 Chapters

5. Current State

6. Customer Research

7. Market Research

8. Make Sense

The focus during this phase is to really understand the current reality. What actually is – not how we might wish it to be. No matter how much experience we have of the problem we're focusing on, we need much more than just our own perspective.

This phase is about spending time with the people you hope will use and pay for your solution – to deeply understand how they experience the problem, test your risky assumptions, and refine your thinking. By the end of this phase, we want to have reached a point of sharp clarity on the real problem to solve – based on evidence, insight, and meaningful empathy.

The Big Questions

The big question we focus on in Part 2 is, how do I/we:

- Identify our customers, understand what they really care about, and know if they'll buy and use our solution?

Important Note: Before starting on this phase, it's important to have clarity on your purpose and vision. If you feel you're not quite there yet, it might be worth spending a little more time on Chapter 4: Purpose, Vision & Theory of Change. The way you articulate it will evolve over time, but it's critical that you're clear on your "why".

I strongly recommend resisting the urge to skip the People, Problem & Context phase. It's very rare to design, build, and launch successful solutions without having deep insight – and empathy for the people we're designing with and for.

Chapter 5

Current State

Diverge

Converge

Diverge

Converge

Problem
**Are we solving the
right problem?**

Solution

Is it the right
solution?

The purpose of this chapter is to really start focusing on the problem diamond. This is about understanding the current state. What actually is – not how we might wish it to be. Your idea needs to be grounded in reality.

In Chapter 2, we talked about first principles thinking, and how important it is when working on complex problems. We need to break down the problem and its causes into its basic elements. We ask the question "what do we know to be true?" and remove assumptions to get to the set of things we can be confident are true.

The way we'll approach this is to:

- Crystalise and capture your current thinking using the Lean Canvas

- Zoom out to quickly map the system(s) you're working in

- Zoom in a little to see how the external forces and trends are likely to impact your organisational context and idea

- Simplify your focus on the people and the problem

Where Are You At?

In the last chapter, you explored and articulated your purpose, the change you want to create, and some of your ideas to get there. Most people I work with already have an idea, even in the earliest days, which usually includes a lot of expectations on what the solution will be.

Many already have some version of their solution launched, and might even be making some revenue. Or you might be at the stage where you don't have a specific idea, and there's a problem you really care about and want to explore.

No matter where you're at, the next couple of actions are important to articulate your current thinking. They will form an important foundation that we'll build on and iterate as we move through this together.

In Chapter 2, I briefly mentioned the Business Model Canvas and the Lean Canvas. They're both great tools that I've used for years in many contexts. The reason I love these two tools is that they're a quick and simple way to prototype nine key building blocks of your business model on a page.

It's a simple way to explain how your idea helps people with the social, environmental, and economic value that you create. It's a powerful way to bring the key elements of your story together. In many cases, people won't risk their time, money, or reputation if they don't believe you're clear about how your idea works.

Lean Canvas

I find the Lean Canvas is generally better suited to early-stage ideas. A key reason for this is it includes blocks for the problem, solution, and key metrics – which is a natural place to include our output and outcome measures from our theory of change. If you're already using the Business Model Canvas, feel free to keep using it.

The Lean Canvas by Ash Maurya is adapted from The Business Model Canvas (BusinessModelGeneration.com) and is licensed under the Creative Commons Attribution-Share Alike license.

I'll explain the nine blocks quickly. I find this sequence makes sense for most people.

Customer Segments/People & Early Adopters

When defining terms in Chapter 2, I mentioned that we'd differentiate between customers and users in contexts where it matters. This is one of those cases.

I recommend thinking about this as the people – the who. These are the people and groups you're focused on helping. They are the recipients of the value that you create. You might refer to them (or some of the groups) as something other than customers. Not all of them will be people who pay for your solution.

What happens quite often in a social enterprise context is that the end user or beneficiary of the value you create isn't necessarily the person paying. There might be an intermediary who is paying on behalf of the end users.

An example of this is where an organisation, like an NFP or government department, pays for the solution (the customer) – that a group of people use at no cost (the beneficiaries or users). This forms a triangular value relationship where we need to understand the needs of both the paying customer and the beneficiaries or users. There are many more possible models, but let's keep it relatively simple.

It starts with identifying these different groups of people and making a note of the role they play. You'll do more of this in a

moment, when you zoom out to see the system. Also, keep this in mind in Chapter 6 when thinking about who the right people to talk to are.

Early adopters are the ideal customers and users you believe you can get to early, where there's a very high likelihood they'll adopt your solution. They recognise the problem, and you have evidence they're ready and able to do something about it. What are the key characteristics of these people? How will you identify them?

Problem & Existing Alternatives

What is the problem your target customers are experiencing? What goals are they trying to achieve? What jobs are they trying to get done? What triggers this? Describe the problem from their perspective. Be clear on which group of people is experiencing each of the problems. Don't confuse this with your organisation's problems.

How are your early adopters currently solving the problem? This might be a competitor, their own workaround, or maybe they aren't doing anything about the problem. What about these existing alternatives works well for them? What doesn't work well for them and is the cause of frustration? We'll build on this more in Chapter 7.

Unique Value Proposition

What's the value and the benefit that you create for these different groups of people? What's the social and environmental value that you create?

Solution

How do you (or will you) solve the problems you've identified?

Channels

Think about all of the touchpoints used during the full lifecycle. How do people find out about you, evaluate, and buy your solution? How do you deliver your value and solution to your customers? How do you provide support?

Revenue Streams

How do you make money? What are the sources and types of revenue (fee for service, product purchases, subscriptions, grants, donations)?

Be more creative than just financial transactions. What are the other types of value exchange where you receive value?

Cost Structure

What does it cost to design, build, launch, and run your solution? What does it cost to keep your organisation running? What costs are fixed? What costs are variable? Wherever you see something in most of the other blocks, there's often a financial and/or time cost associated.

What are the other types of value exchange where you provide value?

Key Metrics

What are your business metrics that let you know you're on the right track? What are the metrics for your social and environmental outputs and outcomes?

Unfair Advantage

Why you? What's your secret sauce? What have you got that nobody else can easily replicate? How do you differentiate?

Unfair advantage is one a lot of people struggle with. There will always be something though, because no one else can be you. Your personal why and Ikigai from Chapter 4 should provide some inspiration.

Lean Canvas

PROBLEM	SOLUTION	UNIQUE VALUE PROPOSITION	UNFAIR ADVANTAGE	CUSTOMER SEGMENTS
	KEY METRICS		**CHANNELS**	
EXISTING ALTERNATIVES		HIGH-LEVEL CONCEPT		EARLY ADOPTERS

COST STRUCTURE	REVENUE STREAMS

Your Current Lean Canvas

The purpose of using the Lean Canvas right now is to capture your current thinking. It's ok to leave blocks empty. Bullet points are good if you're working on a screen or notebook. Sticky notes are great if you're working on a wall, especially with other people.

Take 15-20 minutes to capture your thinking on the current version of your idea. Don't worry about the future or the many possible shapes the idea might take.

I find this sequence makes sense for most people. Feel free to jump around as things come to mind. The key is to keep moving, and don't stop if you feel stuck. Just skip that block, and maybe come back to it later. Something is better than nothing though, and the intent is for it to be a reminder of your thinking, not for it to be polished.

- Customer Segments/People & Early Adopters
- Problem & Existing Alternatives
- Unique Value Proposition
- Solution
- Channels
- Revenue Streams
- Cost Structure
- Key Metrics
- Unfair Advantage

Coaching Questions

- What are the riskiest assumptions that you've identified? Why? Have you updated your Assumptions Log?
- What does this mean for the assumptions you've already identified?
- How does your Gaddie Pitch refine from doing this? Have you updated it and tested it with anyone?

Zoom Out to See the System

Social enterprises and purpose-driven organisations usually work on very complex problems, and are often focused on systemic change. Complex systems have many possible cause-and-effect pathways with a lot of people and interconnected moving parts to the system.

Systems thinking is a holistic approach to understanding the system you're focusing on. Rather than breaking the system down into separate components and analysing the parts at a point in time and in a vacuum, it looks at how things work in their actual context over time.

Why apply systems thinking? It helps us zoom out to understand the context we're focused on. It's easy to get lost in the detail but pausing to zoom out to see the whole gives us a better perspective, which often results in us seeing things in new ways. It's also important because it helps us see how some of the decisions we make will impact other parts of the system or interconnected systems. Some of these impacts may be unintended consequences that cause harm. With these insights, we can make better decisions.

I deliberated including this action because systems thinking is a massive field that can be very complex and is usually written about in very academic ways. There are so many key concepts and tools that are really powerful here, but at the risk of oversimplifying the topic, I'm just going to guide you through some basics to create a simple map of the system you're focused on.

What the map looks like isn't the important thing. It's the process of thinking it through (collaboratively with your team if you have one) and identifying where you need to do more research to understand the system.

Visit dynamic4.com/sptm for links to some other useful resources, including more detailed guides.

171

Guidance on Your Systems Map

A systems map is a visual way to articulate the moving parts of the system and their relationships. A popular way to draw this is as a cluster map – which can look similar to a mind map.

Some basic guidance:

- A whiteboard or a big sheet of paper is great for this, especially if you're working with other people. If you're working on a screen, an online whiteboard like Google Jamboard, Mural, or Miro is good

- This will be messy, and that's good. Don't try to make it neat

- Start by writing the problem you're focused on in the middle of the page

- Explore the different components that make up the system. Write down what comes to mind, and don't edit yourself at this point. I've listed some questions to help get you started

- Draw connections between the components you identify. Draw the direction of the connection or interaction where it's relevant – like processes, power dynamics, and feedback loops

- Refer to your system map as you progress. Keep adding and iterating as you think of things. This may happen over a period of days or weeks

- I recommend saving a version after each session (by taking a photo or saving a new file). This will allow you to see how your understanding changes over time

Your Systems Map

Take 30-45 minutes to capture your understanding of the system. Here are some questions to get you started:

- What system and context are you focusing on?

- Where is the boundary of the system you're focusing on, and where does the system interact with other systems?

- Who are the groups of people (actors) in the system?

- What do these people and groups care about, and what are their goals?

- What are the nodes, connections, interactions, power dynamics, key processes, incentives, and feedback loops between the components of the system?

- Which feedback loops create a positive impact, and which reinforce the negative?

- What are the root causes of the problems you've identified? A couple of useful methods for this are the 5 Whys and a Fishbone Diagram

- How has the system changed over time? What are the big patterns and trends?

- What might some unintended consequences you need to be mindful of be?

Coaching Questions

- As you map the system, what do you see differently? Why?

- What additional research do you need to do?

- What are the riskiest assumptions that you've identified? Why? Have you updated your Assumptions Log?

Zoom In on Your Organisational Context

We've just been zooming out to explore the broader system you're focused on to get a better perspective. Let's zoom in a little now to your specific organisational context. This is still thinking bigger than your business model, and we're looking to identify the external forces, patterns, and trends – similar to the system level.

We do this to understand how these external forces are likely to impact us directly, the constraints, and where things are trending. These insights help us design and iterate our business model.

There are a few tools that are useful for this, like Porter's 5 Forces, PESTLE, and DEEPLIST – but my favourite is the Business Model Environment tool from *Business Model Generation* by Alexander Osterwalder & Co. This tool was designed to use with the Business Model Canvas, but I've found it works just as well with the Lean Canvas.

A business model is designed and operates within a specific context. The Business Model Environment tool helps us identify and map what that context is. This model looks at four types of external forces. I'll outline the four forces and the elements that make them up.

Market Forces

What are the market forces in your context? This is mostly focused on your customers – their needs, expectations, and behaviours.

Market Issues. What market trends are you observing?

Market Segments. What are the most important customer segments? Which segments are emerging, growing, or shrinking?

Needs & Demands. What do customers want? Where is demand increasing or shrinking? Is there unmet demand?

Switching Costs. Is it easy for customers to switch to new solutions? What are the barriers? (These might include money, time and attention, regulation, etc)

Revenue Attractiveness. How competitive is the market? What are customers willing to pay? What solutions have margin?

Macroeconomic Forces

What are the macroeconomic forces in your context? This includes regional, national, and global economies.

Global Market Conditions. What's the general market sentiment? What's the current unemployment rate? Are economies growing, shrinking, or stagnating?

Capital Markets. How easy is it to get access to the funding you need? How expensive is funding currently? Where is the cost of capital trending?

Commodities & Other Resources. How easy is it to access the resources you need? What is the talent market like? Where are prices trending?

Economic Infrastructure. How good is public infrastructure in your context? (This might include health, education, transportation, trade, and access to the market.)

Industry Forces

What are the industry forces in your context? These include the different stakeholders who have an impact on your organisational context.

Competitors (Incumbents). Who are the established organisations? What segments do they focus on? What are their strengths and weaknesses? How does their pricing and business model work?

New Entrants (Insurgents). Who are the new organisations entering the market? What segments do they focus on? What are their strengths and weaknesses? How does their pricing and business model work?

Substitute Products & Services. What are the other solutions available that might be an alternative to yours? How easy is it for customers to switch? Think about alternatives in a broad sense. They might even be from another industry, category, or market.

Suppliers & Other Value Chain Actors. What other suppliers in the industry is your solution dependent on? What industry trends are you observing?

Stakeholders. Who are the other stakeholders influencing your industry? What agendas are you observing?

Key Trends

What are the key trends you're observing that impact your context?

Technology Trends. What are the major technology trends? Which of these are opportunities, and what are the threats? What technologies are your customers adopting?

Regulatory Trends. What are the regulatory trends you're observing that impact your industry and market? How might they impact you? How might they impact your customers?

Societal & Cultural Trends. What are the societal and cultural trends you're observing? How might they impact you? How might they impact your customers' expectations and behaviours?

Socioeconomic Trends. What are the socioeconomic trends you're observing? What are the changes in demographics? How high are wage growth, the cost of living, and disposable income?

Visit dynamic4.com/sptm for links to some other useful resources, including more detailed guides.

Your Business Model Environment

A business model is designed and operates within a specific context. The Business Model Environment tool helps us identify and map what that context is.

Take 45-60 minutes to capture your understanding of these external forces and how they relate to your organisational context. Feel free to jump around as things come to mind. If you can't answer these points, it's an indicator of risk, and highlights areas where you probably need to do some more research.

Market Forces

What are the market forces in your context? This is mostly focused on your customers – their needs, expectations, and behaviours

Macroeconomic Forces

What are the macroeconomic forces in your context? This includes regional, national, and global economies.

Industry Forces

What are the industry forces in your context? This includes the different stakeholders that have an impact on your organisational context.

Key Trends

What are the key trends you're observing that impact your context?

Coaching Questions

- What are the key trends, and how have they been changing over time?
- What do these forces and trends mean for your organisation?
- Where did you find this action challenging? Why?
- What additional research do you need to do?
- What are the riskiest assumptions that you've identified? Why? Have you updated your Assumptions Log?

Focus on People & Problem

Human-centred design is the core of my professional life and has been since the early 1990s. For me, this means starting with people. Always.

While we talk about problems that matter, I think it's important that we look at the inherent potential of people, communities, and systems. Please never see people as problems to solve. Deficit thinking is harmful to the people involved – and it doesn't address the real problem and its causes. We need to approach these problems with humility, empathy, and an understanding of the systems at play.

You've just spent some time capturing your current thinking using the Lean Canvas. You then zoomed out to see the systems you're working in – and zoomed in a little to look at the external forces that influence your organisational context. As part of this, you identified the people and groups involved in the system and your context.

With that framing, we're going to build on the work you did on your Lean Canvas by simplifying it, and focusing on the people you want to help, and the problems or challenges they experience. With problems comes opportunity. This is often a matter of mindset and reframing.

The two tools I have used for years are the Lean Canvas and the Value Proposition Canvas. You already know about the Lean Canvas. The Value Proposition Canvas is another great tool from Alex Osterwalder and the Strategyzer team. The right side has the profile of the ideal customer with the organisation's value proposition on the left.

Peter J Thomson remixed this canvas in 2013, and I found his rationale compelling for early-stage ideas – the primary context I work with people on. This simplified Value Proposition Canvas brings more focus to building empathy. This has been the main version of the canvas I've used since 2014. We'll start using this version in Chapter 8.

All of these canvas variants are just tools. I've found that all of them are useful, but some are more tailored to certain contexts. You might be thinking the last thing the world needs is another canvas. I tend to agree, which is why, when I mashed up the People/Problem Canvas in 2019, I didn't promote it and just used it in my own practice and with the people I work with.

Why another canvas? For years I used the Lean Canvas and Value Proposition Canvas with most blocks greyed out to focus on just the elements that are important while we're focused on the problem diamond. It's where I spend a lot of time nudging people away from jumping into solution mode. It's where we are right now. These other blocks were a distraction. Ash Maurya actually published the Leaner Canvas in 2019 for a similar reason.

Another challenge in the early stages is that many people I work with aren't sure who their customers and customer segments might be yet. As I mentioned earlier, there's often a more complex set of stakeholder interactions with social enterprise ideas. Changing customer segments to people simplified this conversation, and brought the focus to identifying who the people involved are and the roles they play. Working out who the paying customer might be and different segments flows from there.

Right now, we need to be focused on the people and the problem. We have those two blocks from Ash Maurya's Lean Canvas. To save switching between different canvases, I put the ideal customer circle from Peter Thomson's Value Proposition Canvas in the centre – and focused it on the early adopters. The People/Problem Canvas was born. Visit dynamic4.com/sptm to download the template.

That's the backstory... how do you use it? I'll explain the seven elements quickly.

179

Dynamic4 People/Problem Canvas

Problem

Existing Alternatives

Early Adopter

Wants

Fears

Needs

People

Early Adopters

Dynamic4 People/Problem Canvas (Ben Ferretti) is adapted from the Lean Canvas (Ash Maurya) and Value Proposition Canvas (Peter J Thomson) and is licensed under the Creative Commons Attribution-Share Alike 3.0 License.

People

The people and groups you're focused on helping. These are the recipients of the value that you create – both paying customers and beneficiaries or end users.

Early Adopters

Early adopters are the ideal customers and users you believe you can get to early, where there's a very high likelihood they'll adopt your solution. They recognise the problem, and you have evidence they're ready and able to do something about it. What are the key characteristics of these people? How will you identify early adopters?

Wants (Early Adopters)

What are the emotional drivers for your main group of early adopters? What do they desire? What's appealing to them? What are the things they actively seek out? We make most of our decisions emotionally, and then find rational reasons to justify them.

Now is a good time to refer to the SCARF model we covered in the Threats, Rewards & Triggers section of Chapter 1. When you successfully identify the wants, it's compelling for your early adopters and creates demand – they're more likely to pull your idea towards them.

Needs (Early Adopters)

What are the rational drivers for your main group of early adopters? What are the things they think they need to do? Needs often feel like obligations. We know we should do certain things, that they're good for us – but we often lack the real drive and motivation to do these things.

With some thought and reframing, you can often find an underlying want or desire for the needs you identify. A way to dig into this is by asking why they feel the need to do certain things. What are they trying to get done, and why? What's the expectation they're responding to? Make a note of the want. If your idea only taps into the rational needs and not the emotional drivers, you're likely to feel you're always pushing your idea toward people who aren't that interested.

Fears (Early Adopters)

What fears might your main group of early adopters have about adopting your idea? Many of these fears are the objections you need to overcome. Common ones include the fear that they'll damage their reputation, that they'll get a bad deal, or that it won't work as expected – the risk of being one of the first people to try something new.

A fear that might trigger people to get involved is the fear of missing out.

Often there are rational reasons given for these fears, but usually there's an underlying reason related to psychological safety and the SCARF model.

Problem

What are the top three problems your early adopters are experiencing? What goals are they trying to achieve? What jobs are they trying to get done? What triggers this? Describe the problem from their perspective. Don't confuse this with your organisation's problems.

Existing Alternatives

How are your early adopters currently solving the problem? This might be a competitor, their own workaround, or maybe they aren't doing anything about the problem. What about these existing alternatives works well for them? What doesn't work well for them and is the cause of frustration? We'll build on this more in Chapter 7.

Coaching Questions

- What evidence and insight do you have for your early adopters' wants, needs, and fears?

- What evidence do you have that your early adopters experience these problems and think they're a problem?

- What are the riskiest assumptions that you've identified? Why? Have you updated your Assumptions Log?

Your People/Problem Canvas

The purpose of using the People/Problem Canvas is to focus your thinking on the people involved and the problems they experience. Bullet points are good if you're working on a screen or notebook. Sticky notes are great if you're working on a wall, especially with other people.

Take 10-15 minutes to identify the people you want to help, the problems they experience, and what you know about your early adopters. Build on the work you've already done on your Lean Canvas.

Start with this sequence, but feel free to jump around as things come to mind. The key is to keep moving, and don't stop if you feel stuck. Just skip that element and come back to it. Something is better than nothing though, and the intent is for it to give you a clear direction on the research you need to do.

People

Who are the people and groups you're focused on helping?

Early Adopters

What are the key characteristics of your early adopters? How will you identify them?

Wants (Early Adopters)

What are the emotional drivers for your main group of early adopters?

Needs (Early Adopters)

What are the rational drivers for your main group of early adopters?

Fears (Early Adopters)

What fears might your main group of early adopters have about adopting your idea?

Problem

What are the top three problems your early adopters are experiencing? What triggers this?

Existing Alternatives

How are your early adopters currently solving the problem?

This chapter has been focused on helping you capture your current thinking and understanding. You hopefully identified some key assumptions and tested that thinking to refine it and get closer to a set of things you can be confident are true. It's important to be aware that this is your understanding and perspective. Other people will have different perspectives.

We talked about adaptive challenges in Chapter 2. We live in a dynamic and adaptive world – full of dynamic and adaptive systems and people. The technical aspects of the problem you're focused on are normally easier to define, and you can break down the problem and its causes to get to first principles.

To get to first principles on the adaptive aspects of the problem and system you're focused on is a lot more challenging. You need to talk with the people involved. That's one of the key reasons we do customer research. We'll now build on the work you've just done to test and refine your understanding of the current state.

Chapter 6

Customer Research

Diverge

Converge

Diverge

Converge

Problem

Are we solving the right problem?

Solution

Is it the right solution?

The purpose of this chapter is to help you prepare for engaging customer interviews and to feel confident doing this research. You can't build meaningful empathy without this, and you need to take the time to build these connections. No matter how much experience you have of the problem, you need much more than just your own perspective.

Building on the work you did in Chapter 5, customer research is critical to test and refine your understanding of the system and the current state. Customer research helps you deeply understand how the people you're designing with and for experience the problem. But it does more than just help you understand. It helps you build meaningful empathy.

In Chapter 2, we talked about the different types of empathy: cognitive, emotional, and compassionate. The neuroscience shows that each activates different parts of our brain, and the three types work together. Customer research will help us build these layers of empathy.

We also talked about mental models and cognitive biases. These shape what each of us believes, how we reason and make decisions, what we remember, how we form relationships, and ultimately how we behave. We've done some work in Part 1 to identify and understand our own. Now it's time to really understand our customers and how they experience the world – and the problem we're focused on.

How do they think about and describe the problem? What motivates them, and what do they find appealing? How do they make decisions? Are we working on a problem that matters to them? We're focused on the desirable lens of the three lenses model.

I'm surprised how many founders and leaders I speak with who have never spoken directly with the people they believe they're solving a problem for – and that they hope will use and pay for their solution. You need to spend time with your customers to build meaningful empathy through human connection.

If you only learn and practice one thing from this book, I hope it's the value and importance of customer research.

The way we'll approach this is to:

- Identify the key things you need to learn from your customers
- Choose the research methods you'll use to learn these things
- Identify the right people to do your research with
- Get the logistics set up to do your research
- Prepare to ask good questions
- Start thinking about how you'll make sense of what you hear

As I mentioned in the intro, I have no desire to duplicate or compete with good work that has already been done by others. My focus is on providing a guided path to design a sustainable business model that has purpose and impact embedded and is financially successful.

There are a lot of books I love covering startups, human-centred design, and innovation. Many of these do a great job of detailing different methods and tools. This is a short list of books I recommend if you're keen to explore more methods to take a human-centred approach to innovation:

- *Running Lean* by Ash Maurya. We've already referred to this book a few times. It's worth following Ash's blog too (blog.leanstack.com)

- *Design. Think. Make. Break. Repeat.: A Handbook of Methods* by Martin Tomitsch & Co. The website includes useful free resources (designthinkmakebreakrepeat.com)

- *Innovator's Playbook* by Nathan Baird

- *This is Service Design Thinking* by Marc Stickdorn & Jakob Schneider

To keep things simple, we're going to focus on customer interviews with individuals (not focus groups) and a couple of basic tools for synthesis. The principles we cover are relevant, and apply to most design research methods.

To get started, visit dynamic4.com/sptm and download the Customer Research Planner Template and the Conversation Guide Template. You'll use both in this chapter.

What Do You Need to Learn?

As we've been working through the last couple of chapters, I've been prompting you to keep track of your assumptions – the Assumptions Log you set up in Chapter 3. Now it's time to talk to people to learn more, understand their perspectives, and build empathy.

A lot of people working on social enterprise ideas have their own lived experience of the problem. Having that personal connection can be powerful and help with credibility. It can also make it challenging to see beyond how we experience the problem. People often experience similar situations in very different ways – in part because of our unique mental models and set of cognitive biases.

No matter how much experience you have of the problem, I encourage you to approach this research with a beginner's mind. Be aware of the natural confirmation bias we all have, and avoid projecting your perspective of the problem onto others.

Think of this as a discovery process and start with exploratory research. We're in a divergent phase. We're exploring, gathering information, opening things up. It's about creating options.

With that framing, what do you need to learn? We need to apply the scientific method we talked about briefly in Chapter 2. We don't seek to validate our thinking – we seek to learn. This starts with an observation or question. A point of enquiry. This focusing question helps focus our research and give it direction.

ACTION

Your Research Objective

Using the Customer Research Planner template, take 5-10 minutes to write your research objective. These questions will help:

- What are the riskiest assumptions you currently have? Refer to your Assumptions Log and focus on the ones you've rated as the riskiest

- What are the different perspectives on what you're trying to learn?

- What are the different groups of people who can help you learn?

Choose Your Research Methods

There are almost unlimited design research methods, and your research objective will guide you on the best ones to use. On your Assumption Log, you hopefully identified the best way to test specific assumptions. As I mentioned though, we're going to focus on customer interviews.

Customer interviews are a qualitative research method. I recommend you also include some quantitative research, like a survey. There's a lot of insight to be gained by combining both qualitative and quantitative research. The core principles that we'll cover now apply to both.

I find it's usually better to start exploratory research with conversations. While you prepare well for them, there's a lot more space for serendipity and being able to adapt, based on where the conversations go. You can't really do that with a survey.

It's great to meet people in their normal context or environment – an ethnographic research method called contextual enquiry. Being able to observe behaviours and the workflow of the people we're doing research with gives us much deeper insight than just hearing about them. This isn't always possible or appropriate, but we'll talk about being observant and I'll give tips for customer interviews in a moment.

A reminder that you're interviewing people one at a time so they can talk through their experience in detail – from their own perspective without it being clouded by what someone in a group says.

Focus groups don't allow you to get the depth and context you need, and it's much harder to connect and build empathy. They also normally result in groupthink, with participants following the most dominant voice in the room. This means you don't get the diversity of thought and experience you need.

These initial conversations can be very useful when creating a survey. At the end of a survey, I like to ask if the person is open to having a conversation to share more about their experience and perspective – and asking for their contact details if they are. It's a great way to recruit research participants and build relationships.

After doing exploratory research and some synthesis – ideally including the results from your quantitative research – you'll probably find you've got more questions. It's good to plan to do a second round of interviews to be able to test your understanding. This is still with the intent of understanding what is, not testing your solution idea. We'll talk about this briefly in Chapter 8.

A simple research approach I recommend is:

- Customer interviews with an exploratory focus – using contextual enquiry where possible and appropriate

- Initial synthesis to identify the key patterns and themes that are emerging. The Empathy Map is a useful tool at this point, and it's also a good time to refine your People/Problem Canvas

- Survey to explore key themes, test some understanding, and get quantitative data from a larger sample size

- Synthesise the survey results with your interview findings to identify the key patterns, themes, and insights. Map your understanding of the current experience and journey using the Experience Blueprint, which we'll cover in Chapter 8

- Another round of customer interviews to test and refine your understanding – including what you've discovered in your market research

- Finalise your synthesis (for now) to produce a clear set of key customer insights that have been tested

- Define a clear problem that matters as a how might we (HMW) statement

- Draft the value proposition statement that you'll test in the solution phase

This approach will take four to six weeks, which is why I recommend you at least start planning for this within the first couple of days of Sprint 1. As I mentioned in Chapter 3, the combination of the learning curve and the time to set up the logistics puts this on the critical path. Each step builds on the one before, but some of this can be done in parallel.

ACTION

Your Research Approach

Take 10-15 minutes to update your Customer Research Planner with your overall research approach and method and the schedule – aligned with your sprint planning.

Research Approach & Method
- What are the key steps for your customer research?

- What methods will you use? Make a note of why you're using the method, and the type of information you expect to get from it

Research Schedule
- What is the timeline? Make sure this is aligned with and included in your sprint planning

Talk to the Right People

The key to valuable customer research is to talk to the right people. The right people to have conversations with are the people and groups you described as your early adopters on your People/Problem Canvas. These are the people you've identified as experiencing the problem you're focused on. The intent of these conversations is to build empathy with your ideal customers.

The information we get from doing research with people who aren't our early adopters or ideal customers might be interesting, but it's often misleading and can be dangerous – or at least it's not helping us learn what we need to. Asking friends and family if they like our idea doesn't count as customer research.

As part of that action, you also answered these two questions:

- What are the key characteristics of these people?
- How will you identify early adopters?

Let's build on this to be even more specific.

People often initially answer these types of questions with demographics: age, gender, where they live, how much money they make, level of education, occupation. These can be good things to understand about your customers, but identifying their attitudes and behaviours is much more important.

Psychographics

Psychographics is the name for the set of attributes that drives customer behaviour. You started identifying some of these with the needs, wants, and fears of your early adopters on your People/Problem Canvas. This is about understanding attitudes and behaviours. What do your early adopters value? What motivates them?

There will be plenty of assumptions here until you've talked to these people and started building empathy. From this work, you have enough to start describing some of the key attributes of the right people to talk with now. Be mindful of where you're making assumptions and add them to your Assumptions Log.

Segments

A segment is a group of people who share a set of these psychographic attributes and have a similar need. You might have a group who will be the end user or beneficiary of your solution, and there might be another who will be the paying customer. These two perspectives would usually be in their own segments.

How many segments do you have? What do you call them?

Screeners

Now that you've built up a picture of the right people to talk to, and have done some basic segmentation, you need to screen potential customer research participants to match your criteria. In design research, we use a screener to do this.

As I mentioned, we're primarily screening for psychographics and behaviours – rather than demographics. We also need to be clear which of our segments they fit into.

To do this, you need a clear picture of the attributes your research participants must have. If they don't have these attributes, it means they're not the right people to be doing this research with, and you won't interview them. These are your eligibility requirements.

It's also common to have some exclusion criteria – attributes that mean the person isn't eligible and you won't interview them. This is often because they're expert users and not representative of your early adopters – unless you're focused on helping expert users, of course.

With a screener, the intent is to filter out people who don't match the eligibility requirements as quickly as possible so you don't waste anyone's time. This means asking a set of precise questions with the must-have attributes first. We'll talk about recruiting research participants in a moment.

Sample Size & Mix

You're probably wondering how many people you need to talk to. There's no absolute answer to this. What I recommend is to start with five or six people from each of your segments. If you're still learning very new things from each conversation and a consistent pattern isn't emerging, you probably need to add more people to your sample size. I recommend you talk with at least 10 people during the two rounds of research.

Your sample mix needs to be representative. What representative means will depend on your context, but think about the people who make up your customer segments – are they represented in the people you're interviewing? This includes thinking about the demographics: gender, ethnicity, age, and other relevant attributes. It's also an opportunity to apply inclusive design principles and include people who've traditionally been underrepresented.

Ethics

We want to be ethical in everything we do. Through design research, we're seeking to understand what really matters to people and their deepest motivations – what triggers certain thinking patterns and behaviours.

Sadly, there are examples of this type of information being used to manipulate people to do things that aren't in their best interests. We have a responsibility to collect, store, and use our design research in ethical ways.

It's not up to me to tell you what's ethical. In certain contexts, the ethical requirements will be documented, and you might need approval. Even if your research has been deemed legal and ethical by an authority, I encourage you to use the test of what your research participants think is ethical and fair. Empathy is a good principle to apply here.

We talked about the three types of empathy in Chapter 2. Design research helps us understand and create a picture of our customers' mental models and language. This is cognitive empathy. Through these conversations, we also need to build emotional and compassionate empathy. Aligned with this, the principle of "nothing about me, without me" is a very good guide.

Visit dynamic4.com/sptm for links to additional useful resources on research screeners, sample sizes, and design research ethics.

Your Research Participant Screening Criteria

Take 10-15 minutes to update your Customer Research Planner to describe the attributes of the people you need to talk to.

Eligibility Requirements (Must-Have Attributes)

What are the attributes the people must definitely have? If a potential research participant doesn't match these attributes, they aren't the right person to talk to, and you won't interview them.

Exclusions

People with these attributes aren't eligible, and you won't interview them.

Sample Size & Mix

What are your different segments? How many people from each segment do you plan to interview? What is your sample mix to be representative?

Recruit Participants & Set Up Logistics

Now you're clear on your research approach, the methods you'll use, and the right people to do your research with – it's time to find those people and set up the logistics.

Recruit Research Participants

Where are the people you want to talk with, and how can you reach them? How will you screen them? If you're already active in a community where your early adopters are, this is much easier. If you're not, now is a good time to identify the places they hang out and join those communities. This might be a physical place or online. A good principle to apply whenever you're thinking about customers is to go where they already are.

Good ways to find your early adopters to participate in your research include networking and support groups, online forums and social media groups, professional associations and clubs, your network and their connections, and partner organisations. In some cases, you might even pay a professional research participant recruiter.

It's important to get beyond your immediate network and people you know well. Your screener plays a critical role in selecting the right people. Using an online screening survey based on your eligibility requirements is a good way to do this efficiently.

Be clear about what you need, how long it will take, if you plan to visit them in their context or meet somewhere else, and if you're paying for their participation. This payment is normally referred to as an incentive.

When recruiting research participants directly, most people won't expect to be paid an incentive, and they're just happy to have a conversation – maybe with a coffee or something.

If you use a professional recruiter, participants usually expect an incentive – and you'll also pay the recruiter for their services. It's important to be clear what if any incentive you're providing.

Interview Logistics

There are a few interview logistics to think about. This is a case of being prepared and thinking through the experience you want to design for your research participants – the whole journey from how they find out about the opportunity to participate, express their interest, set up the interview, the interview itself, and what happens afterwards. Some of these participants may even end up becoming customers – and this first impression will last.

Who?

Who will be in the interviews? There will at least be you and the person you're interviewing. When possible, it often works well to have a lead interviewer and a note-taker. This allows you as the interviewer to stay focused on the person you're interviewing without breaking the connection and looking down to take notes while they're talking. It also tends to help the conversation flow a lot better.

If you're working solo, this might not be possible though. Be mindful that you need to maintain the connection. This might mean not taking lengthy notes, and relying on another form of recording to refer to.

Where?

Where will you do the interviews? If it's possible and appropriate, meeting your participant where they spend their time and experience the problem you're focusing on is likely to give you a lot more insight than meeting in a neutral place. This might be their home, office, or somewhere else.

For some research, it's more appropriate or practical to do the interview in a neutral place or even rooms specifically set up for interviews. These facilities are normally set up with video recording and often an adjoining observation room. Interviews by phone and video calls have become common recently too.

Wherever you're having the conversation, the person you're talking with needs to feel safe and confident to share their thinking and experience.

Each option has constraints and logistics to organise. What they are will depend on your specific context. It's always good to have a backup plan too.

Recording

How will you record the interviews? To have reliable data to synthesise, you need some form of recording. This might just be notes that you make during the interview or immediately after. It might be a video or audio recording or a combination.

Whatever method you're using to record the conversation – including written notes – you need to let the person you're interviewing know, and get their explicit consent.

I like to at least have an audio recording of the conversation. I normally just use my phone, and within a couple of minutes we've both forgotten that we're recording the conversation, and it doesn't impact the rapport. I don't take many notes but I do write down important numbers, dates, and key phrases that are used. I then rely on the recording to get the quotes correct word for word.

In most physical contexts, it's challenging to set up video recording and get good quality video without it changing the dynamic of the conversation. This has changed with video calls. It's now very easy to record these conversations without it being intrusive – always with explicit consent of course.

From these audio and video recordings, it's easy to get very accurate transcripts which are great for synthesis. Otter.ai is a transcription service I use, and they provide a basic free plan.

When?

What's the interview schedule? This needs to align with your overall research approach and schedule. You also need to agree and communicate this clearly with your research participants.

An important tip for scheduling is to allow a break to reflect and debrief immediately after each interview, especially before your next interview. I recommend 15-30 minutes.

Reflect & Debrief

If you're doing the interviews by yourself, reflect on what you heard and make some brief notes on your observations while the memory is fresh. Include key words, phrases, and quotes – or at least where to find them in the recording. These need to be word for word accurate because the language used is very important. Also, make a note of the body language and facial expressions you observed – with the context. What was being discussed at the time?

If you have a note-taker working with you, take a moment to discuss and compare your observations.

Your Research Participant Recruitment & Logistics

Take 10-15 minutes to update your Customer Research Planner with your plan for recruitment and logistics.

Research Participant Recruitment

Where are the people you want to talk with, and how can you reach them? How will you screen them?

Participant Incentives (If Any)

Are you paying an incentive? If you are, how much are you paying and how?

Who?

Who will be in the interviews?

Where?

Where will you do the interviews?

Recording

How will you record the interviews?

When?

What's the interview schedule?

Ask Good Questions

What does it mean to ask good questions? It starts with talking to the right people. If you're not talking to the right people – your early adopters and ideal customers – then it doesn't matter what questions you ask. The information you get is going to put you on the wrong path.

The intent of these conversations is to build empathy and to get a deep understanding of how they think, feel, behave, what they expect, and what motivates them. Not just how, but why. What triggers certain thinking, behaviours, processes, and workflows?

We're exploring and learning. We're curious and genuinely interested in the people we're talking with. This means we ask questions that will draw these things out. Good questions will result in conversations that help us learn what we need to – aligned with our research objective.

Start a Conversation

Customer interviews are a conversation, not an interrogation. Rapport is important. The sooner you can both feel safe and confident to have an open and honest conversation without judgement, the more enjoyable it will be, and you'll get more valuable information.

Start by getting to know the person. Ask open questions that invite your research participant to share, and show that you're interested. Start easy and on a positive note – remember the power of switching the brain to positive that we covered in Chapter 1.

Everyone has their own style, but I approach these conversations in a casual and slightly playful way. I'm mindful of my energy and how it's perceived. Even when I might be feeling quite drained from doing six hours straight of customer interviews, I lift my energy and enthusiasm because I know the person I'm talking with will feed off that and mirror that energy. If I'm flat, the conversation is very likely to be slow and feel like hard work for both of us.

To start a conversation and encourage stories, we need to use open questions – questions that open up possibilities for discussion, rather than closed questions that shut things down.

Encourage Stories

We all have a gap between what we say and what we actually do. We also tend to be quite optimistic and aspirational when asked what we'd do in the future. If we rely on this stated behaviour, we can end up very disappointed.

A key technique that helps overcome this is to encourage the person you're interviewing to share stories. Ask questions that draw out and explore stories about things they've actually done in the past. Ask them to walk you through specific examples of how they did something and why. The information you get from these stories is a lot more reliable.

Asking hypothetical questions about what they plan to do in the future can give some good clues about what's important to them and how they aspire to behave, but unfortunately that's also likely to be quite different to what they actually do.

Understand How They Make Decisions

Building on drawing out stories, understanding how they made their decisions is the source of great insight.

Ask how they made the decisions or choices in their stories. What triggered the event or decision? What did they hope to achieve? What options did they consider? What information did they use? Where did they get that information? How did they prioritise things? Where were they when they were making this decision? Who else was involved in making the decision?

Getting a clear picture of the key triggers that start this process is one of the most valuable insights you can get. Understanding how they think and feel through the decision-making process is really important and helps build empathy. Then there are the practical steps in the process – what they did, with who, and where.

Ask Clarifying Questions

As the conversation unfolds, you're going to have more questions, and need to check your understanding of things that have been said. There will also be times when you feel like some important parts of the story have been left unsaid. Asking some follow-up questions to draw these points out and clarify your understanding will result in a clearer picture. They're also a natural part of conversation.

The timing of these clarifying questions is also important. If you're constantly interrupting with another question, it stops the flow of the conversation. Sometimes it's better to make a brief note and come back to it towards the end of the interview.

Avoid Closed & Leading Questions

I mentioned closed questions briefly. These are questions that commonly result in a yes or no answer – or at least a very short reply. Closed questions can play a role when confirming your understanding of something, but they shut things down rather than open them up.

Leading questions are a bit trickier. A leading question encourages the person we're interviewing to give a particular answer. Sometimes we ask leading questions just by the way we phrase things, and not because we intend to influence the response. This means we need to be aware of how we're phrasing questions, and it takes practice. I've been doing customer research for decades, and I still catch myself accidentally phrasing some interview questions in a leading way.

Let's put this into practice now by preparing your Conversation Guide. If you haven't already, visit dynamic4.com/sptm and download the Conversation Guide Template.

Prepare Your Conversation Guide

The purpose of the Conversation Guide is to help you prepare and feel confident to do your customer interviews. You will use it to guide the conversation and to have some consistency across the people that you interview – making sure you're collecting a similar set of information.

Think of this as a conversation guide, not a script. We want this to feel like an open conversation, not an interrogation. If you read from a script, it doesn't feel natural and quickly becomes stilted. This isn't good for building rapport and empathy.

Research Objective

It's important to be clear about your research objective. Why are you having this conversation? What are you hoping to learn? This clarity will help as you prepare your conversation guide.

You wrote your research objective on your Customer Research Planner. Copy this to your Conversation Guide. Refine it if you need to.

Topics

Thinking about your research objective, what are the specific topics that you need to learn about? This breaks your research objective down into some more manageable themes. I recommend having no more than five topic areas. How much time do you plan to allocate to each topic?

The template already includes a welcome, final questions and comments, and the interview close.

Questions

Finally, we have the high-level questions that you'll ask for each topic. These will help start and guide the conversation. Remember, this is a guide, not a script.

Your first draft might be very text heavy with a lot of questions. That's ok, and a good place to start. Refine and simplify it to get to a set of questions that will help you feel confident about keeping the conversation moving and covering the key things you need to learn.

Your final Conversation Guide should be glanceable – you can just glance down at the sheet and know which part of the conversation you're up to. If you're looking at big blocks of text, you won't be able to find your place, or you'll probably start reading it like a script.

Your Conversation Guide

Take 30-45 minutes to prepare your Conversation Guide. Remember to keep it glanceable.

Research Objective

- Copy your research objective from your Customer Research Planner. Refine it if you need to

Topics

- What are the specific topics that you need to learn about? No more than five

- How much time do you plan to allocate to each topic?

Questions

- What are the high-level questions that you'll ask for each topic to help start and guide the conversation?

Interview Tips & Recap

You've now prepared for your customer interviews and have set up the logistics. I hope you feel confident and excited about having some interesting conversations. Here are some final tips for the interviews, and a quick recap of what we've covered.

Allow for Silence

Allowing for silence is often one of the most challenging things if you're new to customer interviews. Silence can be uncomfortable. When you ask a question, it's important to give the person time to think and respond. That silence can feel like it's lasting forever. Resist the urge to jump in and fill it.

You'll get more comfortable with silence as you do more interviews.

If the person you're interviewing never pauses to think about their answer, it can be an indication that you're not getting below the surface to what's really going on.

Ask Why

Asking why is important. Sometimes the initial response you get can be at a very superficial level. As you draw them out on why, you'll get a deeper understanding of their motivations and what's really going on. This gives us much richer information.

Take Good Notes

I mentioned a few things about recording and taking notes in the Interview Logistics section. If you have someone taking notes, this advice is for them too. You might also do some of this note-taking from a recording.

It's important to take careful note of the key words, phrases, and quotes that the people you're interviewing use. These need to be word for word accurate. The language people use is shaped by how they think, and it also shapes the way they think. It gives us signals about what they value. Being able to communicate using your customers' language is powerful.

Be Observant

Being curious and observant is critical during customer research. We've talked about taking good notes and observing the language used. You might have heard about a study done at UCLA that concluded that up to 93% of communication is nonverbal. It turns out that that study was flawed, but we do know that a substantial portion of our communication is nonverbal.

What is nonverbal communication? We all send a stream of visual cues to the world expressing who we are, what we care about, our reaction to things, and how we want to be perceived. This includes our body language and facial expressions, how we greet people, our tone of voice, the photos and items we display, what we wear, what we carry with us, and much more – a lot of this we do without thinking.

We can still observe a lot of these things when doing research remotely. Simple things like the profile image people use. Who is in it?

What's the setting? Are they by themselves or with someone else or a pet? Or are they not in the image and are using the default image or an avatar instead? If you're doing an interview by video, what's in the background? Or do they use a virtual background? What tone do they use in written communications? How do they sign off? Is it formal or informal?

When making notes on body language and facial expressions, make sure you include the context of what was being talked about. Making a note that they crossed their arms doesn't mean anything without context. If they crossed their arms when you talked about a certain topic, that might have some meaning.

We can learn so much by being observant. An important note though: when we make these observations, we're giving them meaning based on social norms and our own set of cognitive biases. We're making assumptions. Rather than giving these things absolute meaning, think of them as assumptions to explore and test.

Practice

Customer interviews will feel more natural with practice, and you'll build your confidence. As you prepare for these conversations and start having them, you'll probably find that you've already been doing a lot of these things, and you're just doing them in a more conscious way now.

Recap

There are so many more things I'd love to share, because I love having these conversations. But it's time for me to do a quick recap of what we've covered and get out of the way so you can go and have some interesting conversations with your early adopters and ideal customers.

1. Be clear on who your early adopters are, and what you need to learn from them

2. Get the logistics sorted early and have a backup plan

3. Prepare a few good questions that will guide the conversation, help you learn, and build empathy.

4. Encourage rich stories

5. Be observant and take good notes

Make Sense of What You Heard

Before starting your customer research, it's worth having a quick look at Chapter 8: Make Sense. It's important to have an idea of how you'll synthesise the data and make sense of what you've heard in these interviews.

Do Your Research

You've prepared well for these conversations, and you can go into them with confidence. They will feel more natural with practice.

Remember, the intent of these conversations is to build empathy and to get a deep understanding of how they think, feel, behave, what they expect, and what motivates them. Explore and learn. Be curious and genuinely interested in the people you're talking with.

Build rapport and create an environment where you both feel safe and confident to have an open and honest conversation without judgement. Most of all, have fun and start some good relationships.

This chapter has focused on helping you prepare for engaging customer interviews and to feel confident to do this research. We focused on customer interviews, but most of the principles we covered also apply to surveys and other research methods.

I hope you've been having meaningful conversations with the people you would like to be your customers, and that this is helping refine your thinking. I also hope you're building good relationships as part of this.

Through these conversations, you've probably heard a bit about what your customers see as their options, how they currently solve their problem, and how they make those decisions. This information gives you clues about the market you're operating in and what some of the market dynamics are. We'll now do some research on the market to get some reliable information and data.

Chapter 7

Market

Research

Diverge

Converge

Diverge

Converge

Problem
**Are we solving the
right problem?**

Solution

Is it the right
solution?

The purpose of this chapter is to understand how your ideal customers currently solve their problem, the market dynamics, and the market size and opportunity.

In Chapter 5, you used the Business Model Environment tool to identify how some external forces are likely to impact your organisation and business model. A lot of these elements are related to market dynamics. In this chapter, you'll build on this, and do some market research to know more about what you're dealing with.

This also builds on your customer research. From conversations with your customers, you have some key insights on their desires, expectations, priorities, how they make decisions, and their actual behaviours.

Most of your market research is likely to be secondary or desk research, but I recommend including some of this in your customer research. In this chapter, you'll explore critical questions like:

- What do customers want?
- Where is demand increasing or shrinking? Is there unmet demand?
- What options do customers compare when seeking to solve their problem?
- Who's already in the market?
- How do they approach the problem? Are they successful?

- What's their business model? How do they price things?
- What's the market size and opportunity?

Why do market research? According to research by CB Insights, the top three reasons startups fail are: "ran out of cash", "no market need", and "got outcompeted". No market need and getting outcompeted relate directly to market risk – and both are often the cause of running out of money.

In simple terms, this means people don't actually want to buy and use what they're selling – or that the market isn't big enough for the idea to be financially viable.

Market research starts looking at the intersection of the desirable and viable lenses of the three lenses model. Remember:

- If it's not desirable, we end up with a solution that no one wants
- If it's not viable, we can't afford to make it happen – and we'll run out of money

We do market research – along with customer research – to give us the best chance of identifying a problem that really matters to our ideal customers. A problem that's a priority for enough people – who are willing to pay to do something about it.

Existing Alternatives

To get started, let's talk about "the market". A market is where people buy and sell products and services. You might picture a small local market when I say that. That's a good tangible place to start. In that context, it's a physical meeting place where people who have things to sell meet people who want to buy something. A sale is only made when the customer sees something they want at a price they're willing to pay.

A florist in this market might think they're in the floristry business – but the customer is looking to buy a gift – not necessarily flowers. They're choosing between buying some crafts, a book, or maybe even a potted plant. Flowers aren't their only option. They might not even be their preferred option.

A seller in this small local market is trying to get noticed, and they hopefully have something customers want to buy at a price that works for both. They're also being compared to other options – often in ways that aren't obvious.

Take all of these elements and scale them up. There are now maybe millions of potential customers and thousands of sellers – each offering alternative ways for customers to spend their money, time, and attention.

We can sometimes feel pretty confident about the market we're in. The danger is, we might think one thing, when our ideal customers think something different. They might be comparing us to a very different category of solution.

Your Competitors

You'll definitely have direct and indirect competitors. If you tell people you don't have any competitors, they won't believe you. And they shouldn't. You might feel that you can be different and better, but that's not the same thing as your customers not having other choices.

Think laterally about what your customers' other choices might be. Using the video streaming service Netflix as an example, they have very direct video streaming competitors – but in 2017, Reed Hastings, the Netflix CEO, said that sleep is actually their biggest competitor. Their customers have the choice of going to sleep or to keep watching.

In Chapter 6, I recommended one of the things to explore during your customer interviews is how they currently solve the problem, the options they considered, and how they made the decision. This is often the source of a lot of meaningful insight about the market – as your ideal customers see it.

In Chapter 5, you used the Business Model Environment tool to identify market and industry forces that influence your organisational context – this included competitors. You also identified existing alternatives as part of your current state Lean Canvas.

Bring all of these elements together and build on them. This will help you identify your customers' existing alternatives. This will likely include direct and indirect competitors, as well as some workarounds and do-it-yourself solutions.

In reality, you might find some of the organisations which provide an alternative solution are actually potential partners and collaborators. I recommend starting with that perspective rather than taking a combative approach.

Satisficed

If you're being really honest with what the reality is, you'll identify other ways your customers choose to spend their money, time, and attention – rather than on the optimal solution.

In behavioural economics, there's the concept of "satisfice" – a portmanteau of satisfy and suffice. The term was introduced in 1956 by Herbert Simon, a winner of the Nobel Prize in Economic Sciences. His primary field of research was decision making in organisations.

Herbert Simon said, "decision makers can satisfice either by finding optimum

solutions for a simplified world, or by finding satisfactory solutions for a more realistic world".

The concept is simple, and I'm sure it's a behaviour you've observed in yourself and others. A common example is when we choose things that "will do", but they don't really meet our expectations. When something is only just good enough, but it would take too much effort and money to find or change to a better solution. Or it's just not a high priority.

What I'm saying here is, don't dismiss what appear to be inferior alternatives or workarounds. They might just turn out to be your biggest competitors.

Competition Slide

In the pitch deck section of Chapter 3, I mentioned there's usually a slide on the competition. There are different ways to communicate this information. Some common ways are the 2x2 market/competitor matrix (or magic quadrant), Steve Blank's petal diagram, and a comparison table.

It's probably too early to be comparing your solution to the others, and it would be better to come back to this in Chapter 16 when you're refining your pitch deck.

If you decide to use the 2x2 format, remember to always put your solution in the top right quadrant. It's a rigged slide, and everyone knows it because you're choosing the axis, but it's still one of the most common formats of this slide.

I like Steve Blank's petal diagram in many cases because it communicates a broader view of the market landscape and adjacent markets. Social enterprise ideas are often multidimensional, and bring together hybrid models to address gaps in the market. I find the petal diagram does a better job of communicating this than the standard 2x2.

Visit dynamic4.com/sptm for links to more resources and examples.

Coaching Questions

- Who are the incumbents or the de facto standard?

- Who are the insurgents?

- What market do they identify as or communicate that they're in?

- What market or category do your customers see them as?

- What's their value proposition, business model, and pricing?

ACTION

Your Competitors

Take 15-30 minutes to review your People/Problem Canvas, Business Model Environment, and research findings to list your customers' existing alternatives.

Refine the competitor slide in your pitch deck.

Size Up the Market

Market sizing estimates how big the opportunity is. A key focus is to see if the market is big enough for the idea to be financially viable. It looks at questions like:

- How big is the problem?
- Are there enough people willing to pay to do something about this problem?
- Who will pay?
- How much do your customers already spend each year on this?

Social & Environmental Impact

Traditionally, this has only included the financial opportunity. For social enterprise ideas, or if you want to embed impact in your business model, I also like to see a social and environmental lens on these calculations. This works best as a combination of financials and key insights:

- Who is impacted?
- How many people are impacted?
- How much money is currently spent to address the problem?
- How much of this money could be saved? Who would make these savings? What would they do with the money saved?

- What's the waste created and the carbon impact of the current situation? How much of this could be reduced?
- What's the cost of this problem not being adequately addressed?

There's an opportunity to link this with your theory of change, SDGs, and outcome measures that you identified in Chapter 4.

TAM, SAM & SOM

Evaluating your market size is important at this stage. It will require more market research, and you'll have plenty of assumptions as you calculate this – which is fine. With all of these assumptions, the important thing is to make them explicit and test the riskiest ones.

You'll probably hear about TAM, SAM, and SOM as you do your market research. The numbers put to these sizes are generally the annual spend. Here's a very brief explanation:

- TAM is the Total Addressable Market. It's the big number – the entire potential market
- SAM is the Serviceable Addressable Market. This is the financial value of the market you believe you can actually serve with your solution
- SOM is the Serviceable Obtainable Market. This is the financial value of the market you can serve realistically in the short term

There are two major ways to calculate the market size, especially your SOM. Top-down and bottom-up.

Top-down is common, but usually very inaccurate. The rationale and assumptions used for this approach generally aren't very useful. Because market size numbers tend to be fiction, the most valuable part of the exercise is to have solid rationale and assumptions to test.

Unfortunately, it's common to see founders make up a big number for TAM, based on questionable research, and then arbitrarily say that they'll capture 1% of that very large market. Which results in a big number. A big number that no one believes, and actually damages the credibility of the founder making the claim. I recommend not doing that.

The other way is to do a bottom-up calculation. I prefer this approach because it ties into pricing and financial modelling – which we'll cover in Part 3. With the bottom-up approach, you make some assumptions on the price of your solution, and multiply that by the number of paying customers each year to get your SOM.

These numbers are going to be dependent on what your solution is, the price, and the volume of sales you expect to achieve. Start with assumptions now, and you'll test and refine this in Part 3. As you get better information from this testing, you'll refine your market size calculations.

It's very rare that a single source will provide you with a relevant and reliable market size number. You'll normally need to bring together data from a few sources. It's really important to keep track of these sources and your rationale of how you've aggregated numbers to arrive at your conclusion.

I'll briefly cover a couple of methods that can be useful for these calculations. Visit dynamic4.com/sptm for links to more resources.

Keyword Research

Doing some keyword research can be a good data source to help in estimating your market size and to also identify trends. You wouldn't want to rely on it as your only source of data, but it can help to sense check some of your other research.

This method relies on mass data to be useful, so it makes sense to use the dominant search engine and social media platforms for your region or the region that you're researching.

If Google is the dominant search engine for the region you're researching (it is for most), it's worth having a look at Google Trends (trends.google.com) to see how search terms relevant to your idea are trending. You can view this data by geography, time range, categories, and more.

The year in search section also provides some interesting insights like "the world searched for how to start a business more than how to get a job in 2021".

Customer Lifetime Value (CLV)

CLV can be another useful metric when calculating the market opportunity and pricing. It predicts how much a customer will spend with your organisation from first purchase until they stop purchasing from you.

The formula to calculate CLV is simple: (annual revenue per customer x customer relationship in years) – customer acquisition cost

If you're retaining customers, you don't need to acquire as many new ones to achieve the SOM calculation. If you have a high customer turnover (churn), you need to acquire a lot of new customers each year to achieve your SOM. This can drive some key decisions in your business model and the service you provide.

Your Market Opportunity

Take 45-60 minutes to research the size of the market and the impact of the problem you're focused on.

Describe how big the problem is and why it matters.

Calculate your SOM and make your research sources, rationale, and assumptions explicit.

Update the market opportunity slide in your pitch deck.

Coaching Questions

- How big is the market?
- Are there enough people willing to pay to do something about this problem?
- How do you know? What's the research and evidence to support your position?
- Is the market growing or shrinking? At what rate?
- What are the unique attributes of your market?
- What's the size of the social and environmental problem?
- What has been the most surprising insight from your market research?

Your market research has given you a clearer picture of the market. You know how your customers currently solve the problem, the alternatives that already exist, and the size of the opportunity.

We'll now bring all of your research findings together to make sense of things.

Chapter 8

Make Sense

Diverge

Converge

Diverge

Converge

Problem
Are we solving the right problem?

Solution

Is it the right
solution?

The purpose of this chapter is to help you make sense of your research findings. This includes synthesising and integrating your original thinking and internal perspective with your increased understanding of the systems involved, the empathy and insights from conversations with your customers, and a clearer picture of the market.

And it means your thinking will evolve.

Making sense is a convergent process to narrow your focus and get clarity on the real problem to solve. A problem that really matters to the people you want to help. This can be quite a confronting and emotional process. If you're not feeling challenged by what you've learnt in your research, and it's all confirming what you already thought... I encourage you to dig deeper. And be very aware of your confirmation bias.

You did some synthesis and sense-making as you did your research, but now is the time to bring all of your research findings together to find the patterns, themes, and insights.

By the end of this chapter, you want sharp clarity on the real problem to solve – based on evidence, insight, and meaningful empathy.

The way we'll approach this is to:

- Identify the patterns and themes in your research data
- Build empathy by refining your People/ Problem Canvas and creating an Empathy Map
- Map the current experience and journey
- Draft your insight statements
- Test your thinking captured in your draft insight statements and current state experience blueprint
- Define a clear problem that matters as a how might we (HMW) statement
- Draft the value proposition statement that you'll test in the solution phase

Synthesise the Research Data

You've been gathering information and building empathy... you might feel like you're swimming in possibilities. That's a good thing, and a sign that you're learning and hopefully not holding on to the thinking you started with too tightly.

You've been doing some synthesis as you did your research. Now it's time to take a step back and look at the bigger picture. We do this to see the patterns and themes that have emerged from all of your research data – both from qualitative and quantitative methods.

There will be patterns and apparent contradictions from what you've heard from individual people – and that will be the case across your research participants as a whole. Synthesis is part science and part art. We always need to be mindful that we're filtering what we've heard through our cognitive biases and perspective.

In the Integral Theory & Sense-Making section of Chapter 2, we talked about AQAL from Integral Theory as a simple framework to think about the four different but interrelated perspectives that apply to all human experience – on the axis of individual and collective, internal and external.

We also talked about abductive reasoning and first principles. "Abduction is the process of forming an explanatory hypothesis... suggests that something may be", as CS Peirce said.

We need to really understand what is – the current reality. This means getting down to first principles rather than building on faulty assumptions. We use abductive reasoning to generate hypotheses about "something that may be". We then test our hypotheses and ideas using approaches consistent with the scientific method.

With that framing, and doing your best to stay open to seeing what's there rather than what you want to see... what are the patterns in the research data? You need patterns across the full dataset to build up a reliable set of insights.

How do we do this?

Affinity Mapping

Affinity mapping (or affinity diagramming) is a simple and intuitive method to sort through and start making sense of large amounts of data. It works well even when you have different types of data from various sources and methods.

I'll outline a simple explanation, but if you need more guidance on affinity mapping and other synthesis methods, I recommend Jon Kolko's *Exposing the Magic of Design* and *Design. Think. Make. Break. Repeat.* by Martin Tomitsch & Co. Visit dynamic4.com/sptm for links to more resources.

The process is simple, and you've probably already used this method in the past, especially if you've ever worked with sticky notes. Sticky notes are great if you're working on a wall, especially with other people. Online whiteboards also work well for this. You can also use index cards. Whatever you use, the critical thing is you can rearrange them easily.

This is a critical time of convergence. It's about bringing together and integrating all of the research you've done in Chapters 5, 6, 7, and beyond. Your data sources are likely to include:

- Transcripts from your customer interviews

- Comments from your surveys

- Numerical data from your surveys

- Market size and opportunity findings and statistics

- Alternatives in the market and who uses them

- Market trends and other observations from your Business Model Environment

- Statistics and key pieces of information about the impact of the social and environmental challenges

- Root cause analysis

- Observations about feedback loops, incentives, and other components of the system

With synthesis, we're working at a couple of levels of detail at the same time, but we need to be careful not to conflate them. We're looking at the big picture to see patterns and themes across all of the research and the many perspectives involved... and we're also seeking to understand and build empathy with the individuals and our segments within that bigger picture.

This comes back to the key things we covered in the Talking to the Right People section of Chapter 6, and we'll look at this a little more in the next section on Build Empathy.

Some really important notes:

- Write one piece of data or information on each sticky note because you're going to be moving them around

- Make a note of the data source so you can refer to each piece of data in its original context. This includes the segment the person is in or represents

- Words, phrases, and quotes noted need to be word for word accurate. Where you have notes on body language, facial expressions, and other observations – don't lose the context

With these data sources collected and those points in mind, the process itself is simple:

- Write one piece of data on each sticky note and lay the notes out randomly

- Take a moment to scan through them

- As you see sticky notes that are related, move them next to each other to create clusters or groups – but keep each sticky note visible. If you're doing this with other people, explain why you're moving them together

- Work through all of your sticky notes identifying patterns and connections, but don't let any cluster become too big. Split them into smaller groups where it makes sense

- When your clusters are stable and not being moved around any more, give each a name. This label is the theme of the cluster, and it's good to use a different size or colour sticky note, so it stands out

- For each theme, add a few sentences describing what it is and why it has been identified as a key theme

- You might want to create connections between clusters depending on what you've found

Synthesise the Research Data

Take 45-60 minutes to do your affinity mapping of the research data. This will result in your research themes and findings.

You'll build on these, take a position, and crystallise some key insights with the next few actions.

Coaching Questions

- What patterns and themes really stood out for you?

- What language did you hear from your customers, the key words and phrases that they used?

- How do your ideal customers describe the problem?

- How do your ideal customers currently solve the problem? What are the alternatives that they use?

- Who buys the solution? How are buying decisions made?

Build Empathy

Your affinity mapping has resulted in some research themes and findings. Some of these are going to be at the big picture level, which gives us important context. We also want to build empathy with the individuals and our segments within that bigger picture.

A couple of tools for this: the first is to build on the work you've already done on your People/Problem Canvas. If you want to dig a bit deeper, which I recommend, the Empathy Map Canvas created by Dave Gray is a well-known tool and very useful.

Refine Your People/Problem Canvas

If you haven't already, you now need to create a People/Problem Canvas for each of your segments. We want to build a very clear picture of each segment individually.

Your thinking might change significantly depending on your research findings, or it might involve smaller things like the language people use or how they talk about it.

Remember to look for patterns in what you heard from individual research participants and from multiple participants in the same segment. It's also worth noting where your segments have very different perspectives on the situation.

As we said in Chapter 5, pay special attention to the events that trigger the emotions and behaviours that you've identified. You can use affinity mapping for this too.

The final step is to identify key insights focused on building empathy, and how the people in each segment experience the problem.

ACTION

Refine Your People/Problem Canvas

Take 15-30 minutes to refine your People/Problem Canvas with your research findings.

Create a set of insight statements focused on building empathy for each segment.

Empathy Map Canvas

Dave Gray from XPLANE created the Empathy Map Canvas in the late 2000s but updated it in 2017. It's a simple and powerful way to build empathy with your ideal customers and segments. The canvas is self-explanatory and asks good questions to reflect on for each of the sections.

Again, it's important to use a separate canvas for each of your segments.

You can download the Empathy Map Canvas from gamestorming.com/empathy-map or visit dynamic4.com/sptm for links to more resources.

Personas and proto-personas can be great tools to build up a much more detailed profile of your ideal customers and segments. It takes a lot of research to do personas well.

Proto-personas are based on lighter research and a lot more assumptions. They can be valuable, but they also have a history of being misused. Visit dynamic4.com/sptm for links to more resources.

─── ACTION ───

Your Empathy Map

Take 15-20 minutes to create your Empathy Map using one for each of your segments.

Create a set of insight statements focused on building empathy for each segment.

"The biggest communication problem is we do not listen to understand. We listen to reply."

Stephen Covey

Empathy Map Canvas

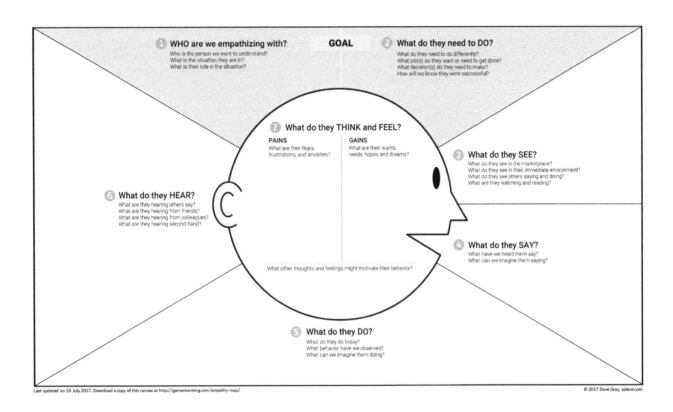

GOAL

① WHO are we empathizing with?
Who is the person we want to understand?
What is the situation they are in?
What is their role in the situation?

② What do they need to DO?
What do they need to do differently?
What job(s) do they want or need to get done?
What decision(s) do they need to make?
How will we know they were successful?

⑦ What do they THINK and FEEL?

PAINS
What are their fears, frustrations, and anxieties?

GAINS
What are their wants, needs, hopes and dreams?

What other thoughts and feelings might motivate their behavior?

③ What do they SEE?
What do they see in the marketplace?
What do they see in their immediate environment?
What do they see others saying and doing?
What are they watching and reading?

⑥ What do they HEAR?
What are they hearing others say?
What are they hearing from friends?
What are they hearing from colleagues?
What are they hearing second-hand?

④ What do they SAY?
What have we heard them say?
What can we imagine them saying?

⑤ What do they DO?
What do they do today?
What behavior have we observed?
What can we imagine them doing?

Last updated on 16 July 2017. Download a copy of this canvas at http://gamestorming.com/empathy-map/

© 2017 Dave Gray, xplane.com

Map the Current Experience

An Experience Blueprint maps the end-to-end journey of your customers as they go through the full lifecycle. The version I've created, and call an Experience Blueprint, is an amalgamation of a journey map and a service blueprint.

It shows the major stages of the journey, what the customer does at each stage, and the various touchpoints and channels the customer interacts with. And finally, the activities that need to happen in the background to deliver the experience and value through the touchpoints – the customer does not usually see this.

We often include an emotion line to show how the customer is feeling through the journey – and where there are key pains or gains for the customer.

You'll use the Experience Blueprint to map **the current experience**. The focus for now is to map what actually happens, not what we think should happen. You'll build on this current state Experience Blueprint in Chapter 9 when you start exploring possible solutions.

We always look at the journey from the customers' perspective first. The full lifecycle normally includes these major stages. Your stages will be specific to your context.

- **Awareness**. How do customers find out about their options?

- **Research & Comparison**. How do customers research and compare their options?

- **Purchase**. How do customers buy the solution?

- **Onboarding & First Use**. What is involved in the customer using the solutions for the first time?

- **Ongoing Use & Support**. What is involved in the customer using the solution over time, and what happens when things go wrong and they need support?

- **End of Life**. What happens when the solution reaches the end of its useful life? What does the customer do? How is the solution decommissioned?

The simplest way to use the Experience Blueprint is to create one for each role that you're focusing on. So if you have a paying customer with a different group of people who use the solution, they will each have their own Experience Blueprint. I normally combine these with journey rows for each role, but let's keep it simple for now.

Some basic guidance on the Experience Blueprint:

- **Early Adopter Characteristics**. Which early adopter or role are you focusing on, and what are some of their key characteristics?

- **Main Problem**. What's the main problem your early adopter experiences?

- **Key Insight/Riskiest Assumption**. What are the key insights you're working with? What are your riskiest assumptions?

- **Journey Stage**. What are the major stages in their current journey? I listed some stages that are common to a lot of journeys

- **Customer Journey**. What is the customer doing and experiencing at each stage in the journey? Turn it into a brief story or narrative from the customer's perspective

- **Touchpoints & Channels**. What are the various touchpoints and channels the customer interacts with at each stage of the journey?

- **Feelings**. How is the customer feeling at each stage of the journey? What are the pain points? What are the delight points?

- **Background Activities**. What needs to happen in the background to deliver the experience and value through the touchpoints? Who does it?

Map the Current Experience

Take 30-45 minutes to map the end-to-end journey of the current experience with the touchpoints and channels and key pain and delight points for the customer.

What do you know about what happens in the background to deliver the solution?

Ash Maurya's Customer Forces Canvas is another tool I like to map aspects of the current experience, especially as a way to capture what the triggers are. Visit dynamic4.com/sptm for links to more resources.

Dynamic4 Experience Blueprint

Early Adopter	Early Adopter Characteristics	Main Problem	Key Insight/Riskiest Assumption

Journey Stage	Stage 1	Stage 2	Stage 3	Stage 4	Stage 5	Stage 6
Customer Journey						
Touchpoints & Channels						
Feelings						
Background Activities						

Take a Position

As we progress through the synthesis process and the convergence phase of the problem diamond, we need to take a position. We do this with the best information we have. We also know this information is incomplete, and to some degree, inaccurate. We'll never have perfect information.

Every aspect of this process is biased – no matter how much we try to remove bias. You've spoken to a relatively small number of people. You're filtering what you've heard through your experiences and cognitive biases. This introduces risk. But they're risks you need to take to have any chance of progressing.

There's no point pretending reality is something other than it is. Being mindful of that reality and managing the risk is what matters.

As you've synthesised the research data, refined your People/Problem Canvas, created your Empathy Map, and mapped the current experience – you've been generating and capturing your insights.

It's time to review all of these insights and refine them. Don't ignore the outliers. Dig deeper into them. That's often where the real learning is.

I love the way Jon Kolko talks about this... "these insights are provocative statements of truth about human behaviour. They're framed as universal truths... we spoke to 16 people, and we're making sweeping generalisations about the world, and I don't care". It's what happens next that's really important.

They pose the question "why?" over and over, and answer it as a way to refine and sharpen the insight statements. Then they use these insights as scaffolding to create value proposition statements, which we'll do in a moment.

ACTION

Your Customer Insights

Review all of the insight statements you've been creating. Identify the key findings, patterns, themes, and opportunities.

Frame what you feel are the most important ones as statements of fact, but treat them as a provocation. Challenge your own statements to refine them.

Congratulations. You've taken a position. You've crystallised some key insights to make sense of what you've heard from your research. Now it's important not to hold that position too tightly. Let's keep testing your thinking to learn and manage the risk.

Test Your Thinking

You've done a lot of work to synthesise your research to make sense of what you've heard. This has resulted in your refined People/Problem Canvas, an Empathy Map, a current state Experience Blueprint, and your insight statements.

You're now at the pointy end of the problem diamond, converging on the mid-point – which is where we want sharp clarity on the real problem to solve – based on evidence, insight, and meaningful empathy.

As we just talked about in Take a Position, there's still a lot of risk. You'll still have incomplete and inaccurate information. You'll be making assumptions, and some of those will be risky.

In the Choose Your Research Methods section of Chapter 6, I recommended another round of customer interviews to test and refine your understanding – including what you've discovered in your market research. This is followed by finalising your synthesis (for now) to produce a clear set of key customer insights that have been tested.

The preparation for the second round of customer interviews is the same as your first round. The purpose is slightly different though. The first round was exploratory and about opening things up to learn as much as possible. The purpose of this round of research is to test and refine your thinking to continue converging.

As we covered in Chapter 2, when we apply the scientific method, we don't seek to validate our thinking – we seek to learn and improve. **We test to see where our thinking is wrong. And why. Then use this information to refine it.**

I really like the way David Bland and Alex Osterwalder talk about the concept of strength of evidence in *Testing Business Ideas*. Not all evidence and insights are equal. They talk about the type and strength of evidence and the number of data points. These three dimensions should drive our confidence level.

ACTION

Test Your Thinking

Prepare for your second round of customer interviews following the same process you used in Chapter 6.

Do your customer research.

Synthesise your findings and refine your People/Problem Canvas, Empathy Map, current state Experience Blueprint, and your insight statements where needed.

Clarity

Congratulations, you've reached the end of the problem diamond! You now have a beautiful clarity on the people and their context... and the real problem to solve – based on evidence, insight, and meaningful empathy. The fog of uncertainty is lifting.

We're now heading into the next phase of the double diamond. The solution diamond.

There are a couple of things that we'll now frame up to provide a solid place to start exploring possible solutions from. A how might we statement and a draft value proposition statement.

HMW statements build on the insights you've gained from your research and time spent exploring the people, problem, and context. They reframe your insight statements to HMW questions that help identify design challenges and opportunities to explore solutions for.

A good how HMW doesn't dictate a specific solution, but keeps the focus on the real problem to solve, and a point to explore from. The framing needs to open up the possible, rather than narrow choices. We're about to head into the divergent phase of the solution diamond.

Are we solving the right problem?   Is it the right solution?

Clarity

The process is simple, but resist jumping straight into solution brainstorming as you write... because that's their actual purpose – to be compelling statements that help generate solution ideas.

ACTION

Your How Might We Statement

Review your tested insights statements, and rephrase them as questions starting with how might we.

Write as many HMW statements as you can. It's good to then synthesise to a small number to take forward. Personally, I like to have one focusing HMW question supported by a few sub-questions.

Your Value Proposition

Drafting your value proposition statement is our final step as you transition into the solution diamond. You'll draft it now, but test it in Chapter 9: Explore Possible Solutions.

You already have a version of your value proposition from your Lean Canvas. The questions you answered with that version were:

- What's the value and the benefit that you create for the different groups of people?

- What's the social and environmental value that you create?

These are still the right questions to focus on, but you've done a lot of research and synthesis since you drafted them for your current state Lean Canvas in Chapter 5. A value proposition is the promise of the value that you'll deliver. If that promise doesn't resonate with your ideal customers, you need to find what does.

We've been using the ideal customer circle from Peter Thomson's version of the Value Proposition Canvas at the centre of the People/Problem Canvas. This has been to keep the focus on the customer rather than our ideas for the solution. Let's bring in the full canvas now.

You've already done the right side of the canvas as part of the People/Problem Canvas. And if you did your Empathy Map as part of the Build Empathy section of this chapter, you've dug into this even more.

Let's switch focus to the left side. The three blocks are experience, benefits, and features. Again, you've already mapped the current state experience, and identified where there are key pain and delight points. In Chapter 8, you'll use the full canvas to describe the desired future state.

With your insight statements and HMW statement, I'm sure you've already started identifying some of the benefits and outcomes that need to be part of the solution. I hope these include the social and environmental impacts too.

Considering all of these pieces, what's the promise you want to make to your ideal customers? A promise you think they'll find compelling. Don't think about the specific solution yet. The first challenge is to draft a value proposition statement that grabs their attention, and will result in immediate action.

One way of doing this that Jon Kolko talks about is to reshape your insight statements – especially when they describe a problem, pain, or gap that currently exists – to be a promise about the benefit your solution will create in response to that insight.

Value Proposition Canvas

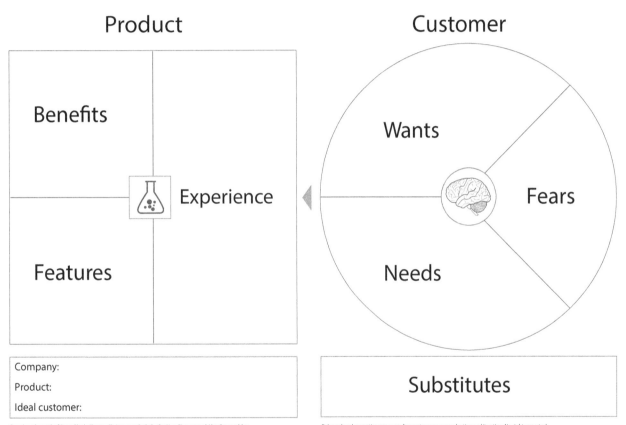

Product

Customer

Benefits

Experience

Features

Wants

Fears

Needs

Company:

Product:

Ideal customer:

Substitutes

Based on the work of Steve Blank, Clayton Christensen, Seth Godin, Yves Pigneur and Alex Osterwalder

. Released under creative commons license to encourage adaption and iteration. No rights asserted.

Another couple of resources that are useful here are Clay Christensen's Jobs to Be Done framework and *Value Proposition Design* by Alex Osterwalder & Co. Visit dynamic4.com/sptm for links to more resources.

ACTION

Your Draft Value Proposition

Take 15-30 minutes to draft one or more value prop statements as a promise of the value that you'll deliver for your ideal customers.

Your draft value proposition statements, along with your HMW statement will keep you focused on the real problem to solve, and drive solution design as you now move into Part 3.

Coaching Questions

- How has your value proposition refined since your current state Lean Canvas in Chapter 5?

- How has your Gaddie Pitch and pitch deck refined with your customer insights and value proposition?

- How are you going with your sprint rhythm?

Now is a critical time to reflect on the journey so far. It's also a good time to refer to the 90-Day Plan & OKRs section of Chapter 3.

By this point, you want to have reached a point of sharp clarity on the real problem to solve – based on evidence, insight, and meaningful empathy.

During Part 2: People, Problem & Context, you've covered a lot of ground. You've increased your understanding of the systems involved and spent time with the people you hope will use and pay for your solution.

You now have more empathy and a deeper understanding of their mental models and the language they use to describe how they experience the problem. You've tested your riskiest assumption to refine your thinking and have a clearer picture of the market.

You've spoken with at least 10 people who you believe you're solving a problem with and for – and who you hope will use and pay for your solution. Ideally, you have insights from tens or even thousands of potential customers by doing quantitative research.

All of this insight has resulted in a simple and compelling HMW statement – as a clear articulation of the problem and opportunity – and also your draft value proposition statement.

With this sharp clarity on the problem that matters, it's time to move into the next phase. Our focus in Part 3: Solution & Business Model is the solution diamond.

Solution & Business Model

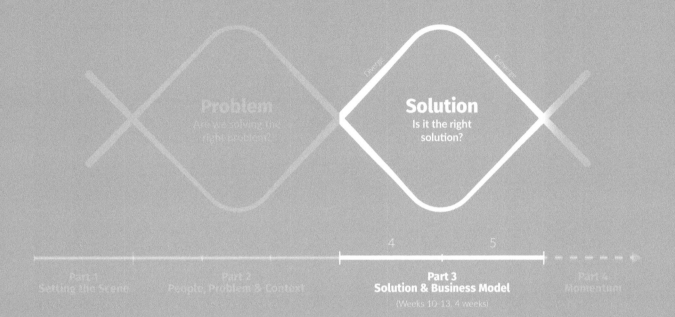

Diverge   Converge

Problem
Are we solving the
right problem?

Solution
Is it the right
solution?

4   5

Part 1
Setting the Scene

Part 2
People, Problem & Context

**Part 3
Solution & Business Model**
(Weeks 10-13, 4 weeks)

Part 4
Momentum

Weeks 10-13. Sprints 4 & 5

The standard program allows four weeks for this phase – two sprints.
This is primarily focused on the strategic design of your solution and
business model. This is the beginning, not the end.

Part 3 Chapters

12. Financials

13. Legals

Part 3: Solution & Business Model

The focus during this phase is to build on the sharp clarity we've achieved during the People, Problem & Context phase – based on evidence, insight, and meaningful empathy.

We'll prototype and test possible solutions and your business model. The focus is on ways to design, build, and launch your social enterprise idea in a way that reduces the risk of overinvesting time, money, and energy in a solution no one will use or pay for. A way of rapidly learning and refining to create a solution that people want, that's financially sustainable, and that you can make happen.

The Big Questions

The big questions we focus on in Part 3 are, how do I/we:

- Communicate our purpose, theory of change, and the social/environmental value we'll create?

- Identify our customers, understand what they really care about, and know if they'll buy and use our solution?

- Design, build, and launch our solution as an end-to-end experience, and test what our customers will pay for it?

- Calculate how much money we need, and when we'll break even?

Important Note: If you haven't spoken directly with at least 10 people who you believe you're solving a problem with and for – and hope will use and pay for your solution – you're not ready to be focusing on this phase yet. Please spend more time focusing on the People, Problem & Context phase before starting work on your solution and business model.

Chapter 9

Explore Possible Solutions

Are we solving the
right problem?

Diverge

Converge

Diverge

Converge

Solution
Is it the right
solution?

We're now starting on the first part of the solution diamond. Exploring possible solutions is a divergent process to open up and create options on the many different ways to solve for the problem you've identified. A problem that really matters to the people you want to help.

We often fall in love with our ideas very quickly, and the temptation is to just dive straight into the original solution idea – which you probably had on day one. I encourage you to resist that urge.

The purpose of this chapter is to help you start exploring possible solutions to get clarity on your solution concept, describe how it works, and design the experience. This flows directly from the work you've just done on making sense of what you heard during your customer and market research in Chapter 8.

The way we'll approach this is to:

- Test and refine your draft value proposition statement with your Value Proposition Canvas

- Generate multiple ideas on how to solve the problem and describe how it works

- Refine your Value Proposition Canvas to describe your ideal customers and the value you intend to create as part of your business model

- Blueprint the desired experience

By doing this, you'll create the early prototypes of your ideas for the solution and business model. We'll refine this thinking in Chapter 10: Prototype, Test & Learn and look at pricing in Chapter 11 with what that means for your financial model in Chapter 12. In reality, these four chapters all go together as part of a rapid and iterative process.

The Right Solution?

How do we know when it's the right solution? Let's revisit the three lenses model we covered in Chapter 2, and have referred to regularly since.

Through your customer research, you started with the desirable lens. With market research, you started looking at the intersection of the desirable and viable lenses. From this point forward, you keep those two lenses and add in the feasibility lens.

From your organisation's perspective, what's feasible? Do you have or can you get the skills to design, build, launch, and run this solution? Can you realistically make it happen? Are you the right people to be doing it?

The sweet spot of success is at the intersection of these three perspectives. The bigger the overlap, the more likely you're onto a good idea. An idea that people love, that delivers real value, and solves a problem that matters... you can afford to do it and be financially sustainable... and you have the skills to design, build, launch, and continue to run it. That's the happy place.

This is why we test our thinking. If we get it wrong, it's easy to see how everything else in our solution and business model falls apart:

- If it's not desirable, we end up with a solution that no one wants

- If it's not viable, we can't afford to make it happen – and we'll run out of money

- If it's not feasible, we can't design, build, launch, and run the solution – which means we can't deliver the value even if people want it

The objective is to learn as quickly and cheaply as possible – so you can create a solution that people want, that's financially sustainable, and that you can make happen. This is absolutely critical in reducing the very real risk of overinvesting time, money, and energy in a solution no one will use or pay for.

Test & Refine Your Value Proposition

In Chapter 3, I recommended setting up the logistics for some customer interview sessions a week or two before you plan to start this phase. This might include people you spoke with during your customer research.

These interviews are to test the draft value proposition statements you created in Chapter 8. Your value proposition is the promise you're making to your customers about the value that you'll deliver. It will help keep you focused on the real problem to solve – and drive solution design.

If that promise doesn't resonate with your ideal customers – you need to rapidly iterate to find what does – before starting on solution concepts.

Working on your value proposition might sound like a marketing thing, and maybe not that important. But when done well, the value proposition drives the design of the actual solution, and the promise is authentic. It's not a false promise trying to con customers into buying a solution that you made up without them – intent matters.

The preparation for this round of customer interviews is the same as your last two – in Chapters 6 and 8. You're doing two things at once with this round of research.

You're testing and iterating your value proposition statement, which is a convergent process. At the same time, you're exploring and opening up possible ways to solve for the problem – and to deliver on the promise.

When you've tested and iterated your value proposition statement, you want to have confidence based on strong evidence that it resonates with your ideal customers. Customers buy the promise of how their situation is going to improve, often more than the solution itself.

ACTION

Test & Refine Your Value Proposition

Prepare for your customer interviews following the same process you used in Chapter 6. Be clear on what you're trying to learn from these conversations.

Do your customer research.

Synthesise your findings and refine your value proposition statements where needed.

Generate Solution Concepts

I've mentioned a few times that this part of the solution diamond is a divergent process to explore many possible solution concepts. This is the time to resist the temptation to just dive straight into your original solution idea – which you probably had on day one.

During the process of generating multiple solution concepts and testing them, there's a good chance you'll have even better ideas – or you might find it just makes aspects of your original idea better. The tricky thing is to not fall in love with your idea and be open to learning. You might even start co-designing some solution concepts with your customers.

It's important to focus on the journey, experience, and business model first – not detailed solution features or the technology.

In Chapter 8, you created one or more compelling HMW statements that will help generate solution ideas. They don't dictate a specific solution, but keep the focus on the real problem to solve and a point to explore from. They open up the possible.

Your HMW statement, along with your tested value proposition statement, and customer insight statements, will help you generate solution concepts. They provide a clear articulation of the people involved, the problem as they experience it, and the opportunity. Use these assets as the catalyst to generate solutions concepts.

There are many methods that you can use to generate ideas, but it's the area where I find people tend to be the most comfortable in the whole process. What does tend to happen though is that people don't stay in the idea generation process long enough, and quickly fixate on one idea.

If you need guidance on methods, I recommend having a look at *Design. Think. Make. Break. Repeat.* by Martin Tomitsch & Co, and Nathan Baird has a great section in the *Innovator's Playbook* on incubating ideas, boosting your team's creative confidence, and idea generation.

I like crazy 8s and sketchstorming as a couple of simple methods to generate ideas rapidly. Visit dynamic4.com/sptm for links to more resources.

Generate Solution Concepts

Review your HMW statement, tested value proposition statement, and customer insight statements as catalysts to generate solutions concepts.

Take 15-20 minutes to rapidly generate at least eight different ideas. Don't filter or critique the ideas while you're generating. There's a lot of value in involving other people in this process – including co-designing with your ideal customers.

Use your HMW statement and value proposition to filter and prioritise the solution concepts generated. You might find that combining elements from different concepts has the potential to work well.

In most cases, I find it's really valuable to do a second round of idea generation – especially when working with other people – so you can build on each other's ideas.

Blueprint the Desired Experience

In Chapter 8, you mapped the current experience – the end-to-end journey of your customers as they go through the full lifecycle. While you were mapping the current state, I'm sure you had plenty of ideas about how you'll design for a better experience. Now's the time to describe what that looks like.

We'll break this into a few steps.

How Does It Work?

You might still have a couple of solution concepts that you feel are worth testing more. Describing how the idea works and the benefits created for your ideal customer and users is a quick way to prototype it as a thought experiment.

This might even form an early prototype and something you can use to run experiments. We'll talk about that more in Chapter 10.

This action is designed to help you articulate the idea and iterate to the point of sharp clarity and simplicity. With the final step, you have a 30-second description of your idea that you can share with people to see if they understand it. Do this action for each of the solutions concepts that you want to test.

How Does It Work?

Take 15 minutes to write a few sentences outlining how the solution works. Think of it as a journey from the customers' perspective – the full lifecycle from how they find out about your solutions through to ongoing use and support.

This will form the brief story or narrative of the customer journey on your desired future Experience Blueprint – as you did for your current state version.

What are the benefits created? They can include the value created for your customers and users as well as positive social and environmental outcomes.

Take 5 minutes to outline the steps in the journey. Are they the same as the current state journey, or has something changed? Why?

Take 10 minutes to simplify this story to three or four steps. Describe it as being as easy as 1, 2, 3 – key information you would include on a website landing page to communicate quickly and simply.

Map the Desired Experience

Build on the work you've just completed to create your desired future Experience Blueprint. If you haven't already, now is also a good time to review the current state Experience Blueprint you created in Chapter 8.

ACTION

Map the Desired Experience

Take 15-30 minutes to map the end-to-end journey of the **desired future experience**. Use the journey stages and the brief story or narrative of the customer journey you outlined in the How Does It Work? action.

Add the touchpoints, channels, and interactions for each step in the journey.

Add the key pain and delight points for the customer. Where have they changed compared to the current state journey? Why?

What would you need to do in the background to deliver that experience and value through the touchpoints you've identified?

Your Value Proposition Canvas

You started work on your Value Proposition Canvas in Chapter 5 because we've been using the ideal customer circle at the centre of the People/Problem Canvas. I briefly introduced the full version of Peter Thomson's version of the Value Proposition Canvas in Chapter 8.

The left side of the canvas has three blocks: experience, benefits, and features. In this chapter, you've outlined the desired future experience, the benefits you believe your solution will create, and some detail on how it works. This gives you the ingredients to complete the left side of the canvas now.

Visit dynamic4.com/sptm to get more detail on how I use the Experience Blueprint to map specific features, content, website/app screens, data, and user stories.

ACTION

Iterate Your Value Proposition Canvas

Take 15-30 minutes to add a brief description of the experience, benefits, and key features to your Value Proposition Canvas.

This chapter has been focused on helping you explore possible solutions to get clarity on your solution concept, describe how it works, and design the desired future experience.

The next step is to create the early prototypes of your ideas for the solution and business model, and run some experiments to test your thinking. As I mentioned, Chapters 9, 10, 11, and 12 all go together as part of a rapid and iterative process.

As your idea iterates, return to this chapter and refine your desired future Experience Blueprint and maybe your Value Proposition Canvas too.

Chapter 10

Prototype, Test & Learn

Are we solving the
right problem?

Diverge

Converge

Diverge

Converge

Solution
**Is it the right
solution?**

As I mentioned, you already started prototyping your ideas for your solution and business model in Chapter 9. The purpose of this chapter is to build on that as part of a rapid and iterative process to refine your prototypes and use them to test your thinking.

The primary objective here is to learn as quickly and cheaply as possible. This is absolutely critical in reducing the very real risk of overinvesting time, money, and energy in a solution no one will use or pay for.

It's really important that you're clear on why we prototype and test. It's not to validate your idea. As we covered in Chapter 2, we're applying the scientific method. We test to see where our idea falls down. And why. Then use this information to improve it. This is a really important time to be aware of our confirmation bias and not let it drive our decisions.

The way we'll approach this is to:

- Use the Lean Canvas to prototype, test, and refine your business model

- Prototype, test, and refine your solution

- Sell before you build

- Launch and iterate your solution

"Prototype like you're right, test like you're wrong."

Unknown

Prototype & Experiment

You're probably not going to design and build a completely new solution in four weeks (two sprints). You might already have a solution in the market, or you might already be well into the process of building your solution – a lot of people I work with are in these situations.

There's often a rush to design and build the first working version of the solution – and there are usually very high expectations about how perfect and polished it will be too. This is an area where it can be easy to confuse activity with meaningful progress and momentum.

The most common trap we tend to fall into is trying to solve business model problems with solution features. The feeling that if we just add this one feature, then people will buy it. Which is usually followed by just one more feature. And another. Before you know it, you've run out of money and still don't have any paying customers.

Unfortunately, I've been through this cycle myself many times. It hurts. On reflection, I think it would be safe to say every solution I've designed and built was too soon. Even when it's worked out, it was a higher risk than needed.

The approach we'll take is focused on learning as quickly and cheaply as possible. This means prototyping, running experiments to test your thinking, and refining. It's critical that we do this not just for the solution, but also for your business model. Most of the risk is generally in the business model, and it's important to test your riskiest assumptions first.

The specific kinds of prototypes and experiments that are right for you depend completely on where you're at, your ideal customers, your context, your riskiest assumptions, and the resources you have access to. I have a lot more of this information in a coaching context, and can help with more direct advice.

I don't have that information, so I'll cover some key principles and direct you to other useful resources. The focus of this section is to plan the prototypes you'll create and the experiments you'll run.

Visit dynamic4.com/sptm for links to more resources on prototyping and experiments.

Prototypes

What do I mean by a prototype? Prototypes can take many forms, and the best method depends on what you're trying to learn and the experiment you want to run. The critical thing is to make your idea tangible and testable. As you learn more and progress, the best methods to use will also change.

The purpose of a prototype is to help you test specific assumptions.

Prototyping means taking a position based on the current evidence, and then actively testing it to see where you're wrong and why. With these insights, you'll refine your prototypes and test again – a continual process of testing and experimentation.

In Chapter 9, you started prototyping your solution concept and value proposition using the Experience Blueprint and Value Proposition Canvas. These, along with your Lean Canvas, are foundational, and you'll continue to build on them in this chapter.

Your early prototypes will probably be things like your value proposition statement and sketches of how the solution will work. Low-fidelity prototypes – like rough storyboards – that you can use when talking with your ideal customers and iterate rapidly.

A key principle is when prototypes are low-fidelity and not polished – like a sketch – people tend to be more open with their

feedback, and feel they're co-creating the solution with you. Because they are. Not everyone is comfortable working at this conceptual level though, so be mindful of different preferences.

As prototypes refine and become more polished, people often start tempering their feedback. Another tendency is that some will fixate on specific parts of the prototype that might not be focused on the things you want to learn.

Just as you went into your customer research interviews with a clear plan, it's worth having that same level of clarity on what you're trying to learn and a plan when you're testing prototypes.

What prototypes will you create to test and refine both your business model and solution?

Experiments

Experiments help us learn. But not all experiments are equal. Some really important concepts are testable hypotheses, the strength of evidence, and safe to fail experiments – which we'll cover in a moment.

The sequencing also matters. You need to run experiments that help you learn the right thing at the right time – and it's best when they build on what you've already learnt, so you can keep progressing.

Most experiments will require a prototype or something to test. This is why matching your planned experiments with your prototypes is important. The right set of experiments depends on what you need to learn – which is driven by what your riskiest assumptions currently are.

You'll probably run different experiments to test assumptions about desirability, viability, and feasibility. As you plan your experiments, it's a good time to review your Assumptions Log and how you've categorised your assumptions.

Testing Business Ideas has a great set of experiments with detailed techniques to try.

Testable Hypotheses

A hypothesis states an expected result based on current information. Creating testable hypotheses and well-formed experiments helps bring more rigour to the process and will help you be less reactive.

With a hypothesis, we're taking a position but holding it lightly. We're testing it to see where we're wrong and why. It's important to remember where the hypothesis fits in the scientific method. It comes after you've asked a question and done some research. Your hypotheses need to build on the insights from the research you've already done – or you may need to do some more specific research.

There are different ways to structure a hypothesis, but it's important that they're:

- Brief, specific, and easy to understand – there's no ambiguity

- A statement about the expected relationship between two things or variables – it's not a question

- Testable and falsifiable – it's possible to show the hypothesis is true, and also possible to show the hypothesis is false

- Repeatable – you can repeat the experiment and get the same result

A common structure is a simple prediction in an "if... then" format. Don't take this structure or grammar too literally and force-fit all of your hypothesis statements to start with "if", and have a "then" in the middle.

The first part (if) states the independent variable – the cause, which is what you control, and will do or change. The second part (then) states the dependent variable – the effect you'll measure.

Another format you might want to try is "because we believe x, if we do y, we expect z to happen".

The Experiment Board by Javelin is a good tool I've used a lot to help structure, prioritise, and track experiments.

Safe to Fail Experiments

Running experiments requires time and often money. Some also have other risks involved, including reputational damage.

Safe to fail experiments are small scale, and don't create damage when they don't go as expected. Being mindful of the impact of our experiments is important in all contexts, but especially when dealing with social and environmental challenges. We need to be careful not to create unintended negative consequences.

Strength of Evidence

As I mentioned in Chapter 2, I really like the way David Bland and Alex Osterwalder talk about the concept of strength of evidence in *Testing Business Ideas*. Not all evidence and insights are equal. They talk about the type and strength of evidence and the number of data points. These three dimensions should drive your confidence level.

What experiments will you run to test and refine both your business model and solution? Now it's time to create your plan.

Plan Your Prototypes & Experiments

Your planned prototypes and experiments go together. Remember, the purpose of a prototype is to help you test specific assumptions. What you need to learn determines the right methods.

Based on where you're at, your ideal customers, your context, your riskiest assumptions, and the resources you have access to – what type of prototypes will you create, and what experiments will you run to test them?

This action is very similar to what you did when you put together your research approach in Chapter 6.

Ash Maurya has great advice on solution interviews in *Running Lean* if you need more inspiration. This includes ways to test pricing in these conversations. We'll cover this more in Chapter 11: Pricing.

As you do this planning, make sure you're testing both your business model and your solution. They're distinct, but need to come together and iterate in lock-step. And remember, don't try to solve business model issues by putting all of your attention into creating new solution features.

Plan Your Prototypes & Experiments

Take 30-45 minutes to plan your prototypes and experiments – with the methods you'll use and the schedule. This plan will likely go beyond the 90 days of this program, and extend into the ongoing phase.

Objective

- What are your riskiest assumptions? Refer to your Assumptions Log, and focus on the ones you've rated as the riskiest

- What are the key things you need to learn?

Prototype & Experiment Methods

- How will you prototype, test, and refine your business model?

- How will you prototype, test, and refine your solution?

- How will you set and test your pricing?

- What specific methods will you use? Make a note of why you're using the method and the type of information you expect to get from it

- Do your experiments cover risks related to desirability, viability, and feasibility?

- What's the strength of evidence from each of your experiments?

Prototype & Experiment Schedule

- What is the timeline? Align this with your sprint planning, although some of your experiments will probably run for several months

Prototype Your Business Model

The primary tool we're using to prototype your business model is the Lean Canvas. You used it to capture your current thinking at the start of the program in Chapter 5. You then zoomed out to map the system and used the Business Model Environment tool to understand the forces at play in your context.

You explored your customer segments and early adopters and the problem with existing alternatives in detail, using the People/Problem Canvas and your research with your ideal customers and the market. This led to your value proposition that you've tested and refined.

In Chapter 9, you explored your solution concept with how it works and mapped the desired experience. You also iterated your Value Proposition Canvas to outline your solution's experience, benefits, and features.

As part of your desired state Experience Blueprint, you identified your channels.

We talked about key metrics briefly in Chapter 3 as part of your pitch deck, and covered measuring outcomes and impact in Chapter 4.

You did some work on your unfair advantage by reflecting on your strengths and assets in Chapter 1, as well as your personal why and Ikigai in Chapter 4. How are you different and better than the existing alternatives?

We'll talk more about your revenue streams and cost structure in Chapters 11 and 12.

What I'm highlighting here is that you've been researching and prototyping your business model all the way through this program. You have the ingredients, so it's now time to bring it all together. This is a synthesis process, and a time to see how the pieces fit together.

If you need more guidance on the Lean Canvas, please refer to Chapter 5.

ACTION

Prototype Your Business Model

Take 15-30 minutes to bring all the ingredients together and create a new version of your Lean Canvas.

Coaching Questions

- Did you identify any other ways to prototype your business model in your Prototypes & Experiments Plan?

- What are the riskiest assumptions that you've identified? Why? Have you updated your Assumptions Log?

- How does your Gaddie pitch refine from doing this? Have you updated it and tested it with anyone?

Prototype Your Solution

When you planned your prototypes and experiments, you identified the methods you would use to prototype your solution. It's now time to put that plan into action and create your first prototype.

This is an ongoing activity, and as you progress, you'll execute your plan and adapt based on what you learn.

ACTION

Prototype Your Solution

Create the first prototype in your Prototypes & Experiments Plan.

The next step is to test your prototype and run the experiments.

Continue iterating and refining your prototypes.

Test & Refine Your Solution & Business Model

When you planned your prototypes and experiments, you identified the methods and experiments you would use to test your solution. It's now time to put that plan into action and run your first test or experiment.

This is the hypothesis, experiment, results, conclusion part of the scientific method. Follow the evidence and be wary of your confirmation bias. The skills you built while doing your customer research and synthesising the findings apply at this stage of the journey too.

As you run and review your experiments, take careful notes of your findings. Analyse the results to find the patterns and themes. Synthesise these to identify the key insights. Use these insights to drive your conclusions, and decide how you'll iterate your business model and solution.

Just as you did when making sense of your customer research findings, it's critical to get enough reliable data to find patterns. Reacting to individual data points – including feedback from individual customers – usually results in chasing shadows that cause you to zigzag or go around in circles.

In Chapter 2, I introduced the build, measure, learn loop from lean startup. This is the ongoing cycle of iteration you're in now. It never ends.

Continual innovation is required to find your sustainable business model and solution – and then remain relevant. You'll build improvements based on robust hypotheses, measure the results, and learn. And then repeat.

Coaching Questions

- Does the evidence show that your hypothesis is true or false? Why?
- What is the strength of evidence?
- What have you learnt from your experiment?

ACTION

Test & Refine Your Solution & Business Model

Run the first test or experiment in your Prototypes & Experiments Plan. Take careful notes of your findings.

Analyse the results to find the patterns and themes. Then, synthesise these to identify the key insights.

Use these insights to drive your conclusions, and decide how you'll iterate and refine your business model and solution. Prototype the prioritised improvements.

Continue running your experiments to test and refine your prototypes.

Your Go-to-Market Strategy

A go-to-market (GTM) strategy outlines how you'll launch your solution. It's sometimes confused with a marketing strategy. There are similarities, but your GTM strategy goes beyond marketing to look at the whole lifecycle, and is focused on launching a new solution rather than ongoing marketing. We'll briefly touch on your marketing plan in Chapter 14.

What are the elements of a GTM strategy? There isn't a standard format, but there are some common elements, and the good news is you've already done most of the work. This is a synthesis process, and a time to see how all of the pieces fit together to launch your solution.

I recommend a 12-month time horizon for your GTM strategy. Launching and getting to market isn't a singular event. It's progressive and will happen over time – and we take a sell before you build approach. Your GTM strategy will help you plan for these, and we'll cover them in the next two sections of this chapter.

Using the Experience Blueprint in Chapter 9, you've mapped out the desired experience and this covers the whole lifecycle, including the buying journey. Your GTM strategy will add more detail for each of the phases you'll go through as you iterate your business model and solution, trial sell to your ideal customers, and test your pricing.

Visit dynamic4.com/sptm for links to more resources.

Organisation Objectives

What is your objective with this launch? Treat your GTM as an experiment, and be clear about what you expect, and what you want to learn. This will change in the different phases. What you want to learn will be different for a trial sell and for your public launch.

People & Problem

We always start with who. You've already identified your ideal customers and early adopters – including your segments and the difference between paying customers and people who may use your solution, but not pay for it.

From your customer research and making sense of it in Chapter 8, you've built empathy with the people involved, and a deep understanding of the problem as they experience it. This includes their pain points. You understand their psychographics, how they make decisions, and who is involved in buying decisions.

You will also have insights into where your customers go to find out about new solutions and the information they consider when making purchasing decisions.

Value Proposition & Solution

Your Value Proposition Canvas clearly outlines how your solution addresses your customers' pain points and your value proposition statement has been tested and refined. This will help you have clarity of message.

Your unfair advantage from your Lean Canvas will help you communicate why you, and establish credibility.

Existing Alternatives, Competitors & Demand

From your market research in Chapter 7, you know the existing alternatives and who your competitors are. Your value proposition and unfair advantage help you describe how your solution is different and better than the customers' other alternatives.

Where does your solution fit in the market? How are you positioning it?

You've also sized up the market. As you test your GTM strategy, you'll learn more about the market. Remember to update your market size calculations and competitor slide in your pitch deck as you get more market insight.

Offer & Pricing

Through your prototypes and experiments from Chapters 9 and 11, you've tested different solution concepts and pricing. For each phase of your GTM strategy, which version of your solution are you taking to market and at what price point?

What do you need to have these sales conversations?

What do your customers need before they're ready to make a purchase decision? How long do you expect this sales cycle to take? What payment method will you use for each phase of your GTM strategy?

Channels & Touchpoints

What channels will you use? This is at the awareness, and research and comparison stages but doesn't stop there. The purchasing, onboarding and first use, and ongoing use and support steps, will probably be different for the early phases of your GTM strategy compared to when you've iterated to a more mature business model and solution.

At the awareness, and research and comparison stages, how will you reach your ideal customers and create demand? What channels and touchpoints will you use? The key piece of advice here is to go where your customers are. Align your marketing channels to meet your ideal customers where they are.

Messaging & Marketing Plan

Drawing all of these pieces together, what are your core messages, and how will you communicate them? You've been doing a lot of work since Chapter 3 on crafting and sharing your story. This is an extension of that. Use the same approaches to test and refine.

In Chapter 14, I recommend The 1-Page Marketing Plan Canvas because it takes a lifecycle and journey approach that's aligned with the work you've already done. You might find it useful at this point.

Metrics

How will you measure the success of your GTM strategy? This aligns with your objectives – what you expect and what you want to learn. You identified your key metrics on your Lean Canvas in Chapter 9.

Dave McClure's startup metrics – AARRR, so they're known as pirate metrics – provide a simple way to think about the end-to-end lifecycle. Acquisition, activation, revenue, retention, and referral. Depending on what you want to learn and measure, you might want to identify a metric for one or more of these.

Your GTM strategy metrics need to align with your OKRs, and outputs and outcome measures.

Launch Schedule

What's the timeline for each phase of your GTM strategy? Your launch timeline needs to align with your 90-day plan, sprints, and longer-term planning.

The approach we're taking has at least three phases:

- Sell before you build – when you'll also test your pricing
- Soft launch – an early release as part of launching and iterating
- Public launch – the full public release as part of launching and iterating

You might want to use the evergreen launch approach too. I'll cover this in more detail in the Launch & Iterate Your Solution section of this chapter.

Budget

What is your budget for each phase of your GTM strategy, and for your GTM strategy overall? This is part of your financial modelling in Chapter 12.

Your
Go-to-Market Strategy

Take 45-60 minutes to bring all the ingredients together and create your GTM Strategy document.

I recommend a 12-month time horizon with at least three phases: sell before you build, soft launch, and public launch. Be explicit about each of the GTM elements for each of these phases. They come together as one overall strategy, but you might want to treat them as three distinct plans.

Sell Before You Build

Selling before you build is one of your most critical experiments, and part of the first phase of launching your solution in your GTM strategy.

Why Sell Before You Build?

In most cases, selling before you build is the best approach. At this point in the journey, there's still the very real risk of overinvesting in a solution that no one wants, will use, or will pay for. One of your riskiest assumptions to test with safe to fail experiments is that your value proposition and solution resonates with your ideal customers, and that they will buy it.

By taking the approach of selling before building – prototyping or building just enough to communicate and demo the solution – I've often learnt that there wasn't any real demand, even though research showed we were working on a real problem that mattered to people.

Early solution conversations "validated" that they'd buy it, but when we asked them to use the solution – sometimes for free – or pay, then the real conversation would start. All of the reasons why not or why the timing wasn't quite right started coming out.

When you're selling before building, this is all valuable information and helps you learn quickly and cheaply. With this insight, you can keep iterating and testing if you can sell it – or in some cases, it means it's time to stop and spend your time, money, and energy on something else.

This might feel like failure, but not all failures are equal. If it's not going to work out, you want it to happen early, and before you've wandered down a path of overinvesting in the wrong thing.

If you're having these conversations after spending months and a lot of money on designing and building what you think is an amazing solution – one that does all the things your ideal customers told you they wanted – you're in a different position. From that place, the default path is to chase sunk cost fallacy to the bottom of an empty bank account. And still have nothing to show for it.

This means being disciplined and honest with yourself. Don't ignore the red flags. There's a fine line here between listening to the feedback and giving up when you don't meet with immediate success. You need resilience and perseverance, but you also don't want to ignore what the market is telling you.

It's often confronting and uncomfortable, so it's tempting to skip this step or to do a couple of trial sales that don't go well and tell yourself that it will all work out. Maybe rationalising why it wasn't the right customer or the solution needs to be more polished with some extra features – and stubbornly march on to build the solution without successfully achieving any sales first.

I know because I've done it. More than once. I suspect you can hear the residual pain and see scars as I write this. None of the social enterprises or startups where we did that are still running today.

Over the past few years, I've been a lot more disciplined with myself when working on new social enterprise ideas – if that's a whole new organisation or just a new product. I won't build a solution until I've got at least one paying customer. This approach has saved me investing in ideas where the timing wasn't right or it was the wrong thing many times.

How to Sell Before You Build

What does it mean to sell before you build? This will iterate as you progress with prototyping and testing your business model and solution. The first thing you're really testing is your business model. Is the way you're talking about your early adopters' pain point and your value proposition resonating? Do your early adopters get the sense that you really know them?

I'm sure you've experienced unpleasant pressure sales techniques with psychological tricks to push you into something you don't want to do. These techniques leave you feeling manipulated and probably with buyer's remorse. Please don't do that. They're ethically questionable at best and don't nurture long-term relationships.

Approach the sales process with empathy and build meaningful relationships with your customers, focused on helping them solve problems that matter. Approach it as a way of learning and improving.

This process is about testing real demand and your pricing.

The best methods to use will depend on your context and type of solution, but to start with, conversations are probably the best way to learn quickly. Some of the people you've been speaking with as part of your research are obvious candidates. They've been on the journey with you and have effectively been co-designing the solution with you.

Testing your pricing and price sensitivity is an important part of this process. We'll talk about that a little more in Chapter 11.

In your Prototypes & Experiments Plan, you identified the methods you'll use and the schedule, including how you'll test pricing. You've also planned your GTM Strategy for the sell before you build phase.

To sell before you build, you need to be able to clearly communicate what the specific offer is, the price, and be able to demo your solution so your customer knows what they're getting and how it works. In most cases, your prototype is the demo and it doesn't require a working version of your solution.

Your early adopter might say that if it has a specific feature they'll buy it. Others might say they'll buy it when the solution is built. These are promising signs, but not a sale. Turning this into a solid commitment is important. This might be a pledge like a letter of intent, or something more binding like a contract.

The real commitment comes when there's some form of payment – even a small amount gets past the psychological and logistical barriers of getting paid. This likely makes it much easier for future payments too.

Understanding your ideal customer's buying journey and decision-making process, including the triggers, is really important.

As part of your customer research, you built a clear picture of the key triggers and empathy for how your ideal customers think and feel through the decision-making process, as well as the practical steps – what they do, with who, and where. Draw on these insights.

Identifying triggers is really important, and a key ingredient of the Fogg Behavior Model by BJ Fogg. It's one of my favourite models because it's both simple and powerful. The model is B=MAT. "Behavior (B) happens when Motivation (M), Ability (A), and a Trigger (T) come together at the same moment".

More recently, "trigger" has been changed to "prompt" to become B=MAP, but it's the same concept. Visit dynamic4.com/sptm for links to more resources on the Fogg Model.

In Chapter 7, I briefly outlined the concept of satisficed. From my experience, when people have a solution that they're satisfied with, it's really hard to get them to adopt a new solution – even if they acknowledge their current solution doesn't fully meet their needs and that your solution is better. They might not have the required attributes to be one of your early adopters.

Your First Sale

Making your first sale is an amazing feeling. Take a moment and celebrate the win!

Reflect on what you've learnt from making your first sale. Why did the customer decide to buy? Why now? How long did it take? What about the sales process worked well? What didn't work so well? What initial concerns or objections did your customer have, and how did you overcome them? How and where do you find more people like your first customer?

Repeatable Sales

The objective of this phase of your launch is to test real-world market demand for your solution. A repeatable sales process is critical for this.

A market of one is not going to result in a viable and financially sustainable business model. Having only one customer – even if it results in enough revenue to be viable – is a critical risk. If they go away, so does your whole organisation.

Repeatable customer acquisition is generally the first constraint to solve to achieve repeatable sales. Building awareness is usually the first step, and the progressive launch approach we're taking with your GTM strategy gives you time to do this. It's more important to focus on this than designing and building the first working version of your solution.

Have you found a way to achieve repeatable sales? This is the evidence you need to know that you're solving a problem that really matters to your ideal customers, that it's a priority for them, and that they're willing to pay to do something about it. Now.

Sell Before You Build

Take 15-30 minutes to review your Prototypes & Experiments Plan and your GTM Strategy, and refine where needed.

Execute your Prototypes & Experiments Plan and your GTM Strategy to sell before you build.

Launch & Iterate Your Solution

What does launch mean? It doesn't mean what it used to. The traditional approach was to build a solution and then have a big launch event. A grand unveiling.

This is a very high-risk approach. A lot of this time the design and build phase was shrouded in secrecy as organisations operated in stealth mode – fearful someone would steal their idea and do it faster and better. If your idea can't survive contact with the real world, you don't have a defensible business model and solution, and you've already lost. Another high-risk aspect is the pressure this approach puts on a single event.

You might feel some reluctance to launch your solution. It's a process where all of the work you've been doing is tested and judged. It's natural to feel some fear of what people will think. There will be aspects of your solution that aren't yet what you hope them to be. There will always be reasons not to launch just yet.

The important thing is to approach this with a growth mindset. Feedback helps you learn and improve. The reality is this process never ends. Continual innovation. By taking this approach to launching and iterating, it is something you're doing regularly, which means you have the opportunity to get better at it.

The approach I recommend in most cases is a progressive launch rather than a single event. This is what we've been talking about throughout Part 3 of this book. You've already planned for it in your Prototypes & Experiments Plan and your GTM Strategy.

The approach we're taking has at least three phases of launch, and an optional fourth phase.

> "If you are not embarrassed by the first version of your product, you've launched too late."
>
> **Reid Hoffman**
> **LinkedIn Co-founder**

Sell Before You Build

We've just covered this in detail. Selling before you build is about testing real-world market demand for your solution. The objective is to get your first sale and have a repeatable sales process.

This means you need to be able to clearly communicate what the specific offer is, the price, and be able to demo your solution so your customer knows what they're getting and how it works. You'll usually use a prototype as the demo, not a working version of your solution.

The feedback you get from your customers during this process will help you iterate and refine both your business model and solution.

Soft Launch

The soft launch is an early release of your solution, often to a limited audience. The strategy is to release your solution in stages. For the soft launch, you need at least some of the core elements of your solution that deliver value for your ideal customers, but not usually the complete working version.

Minimum viable product (MVP) is a common term used in startups, and you might have noticed that I haven't been using it as part of this approach. This is mostly because it's a term that means different things to different people, and is often misused. It comes with a lot of baggage, but I'll use it now in a very specific context.

A good MVP is one that is designed and built to help you learn specific things as part of solution development. It's a prototype as part of one or more of your experiments to test your riskiest assumptions. This is part of your Prototype & Experiment Plan even if you haven't called it an MVP.

Eric Ries defined an MVP as the "version of a new product which allows a team to collect the maximum amount of validated learning about customers with the least effort". It's not necessarily the first rough and partially working version of your solution – which is how it's often used. Remember the build, measure, learn loop of lean startup.

Using an MVP of your solution with a soft launch approach will help you collect real information and data from feedback and actual use. Synthesise these to identify the patterns and key insights to drive your conclusions and how you'll refine your business model and solution.

The early stages of the soft launch might just be an awareness campaign. Building awareness usually takes time and is a necessary part of achieving repeatable sales.

What your soft launch looks like will depend on your context and the type of solution. This approach can also include pilots.

Public Launch

A public launch is also known as a hard launch. This is the full public release, and the objective is usually to attract the attention of as many of your ideal customers as possible.

It's probably what you were thinking of when I said launch. The difference is, before this launch event, you've already refined your business model and solution based on testing market demand and price, and feedback from real customers who've been using early versions of your solution. You also don't have the risks involved with your solution going live for the first time. All of this reduces the risks involved in a public launch.

You might even choose not to have a major public launch event.

Evergreen Launch

An evergreen launch is an approach to launching, meaning that it's always running. Rather than a launch that happens within a specific time period, it's an ongoing launch. This won't be relevant for all contexts and types of solutions, but it can work very well for digital products.

You can start using an evergreen launch approach before you even do your soft launch. For it to work well, you need to build and leverage a reusable process and materials. For it to work really well, it requires some level of automation.

As I mentioned in the intro, I think of this book as a product rather than a traditional book. The launch process started around the same time that I started writing it, and I'd already had some sell before you build conversations before that. I did a soft launch a couple of months before I finished the book, and I'm planning an evergreen launch over the first 12 months.

With hindsight, I could have done an even more progressive launch. Visit dynamic4.com/sptm for my reflections on how I've applied the process I outlined in this book to the writing of it.

Launch & Iterate
Your Solution

Take 15-30 minutes to review your Prototypes & Experiments Plan and your GTM Strategy, and refine where needed.

Execute your Prototypes & Experiments Plan and your GTM Strategy to continue launching and iterating your business model and solution.

This chapter has focused on helping you prototype, test, and learn with your prototypes and experiments. This is absolutely critical in reducing the risk of overinvesting time, money, and energy in a solution no one will use or pay for.

The Kano Model – a product development and customer satisfaction model by Noriaki Kano – is another of my favourites. It shows how solutions are about much more than features and functionality, they're about our customers' emotions and expectations. And these expectations increase over time. This is why continual innovation is so important. It means an ongoing process of iterating and launching.

You're designing, building, and launching your social enterprise idea, but that journey has only just begun. The thinking and practices you've started in this chapter will continue as you refine your business model and solution over the months and years to come. Innovation never stops.

The next step is to calculate and test your pricing. As I mentioned, Chapters 9, 10, 11, and 12 all go together as part of a rapid and iterative process.

Chapter 11

Pricing

Are we solving the
right problem?

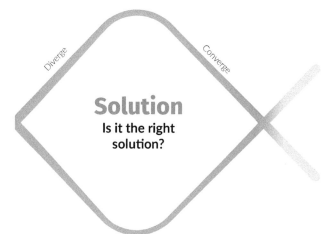

Diverge

Converge

Solution
**Is it the right
solution?**

The purpose of this chapter is to help you work out what your customers will pay for your solution.

In Chapter 5, you used the Business Model Environment tool to look at how other alternatives in the market price their solution, and you built on this with your market research in Chapter 7. As you explore, prototype, and test your business model and solution, you also need to work out what your pricing will be.

The way we'll approach this is to:

- Identify the types of revenue you expect to generate
- Calculate your costs
- Explore possible types of pricing and work out the price for your solution
- Test what your customers are willing to pay for your solution

Price vs Cost

A quick definition of terms. Price and cost are often used interchangeably in general conversation. But in the context of accounting and our financial model, they mean very distinct things.

The price is what customers pay to receive solutions. It's money into the organisation. The costs are the expenses an organisation pays to create, provide, and dispose of their solution. It's money out of the organisation.

Generally, your price needs to be higher than your costs to be financially viable and sustainable. The money left over when all costs have been paid is profit or surplus. You need some level of profit to be able to fund the continual improvement of your organisation and solutions.

It's also important to remember that the costs your organisation needs to pay often continue long after the sale has been made and the price has been paid. Another aspect of cost to remember is any potential social and/or environmental impacts. We'll cover this briefly as part of triple bottom line in Chapter 12.

In summary, your pricing needs to ensure that you're viable not just at the point of transaction, but for the life of your solution. In many cases, this includes disposing of your solution ethically and sustainably at the end of its life.

Your Revenue Streams

Let's start by doing some more work on your revenue streams. I introduced this with the Lean Canvas in Chapter 5, and it was part of prototyping your business model in Chapter 10. Revenue streams are the different sources and types of money coming into the organisation. You might just have one type of revenue, or you might have multiple.

Some common types of revenue include fees for service, product purchases, subscriptions, grants, and donations. Some of these are only possible when you have a certain legal structure.

The term "earned income" relates to revenue generated by customers paying for your solution. The types of revenue this relates to include fees for service, product purchases, and subscriptions. Generally, you have a lot more control of these types of revenue streams than you do for grants and donations – if you're even eligible to receive them.

For these earned income solutions, the amount of revenue is the price of each solution multiplied by the number of sales you make. Setting a price that your ideal customers are willing to pay, and having enough customers willing to pay – your market size – is crucial to generating enough revenue.

This is what you're testing and experimenting with by calculating and testing your pricing and selling before you build. The price of existing alternatives will also provide some guidance here. The information you get from these experiments feeds into your financial model that we cover in Chapter 12.

As I mentioned, Chapters 9, 10, 11, and 12 all go together as part of a rapid and iterative process. You'll need to keep iterating to find the version of your business model and solution that is viable, feasible, and of course desirable for your ideal customers.

This action flows directly into the revenue section of Chapter 12 and will iterate.

As you think about this, be more creative than just financial transactions. What are the other types of value exchange where you receive value?

Your Revenue Streams

Take 15-30 minutes to identify the sources and types of revenue you will generate, and update your Lean Canvas.

Start adding more detail by using a top-down approach and some high-level estimates. How much revenue will each revenue stream generate over the next 12 months? What about the next 36 months?

Try a simple statement like "If we sell x units of our solution at y price, then we will generate z revenue". It's easier to refine this as you get better information than leaving it unsaid. Take a position… then test and refine it.

Make your assumptions explicit, and capture them on your Assumptions Log.

Your Cost Structure

Cost is a critical element when calculating your pricing. As I mentioned, your price generally needs to be higher than your costs, otherwise you'll quickly run out of money. This means being very clear about your cost structure. Again, you've already done some work on this as part of prototyping your business model in Chapter 10.

Build on this now. Keep your estimates for ongoing operational costs separate from your solution design, build, and GTM costs. Remember, the other blocks of the Lean Canvas give you a lot of clues of where there's cost, especially solution and channels.

It's also worth identifying which costs are fixed and ongoing, the variable costs, and you might have some one-time costs too. This action flows directly into Chapter 12 and will iterate.

As you think about this, what are the other types of value exchange where you provide value?

— ACTION —

Your Cost Structure

Take 15-30 minutes to identify the types of cost you will have, and update your Lean Canvas.

Start adding more detail by using a top-down approach and some high-level estimates. How much will you need to spend on each cost category over the next 12 months? What about the next 36 months?

Make your assumptions explicit, and capture them on your Assumptions Log.

You've now used a top-down approach to make some clear statements about the price you think you can set and the number of sales you expect. You're also building a clearer picture of your cost base. These feed into your financial model.

When the numbers are starting to work, it's time to calculate and test your pricing with more rigour. Again, this is an iterative process. The only reason there are separate chapters on the solution, pricing, and financials is to group the information.

These four chapters all go together, and you'll do multiple cycles of learning through all of them as you move from low-fidelity conceptual solution and business model design to more polished versions as you follow the evidence.

Calculate Your Pricing

Calculating your pricing can be tricky, and it takes experimentation and testing to get it right. In the revenue streams section of this chapter, you took a position based on the information you currently have and some assumptions.

Pricing forms part of your GTM strategy in Chapter 10 and is very dependent on the version of your solution, your ideal customers, the offer you take to market, and how you position yourself in the market. Pricing also feeds directly into your financial model in Chapter 12.

There are many pricing strategies, but I'll cover some core concepts and methods. The pricing strategy needs to align with your purpose, theory of change, and what's appropriate for your context. There is no single right answer.

It's also important to remember that costs and prices change over time. This won't be the last time you need to calculate and test your pricing. Visit dynamic4.com/sptm for more resources on pricing.

Cost-Based Pricing

We've established that your price and revenue have to be higher than your costs to be financially viable and sustainable. This means you need to know your cost structure well, and makes cost-based pricing a good place to start. It sets a minimum price that you need to be able to charge – based on a forecast of your sales volume over a specific period.

The cost-plus pricing method simply adds a fixed percentage markup to your total costs. There are variations on this approach, but this is the simplest and is based on your total cost base, not just direct costs.

A key risk to manage with this approach is what happens if you don't make the number of sales you forecast? If the markup percentage isn't high enough, you'll quickly be making a loss.

This approach is very inward-focused, and it doesn't mean the price compares well with the market or what customers are willing to pay. Customers often don't care what it costs you. They care about the value you create by solving their problem and if they feel they can trust you.

Market-Based Pricing

You've done market research including understanding the pricing of the existing alternatives and your competitors in Chapters 5 and 7. How do your competitors position their solutions in the market, and what are their price points?

The market-based pricing method sets prices by aligning your price with similar solutions in the market. Your price might be the same or you might try a slightly higher or lower price.

If the going market price is lower than your cost-based price, you will probably need to refine your business model and solution to be more competitive – or you might be able to change your positioning in the market.

Value-Based Pricing

Value-based pricing is what your customers perceive it to be worth, and are willing to pay. This pricing method doesn't happen in a vacuum though. The market rate is likely to influence what your customer believes is a fair price.

You get a lot of insight by knowing what your customer is comparing you to and possibly price anchoring against. The psychology of pricing is powerful.

How you position yourself in the market, your brand, the version of your solution that you're offering, and the support you provide all have an impact on what your customer is willing to pay.

There are also customer-specific factors like how much it is currently costing them to solve the problem and how painful it is. This pain can be measured in time, lost opportunities, and stress. When you know your ideal customers well, you'll be able to effectively

communicate your value proposition and how you address these pain points.

If most customers perceive the value of your solution to be less than your cost-based price, you probably won't have enough demand. You will likely need to iterate your business model and solution, change your positioning, or reduce the number of sales you expect to make – which means an even higher price.

Sometimes a higher price with a smaller number of customers is a valid approach.

ACTION

Calculate Your Pricing

Take 15-30 minutes to calculate your cost-based price to set the minimum viable baseline.

How does this compare with the draft price you set in the revenue streams section of this chapter?

What is the price range of similar solutions in the market?

What price do your customers perceive it to be worth?

Make your assumptions explicit, and capture them on your Assumptions Log.

Test Your Pricing

How do you know what price you can charge? By running experiments and testing your pricing. This is a key step in selling before you build. It's only when someone actually pays for your solution that you know you have a customer who is willing to pay.

Your Prototypes & Experiments Plan and your GTM Strategy both include testing your pricing. It's time to execute those plans.

While testing price, it's also important to remember that the barrier to the sale might not be the price as much as the time, attention, energy, and learning curve required to switch to your solution. It can be easy to blame price when the real issue is that there isn't really a market demand or it's not a high enough priority for your ideal customers to do something about.

Price sensitivity testing is useful in the early stages of setting and testing your price. The four questions from the Van Westendorp Price Sensitivity Meter can be included in some of your solution interviews as part of your experiments:

- At what price would you consider the solution to be so expensive that you would not consider buying it? (Too expensive)

- At what price would you consider the solution to be priced so low that you would feel the quality couldn't be very good? (Too cheap)

- At what price would you consider the solution starting to get expensive, so that it is not out of the question, but you would have to give some thought to buying it? (Expensive/high side)

- At what price would you consider the solution to be a bargain – a great buy for the money? (Cheap/good value)

What I like about this approach is it gives you a range, rather than a single number. You can then compare this range with what you've heard from different customers. This is more useful than asking customers what they think the price should be.

There's a more complex model that sits behind these questions if you want to use it, but I find just asking these questions gives a lot of insight.

As you get more certainty on your pricing, this will drive your revenue and market size calculations. It will also likely impact your output and outcomes measures.

Test Your Pricing

Take 15-30 minutes to review your Prototypes & Experiments Plan and your GTM Strategy, and refine where needed.

Execute your Prototypes & Experiments Plan and your GTM Strategy. Refine your business model, solution, and pricing until you find a financially viable combination.

Update your revenue and market size calculations.

Review and update your theory of change with output and outcomes measures.

This chapter has been focused on helping you work out the price your customers are willing to pay for your solution. It will normally take a lot of testing and iteration to find your business model and solution that brings together the three lenses of desirable, viable, and feasible. Pricing is a key ingredient.

The next step is to build a clear picture of your financial position, and pricing feeds directly into this. As I mentioned, Chapters 9, 10, 11, and 12 all go together as part of a rapid and iterative process.

Chapter 12

Financials

Are we solving the
right problem?

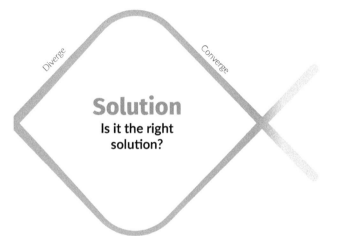

Diverge

Converge

Solution
**Is it the right
solution?**

A quick disclaimer. I'm not an accountant, and I'm not giving you accounting, tax, or financial advice. What I can do though is help you think through the questions and possible implications as you build up your financial model.

The tax law differs by country, and sometimes regions within countries, so I recommend you talk to an accountant who understands your type of organisation – and ideally shares your values. It's worth asking your local network for recommendations and checking the B Corp directory.

As you explore, prototype, and test your business model and solution, your financial model iterates at a high level. As you get more confident – based on evidence – that there's demand for your solution and the price people will pay, you'll develop a more robust financial model.

To develop your financial model, you'll build on the work you've already done on your market size, pricing, revenue streams, and cost structure. You really need to know your numbers – especially what it means to reach monthly breakeven, how long it will take, and how much you will need to invest to achieve it.

A general rule is to be conservative. Plan for the worst-case – not the miracle.

A key focus of this book is to help you design a sustainable business model. Money and your financial model are a critical part of this – but it's also important to think about value, value exchange, and impact in more than just financial outcomes. We also need to think about the outcomes for people and our environment – triple bottom line.

The way we'll approach this is to:

- Calculate the costs to design, build, launch, and get your solution to market
- Calculate what it looks like to achieve monthly breakeven, how long it's likely to take, and the amount of money you'll need to get there
- Calculate if you can achieve net breakeven
- Identify funding options
- Review your triple bottom line

Design, Build & Go-to-Market Costs

What's it going to cost to design, build, and get your solution to market? In reality, these costs have already started. You're at least investing your time in researching the process – and assuming you've been working through the actions in this book, you've been designing and building your idea.

This all involves costs. Even if you've managed to get to this point without spending any money, you've been spending time. The most precious non-renewable resource that we have.

This section is focused on the costs of getting your solution into the real world. This needs to align with your GTM strategy from Chapter 10. As we talked about in the Launch & Iterate Your Solution section, launching and getting to market isn't a singular event. It's progressive and will happen over time.

A common mistake – and one I've made myself – is to plan these costs to the point of a major launch or go-live, without any funds left to keep iterating and marketing after that point. Sometimes this is with the expectation that early revenue will cover costs or the hope that some other funds will turn up.

Please don't make that mistake. It will almost certainly take longer to get to the point of generating revenue than you plan. You need to allocate funding to be able to keep iterating based on what you're learning. It's not a fun position to be in when you have great insights and requests from your customers, but you're stuck with the current version of your solution because you don't have the funds to do anything about them.

I recommend a 12-month time horizon for your GTM strategy – and it's best if you mirror this timeline when calculating your design, build, and GTM costs.

You identified a series of activities in your GTM strategy. All of these will have costs associated – probably some money, and definitely time.

A key consideration is that your pricing and revenue are probably dependent on the version of the solution. The timing of that solution is dependent on the funds and time required to design, build, and get the solution to market. These pieces and expectations need to fit together. This flows directly to your monthly breakeven calculations, which we'll look at in a moment.

You can approach these calculations using top-down or bottom-up methods. I recommend both. Start top-down to get a sense of the overall numbers by making rough estimates on categories of costs over the next 12 months. You started this work in Chapter 11 with your cost structure.

Do they stack up, and can you afford to design and build the solution? Can you afford to run the solution on a monthly basis? This brings the three lenses of desirable, viable, and feasible together.

If the numbers aren't working – and it's common that they don't when modelling the early versions of the budget – it means iterating to find a viable version of the solution. **It's critical to do this before investing in the detailed design and build of your solution**. As I mentioned, Chapters 9, 10, 11, and 12 all go together as part of a rapid and iterative process.

As you go through this process, you need to stay aligned with your purpose and theory of change. Please don't make compromises that create negative outcomes for people and our planet.

This is a point in the process where you might be tempted to take some shortcuts, create waste, not pay fairly, or do other things you promised yourself you'd never do. You might rationalise it as something you'll come back to do right later. Most never do. It's much harder to retrofit and there will always be higher priorities. Live your values now.

When the numbers look like they're in the right ballpark, use a bottom-up approach to calculate the monthly design, build, and GTM costs. It's unlikely that costs are the same every month, so this will give you a forecast of the funding that you need, and the timing of the funding. This is important to help you manage your cashflow.

If going from 12 months to monthly in one step is too much, you can try doing quarterly plans first – and then move to monthly. You probably want to progress to a point of having a three-year forecast.

You're going to be working with a lot of assumptions. That's ok. Make them explicit and write them down.

On the surface, this approach might sound like it contradicts working with sprints and 90-day plans. Your financial planning, 3-Year Picture, yearly planning, 90-day plans, and sprints all need to fit together and align. The finances will often be a constraint that you need to work within. Everything is integrated.

Visit dynamic4.com/sptm for a template spreadsheet and more resources.

Calculate Design, Build, Launch & Go-to-Market Costs

Take 30-60 minutes to calculate how much it will cost to design, build, and get your solution to market over the next 12 months. Align these calculations with your GTM strategy.

Don't forget to include the cost of your time – and that of any team members – even if you're not paying yourself at the moment. I also recommend you include the time you've already spent.

Make your assumptions explicit, and capture them on your Assumptions Log.

Calculate Monthly Breakeven

Monthly breakeven is the point where you have more money coming in every month than you're paying out. It's absolutely critical for a viable and financially sustainable organisation.

Breakeven needs to be achieved within a reasonable timeframe, with a reasonable amount invested. Every month you spend more than you earn increases the total deficit and reduces your runway – the time before you run out of money.

It usually takes longer than we plan to achieve monthly breakeven. Most financial models I see don't include the founders paying themselves – and even then, the numbers often don't stack up. Then there's the harsh reality that well over 90% of startups fail – this applies equally to social enterprise ideas.

This is the context I framed up when talking about your personal sustainability and finances in Chapter 1. It's important that you know both your personal and the organisation's financial numbers to be sustainable – and in the early days, there's likely to be a high cross-dependency.

You started with the top-down method to calculate your revenue streams and cost structure in Chapter 11. Build on that work to build up a monthly forecast of your revenue and costs. The basic structure of the financial forecast spreadsheet is a column for each month and three blocks of rows for revenue, cost of sales, and operating expenses – each with totals and some calculations.

Like your design, build, and GTM costs – you need to keep iterating to find a viable version of the solution where the numbers work. If you can't achieve monthly breakeven on a spreadsheet – or it's going to cost too much to get there – it's very unlikely you'll achieve it in practice. No matter how conservative you think you're being.

It's beyond the scope of this book to get into detailed accounting and financial modelling. If this isn't something you're already comfortable with, it's worth building these skills. In the meantime, I recommend you draw on the support of other team members – using the broad definition of team – and get professional advice.

I'll briefly cover some basic concepts that will help you with this. This is how I approach it, but there are other ways. The most appropriate method will depend on your context, including tax law.

To keep it simple, we'll only look at a basic financial forecast spreadsheet based on a profit and loss statement format using cash basis accounting. This format generally provides a pretty accurate picture of cashflow. As things stabilise, it's probably worth doing a full three-way forecast with profit and loss, cashflow, and balance sheet.

In general, I like to keep indirect costs very lean – and wherever possible I allocate costs as direct costs. This gives a more accurate cost of sale, but reduces gross profit. It also means that the indirect cost base is lower, and if there are no sales, the costs are lower. I'll briefly explain some key terms and provide guidance on how to create your forecast.

Revenue/Sales

Revenue, sales, or income – this is money coming into the organisation. This is the number that needs to be greater than the total of all of your costs. You identified the key sources of this with your revenue streams in Chapter 11.

This is the first block on the spreadsheet. Put each type of revenue in its own row. What's your expected revenue for each month? When do sales start? Will sales be consistent every month? Or do sales fluctuate monthly? Will sales be seasonal? Will there be a ramp-up period?

Add your monthly revenue forecast to each monthly column. Be conservative and remember sales often take longer than expected. I recommend doing this on a cash basis – so you enter the amount of the sale on the month the money is received, not the month the sale is made and invoiced if they are different.

Your revenue depends directly on the version of your solution and pricing. Testing pricing and selling before you build are critical ways of managing risk.

Cost of Sale/Direct Costs

Cost of sale (CoS) – also known as cost of goods sold (COGS) – are direct costs. This is part of the money going out of the organisation, expenses that result directly from creating and delivering your solution. If you don't have a sale, you don't have the cost of sale.

This is the second block on the spreadsheet. Put each type of cost of sale in its own row and add your forecast to each monthly column. There should be a direct relationship between your revenue forecast and your CoS. The cost might not be in the same month as the money from the sale is received – enter CoS in the month you expect to spend the money.

If you still need to pay the expense when you don't have a sale, it doesn't belong in this category. Direct costs can also be variable or fixed.

When your cost of sale is more than your sale, it's probably not viable and you need to look at your pricing, although there are exceptions to this with cross-subsidised models and other factors that are too complex to get into here.

Your direct costs are only part of the picture of your total cost base. There are also your operating expenses, which we'll cover in a moment.

Gross Profit

Gross profit is the money left over from your sales after you've paid cost of sales. A simple calculation: revenue – cost of sales = gross profit.

This is often then expressed as a percentage to be the gross profit margin. The basic calculation is gross profit ÷ revenue x 100%. This can be different with more complex profit and loss statement structures.

Example:
200 revenue – 60 cost of sales = 140 gross profit

140 gross profit ÷ 200 revenue x 100 = 70% gross profit margin

It's important to note that this isn't your total profit or surplus. You still need to subtract your operating expenses. If your gross profit is low or negative, you don't have money left over to pay your indirect costs – including having the funds to be able to continue making improvements.

Operating Expenses/Indirect Costs

Operating expenses or overheads are indirect costs – money going out of the organisation. These are all of the expenses required to keep the organisation running – excluding cost of sales as a direct cost. Whether you're generating revenue or not, you still need to pay these expenses, which include wages, rent, insurances, office supplies, etc.

This is the third block on the spreadsheet. Put each type of operating expense in its own row and add your forecast to each monthly column. There are a standard set of categories, but add any extra that you need.

There isn't generally a direct relationship between your operating expenses, your revenue and CoS. Indirect costs can also be variable or fixed.

Your operating expenses are likely to start well before you start generating revenue. This is where you're probably building a deficit that impacts your net breakeven calculations, which we'll cover in the next section.

Net Profit/Surplus

Net profit or surplus is the money left over from your total revenue after you've paid all expenses, including cost of sales. A simple calculation: total revenue – total expenses = net profit.

Total expenses are cost of sales plus operating expenses.

Net profit is often expressed as a percentage to be the net profit margin. The basic calculation is net profit ÷ revenue x 100%.

Example:
200 total revenue – 140 total expenses = 60 net profit

60 net profit ÷ 200 revenue x 100 = 30% gross profit margin

This is a simplified version and will be different depending on your legal structure, the tax law that applies to your organisation, and some other variables. You may also need to look at the EBITDA calculations. This is where getting professional accounting and tax advice specific to your context is important.

Monthly Breakeven

As you know, monthly breakeven is the point where you have more money coming in every month than you're paying out. According to your forecast, when does the net profit number consistently change from being a negative (a monthly loss or deficit) to a positive (a monthly profit or surplus)? How many months will it take? How does this fit with your personal and your organisation's runway?

You've now got an indication of how long it will take to achieve monthly breakeven. How much money will you need to invest to achieve it? Add up the net profit/loss totals of all the months before the month you identified as the point where you're consistently breaking even. This plus your design, build, and GTM costs is the amount of money you need to invest. Can you afford it? How will you fund it?

These calculations are often confronting. The financial model will often show it's going to take many months or even years and a lot of money to break even. Resist the temptation to rationalise why it will all just magically work out.

As I mentioned, if you can't achieve monthly breakeven on a spreadsheet, it's very unlikely you'll achieve it in practice. Keep iterating your solution and business model, and testing your assumptions until you can make the numbers work.

Calculate Monthly Breakeven

Take 30-60 minutes to do your financial forecast and calculate your monthly breakeven. 12 months is unlikely to be long enough for this forecast. I recommend forecasting the next 24 or 36 months.

Don't forget to include the cost of your time – and that of any team members – even if you're not paying yourself at the moment. I recommend that you include the time you've already spent. You also need to include any loan repayments.

Make your assumptions explicit, and capture them on your Assumptions Log.

Coaching Questions

- What needs to happen to achieve breakeven on a monthly basis?
- How much revenue do you need to earn each month to cover your total expenses?
- How many units do you need to sell at what price each month?
- How much margin do you forecast that you'll earn each month? Each quarter? Each year?
- What will you do to achieve it?
- When do you forecast that you will achieve monthly breakeven?
- How much money is required to cover the deficit between now and when you expect to break even?
- What key assumptions need to be true for this to happen?
- How will you test and refine your key assumptions?
- How are you keeping your organisation's finances separate from your personal finances?
- Are you using accounting software? Do you have accounting support?
- What financial and tax reporting is required?

Calculate Net Breakeven

Net breakeven is the point where, in total, you've earned as much as you've invested from the time you started working on your idea, and it includes paying yourself. Monthly breakeven needs to be achieved before net breakeven.

Like monthly breakeven, many organisations never achieve net breakeven. You might not care about achieving it, but I recommend you make that an informed decision. You need to count the true cost. What are your expectations as a founder, and how does this fit with your personal runway?

This is an especially important point for established NFPs who are starting a social enterprise idea to generate earned income as a way to diversify revenue streams. Is there an expectation that the social enterprise will repay the seed investment?

The deficit you calculated to achieve monthly breakeven plus the total to design, build, and get your solution to market is the amount of revenue you need to generate for net breakeven.

To be truly financially sustainable you need to achieve net breakeven and know that you can sustain monthly breakeven. You actually need to do better than that. You need some funds in reserve for breathing space when (not if) things go wrong – and to be able to continually improve.

ACTION

Calculate Net Breakeven

Take 5-10 minutes to calculate your net breakeven.

Make your assumptions explicit, and capture them on your Assumptions Log.

Coaching Questions

- When will you reach net breakeven?
- How much do you need to invest to achieve it?
- What needs to be true?
- What needs to happen?

Identify Your Funding Options

You've just spent time calculating how much funding you're likely to need to design, build, and get your solution to market... and then cover the gap until you achieve monthly breakeven. Now that you know how much money is required, you need to work out how you're going to fund it.

Maybe you've already got that worked out and you don't have any funding challenges. Well done, that must feel good. I've personally never known that feeling. I'll briefly outline a range of funding options with some key considerations for each.

For many, the desired path is to have some seed money to invest to get their solution to market and start generating revenue from paying customers to achieve monthly breakeven early. Improvements to the solution, business model, and organisational operations and growth are funded by operating profit/surplus. That's the simplest path, but it doesn't often work out that way, and where does the initial seed money come from?

You can't talk about funding without talking about legal structure. Your legal structure is likely to mean you're eligible for some funding options but not others. In Chapter 13, I help

you think through the questions and possible implications of certain legal decisions. I can't advise you on the most appropriate way for your specific context though.

I'll focus primarily on funding options for the early stages rather than the growth and scaling stages. A lot of the same questions and considerations are still relevant at those stages, but there's usually a very different risk profile.

It might sound counterintuitive, but funding constraints and gaps in cashflow during growth periods are often major issues. I won't cover that here, but it's where bridging and invoice financing can play a role.

Funding often comes with conditions and requirements. It's also important to have clear and aligned expectations. Some questions to consider when looking at your funding options:

- Is the funding provided expected to be repaid? If yes, what's the repayment schedule? What happens if it can't be repaid?

- Are there interest payments? What's the interest rate? Does it change over time?

- Is it provided in exchange for a share of ownership?

- Is it provided in exchange for a share of revenue?

- What reporting is required?

- Does it result in a change to organisational control or decision-making?

- Does it result in constraints, conditions of trade, or changes to intellectual property ownership?

- Are there any tax implications?

There's often money available to help you design, build, and get your solution to market. A lot of the following funding options are also available for growth and to enhance your solution. As a general rule, people are less willing to fund your operational expenses – including founder salaries.

Personal Savings & Debt

The initial seed funding is usually invested by the founder(s). In the early stages, there's often a very direct relationship between your personal runway and the organisation's runway. The funding source is often personal savings, or it might be from personal debt by using credit cards, getting a personal loan, or a micro-loan. Be very careful going into debt. In most cases, I'd caution against it.

The principle I strongly recommend is that you only invest and risk what you can afford to lose and you need to cap your downside risk. You don't want to end up in financial hardship. It's important that you know your personal financial numbers to be sustainable, and keep yourself and your household in a healthy financial position. Financial stress is

the cause of a lot of health and relationship issues.

You've already done some work on this. In Chapter 1, as part of your strengths and assets, you identified the resources you have – including money and money you can get access to. You also did some calculations on your personal finances as part of your personal sustainability, and we talked about your risk profile too.

Initial seed funding will normally come from personal savings. There might be some personal debt in the mix, but you can probably see how uncomfortable that makes me feel. In some contexts, the relative risk might mean it's worth it.

Organisational Savings & Debt

If the social enterprise idea originates within an established organisation, it will often invest a specific budget as seed funding from operating profit/surplus.

You may be able to get a loan in your organisation's name. This is unlikely in the early days without a trading history and assets. Lenders want to manage their risk and will normally secure loans against assets.

In some cases, the lender may agree to provide a loan if you personally guarantee the loan and have assets as security. This effectively becomes a personal loan, but in the organisation's name. When you personally guarantee a loan, you're personally accountable, and if the loan can't be repaid, you may lose the personal assets you used to secure it. I've already said how I feel about that.

Some organisations will provide unsecured loans.

Grants

Grants are often only available to organisations with certain legal structures. Grants don't normally need to be repaid. There will usually be very specific eligibility requirements, and there's often reporting required to acquit the grant. In some cases, if you fail to meet the acquittal requirements, the grant may have to be returned.

Grant funding when done well is catalytic and can open up many opportunities – both financially and with relationships and networks.

Sometimes grants are viewed as free money. They aren't. You're likely to have to invest significant time in applying for grants. If you're successful, you'll probably have a fair bit of reporting to do. The value of the time you invest in applying for and acquitting grants can sometimes be more than the value of the grant. It's important to look at the total cost.

Donations

Donations don't need to be repaid. It's very important that it's explicit that the person is making a donation though. This means they're giving the funding without any expectation of being repaid or anything in return. They don't get a share of ownership or have any decision-making rights.

In some jurisdictions, the person making the donation may receive a tax benefit when they donate to an organisation with certain legal structures and registrations. Ensure you set clear expectations and provide accurate information.

Capital for Equity

Capital for equity is only available to organisations with specific legal structures that can issue shares or equity. You receive capital investment in exchange for equity. This means bringing in additional owners. Ownership is part of the picture, but it often also involves voting rights and some decision making.

I won't go into detail on the different types of capital raises and instruments like priced rounds, SAFEs, and convertible notes, but I raise some of the questions to consider in Chapter 13. I also recommend getting professional advice before starting this process. Many of the decisions can have both legal and tax implications – including even asking people to invest.

Raising capital can easily take six to 12 months – if you successfully raise at all. Most investors expect some track record and evidence of traction. In some rare cases, investors will invest in an idea without traction or may close an investment round quickly. You've probably heard about some of these. They're noteworthy because they're rare – not because it's the norm.

Crowdfunding

Crowdfunding has become a popular option over the past 10 years. There are different types of crowdfunding. The most common are rewards-based, donation-based, equity-based, or debt-based. Each of these has its requirements and works in different ways.

A lot of crowdfunding is now done online with platforms that help you launch, promote, and collect the funds from your campaign. One of these is StartSomeGood (startsomegood. com). They're a social enterprise and B Corp, and an organisation I love collaborating with. They're specifically a "crowdfunding platform for social enterprises, nonprofits and changemakers".

I think of rewards-based as pre-purchasing a product, usually a product that doesn't exist yet. Kickstarter and Indiegogo are well-known platforms for these types of campaigns. This can be a good way to get early paying customers for your solution.

Donation-based crowdfunding is self-explanatory. People make a donation to a campaign. GoFundMe is a well-known platform.

Sometimes donation and rewards-based crowdfunding are combined, and you may be given a reward for your donation. While you receive the donations, if you're providing rewards, you will usually have a lot of work to do to deliver on the rewards and packages you promised.

Equity-based crowdfunding is only available to organisations with specific legal structures that can issue shares or equity. This is generally a very regulated form of crowdfunding. You receive capital investment in exchange for equity.

Debt-based crowdfunding is sometimes known as peer-to-peer lending. Kiva and Good Return are a couple of well-known platforms. You need to repay the funds, usually with interest.

Crowdfunding is also often viewed as free money. It isn't.

Using a donation-based method with a reward as an example, I recommend viewing it as at least a three-month campaign. You need at least a month to prepare and launch a good campaign. The campaign will often run for about one month, and you'll be doing a lot of promotion and answering questions. When the campaign is finished, you'll probably be exhausted, but need to deliver on the rewards you promised. It's common for a campaign to become a full-time job for about three months.

Incubator & Accelerator Programs

Some incubators and accelerators will provide funding as part of being accepted into their program. This may be as a grant, for equity, or for a share of the revenue. There will be eligibility criteria to meet, and there will likely be conditions of the funding too. It's important to understand these conditions.

Revenue

The funding we're primarily focused on is pre-revenue, so you probably don't have reserves from customer revenue to fund the initial stages. Progressing to this point is a good ambition to achieve sooner than later.

Blended Deals

Some organisations specialise in helping structure blended deals using two or more funding types. This is often a combination of grants and debt financing, and sometimes capital for equity.

Sefa (Social Enterprise Finance Australia) (sefa.com.au) is a social enterprise and B Corp based in Australia, and an organisation I love collaborating with. They unlock social impact through financial solutions to help "purpose-driven organisations have equal access to finance to be sustainable and maximise impact".

They take the approach of providing access to funding – including blended deals – alongside advisory services and helping build capability and financial literacy.

I hope this highlights a few funding options to consider. They all come with trade-offs. There's no such thing as free money.

Identify Your Funding Options

Take 10-15 minutes to identify your funding options. This will mean different things depending on the stage you're at.

Review your financial forecasts to calculate how much funding you need.

You need to approach funding your social enterprise idea like any investment. You should only invest what you can afford to lose, and you need to cap your downside risk.

Make your assumptions explicit, and capture them on your Assumptions Log.

Coaching Questions

- What can you achieve with the amount of funding you calculated?

- How much runway does it give you?

- What will you do to manage the risk related to the funding?

- Have you updated your pitch deck with your financial forecasts, the ask, and the use of funds?

Review Your Triple Bottom Line

I've been referring to triple bottom line since the opening pages of this book, and it's embedded in the way we've approached everything. John Elkington coined the term in 1994. In his 2018 *Harvard Business Review (HBR)* article, he describes it as "a sustainability framework that examines a company's social, environment, and economic impact".

He goes on to say that the "stated goal from the outset was system change – pushing toward the transformation of capitalism. It was never supposed to be just an accounting system. It was originally intended as a genetic code, a triple helix of change for tomorrow's capitalism".

Triple bottom line is often known as people, planet, and profit. The word profit here is often misunderstood as just organisational profit. What it really means is social impact – a shared prosperity.

In his *HBR* article, John Elkington might have been a bit disillusioned that the "concept has been captured and diluted by accountants and reporting consultants", but the idea has driven a lot of positive change in accounting, management, and reporting. Are any of them

perfect? No, but I believe progress has been made, and that makes me feel optimistic.

Why are we reviewing triple bottom line as part of the chapter on financials? While a lot of people have treated it as an accounting tool, that narrow scope was never its intent. I'm encouraging you to think about your business model and solution beyond just financial terms – but the broader economic impacts, as well as outcomes for people and our planet.

Impact Reporting

Annual reports are an opportunity to communicate your broader economic impacts in addition to your finances – as well as the other social and environmental outcomes you identified in your theory of change.

Social enterprises often produce an annual impact report to communicate their progress with outcome and output measures, which we talked about in Chapter 4. These measures and lead indicators provide a feedback loop that shows us if we're on the right path, and if our solution is having the positive effect we believed it would.

There are also double bottom line and quadruple bottom line. I think these start muddying the waters, and triple bottom line is the concept with the most traction.

Triple bottom line has influenced a lot of accounting and reporting frameworks and also impact measurement frameworks. Some related approaches that I'll mention briefly in case you want to explore more are: integrated reporting, Social Return on Investment (SROI), ESG (Environmental, Social, and Governance), Kate Raworth's Doughnut Economics, Michael Porter's Shared Value, and many others. Visit dynamic4.com/sptm for links to more resources.

Be Climate Positive

I encourage you to design your solutions and business model to have a minimal carbon footprint. Apply collaborative consumption, circular economy, and regenerative thinking and practices. After doing what you can to minimise your carbon impact, I recommend offsetting your remaining emissions. You have the opportunity to be carbon neutral or better from day one.

At Dynamic4, we take this seriously. Since 2010 we've consistently minimised our carbon impact and offset 20% more than our calculated emissions. We're proud to have been climate positive since 2010.

In 2019, we were one of the 533 B Corps who publicly committed to net zero emissions by the year 2030 at the UN Climate Change Conference (COP25) in Madrid. We also encourage our clients, partners, and communities to take meaningful climate action. This is a key consideration for us when selecting our suppliers.

Your Triple Bottom Line

With this framing, take the opportunity now to reflect on your triple bottom line.

─── ACTION ───

Your Triple Bottom Line

Take 15-30 minutes to reflect on your progress through a triple bottom line lens.

- How has your theory of change with output and outcome measures refined as your business model and solution has iterated?
- How are you talking about your triple bottom line as part of your Gaddie Pitch and pitch deck?
- What reporting will you produce to communicate your progress?
- What steps have you taken to minimise your carbon impact and achieve net zero emissions?
- What actions will you take to on these points?

"Every financial decision
should be driven by
what you value."

David Bach

I hope after ongoing iteration and refinement, this chapter has helped you build a clear picture of your financial position.

Exploring social enterprise ideas means taking risks and a lot of those risks have financial implications. We need to manage the risk and cap the potential downside. Safe to fail experiments. This means knowing our numbers.

How we design our business models and solutions today shape organisational culture and the momentum we'll build. While trying to make the numbers work, we never want to lose sight of our purpose, theory of change, and triple bottom line.

Our values need to be codified in everything we do from the beginning – not deferred to some distant more convenient time. Deliver great outcomes for people and our plant – while being financially successful.

Chapter 13

Legals

Diverge

Converge

Are we solving the
right problem?

Diverge

Converge

Solution
Is it the right solution?

A quick disclaimer. I'm not a lawyer, and I'm not giving you legal advice. What I can do though is help you think through the questions and possible implications of certain legal decisions.

The law differs by country, and sometimes regions within countries, so I recommend you talk to a lawyer who understands your type of organisation – and ideally shares your values. It's worth asking your local network for recommendations, and checking the B Corp directory.

The way I recommend approaching the legal and paperwork side of things is to use the process to make things explicit and get to shared expectations – before things go wrong. What another person thinks is fair might be very different to what you think. The purpose of these conversations and agreements is to reduce the risk of disputes derailing your organisation and harming relationships.

There's a good chance that you've already made some key legal decisions. Two that happen very early are the legal structure for your organisation, and following directly from that, who the accountable person or people will be. These decisions often happen by default, based on the path of least resistance and what you're already familiar with. The relative benefits and trade-offs of the different options aren't given much thought.

Some of these decisions are effectively one-way doors – they can't be changed quickly or cheaply, so if you haven't made or executed some of them yet, I recommend pausing briefly to make sure you know what you're getting yourself into.

If you've already got a legal structure for your organisation, I still recommend working through this to make sure you have clarity on what that means for your options and constraints.

Your Organisation's Legal Structure

One of the first decisions is often if you should register your organisation as a standard for-profit company, a not-for-profit (NFP), or in some jurisdictions there are specific legal structures for social enterprise. This decision has major implications for your options on ownership models, the types of funding you can access, reporting requirements, and much more – in some contexts, this includes the perception of what your organisation is focused on.

To avoid overstepping any lines that may be perceived as legal advice – or stating my opinion and experience, which may only be relevant to certain jurisdictions and points in time – here are a set of questions for you to investigate. Getting answers that apply to your jurisdiction and context will help you make an informed decision – or, if that decision has already been made, make sure you have clarity on your options and obligations.

You should be able to get most of this information from some desk research. Just make sure the information source is reliable and applies directly to your context.

For the legal structure options you're evaluating:

- Who is the accountable person or people? Is there a minimum or a maximum number of people required? What are the governance requirements?

- What are the obligations and liabilities of the accountable person or people? Are there specific roles or board officers required?

- Can you ensure pursuing your organisation's purpose is explicit and protected?

- What are the tax, administrative, and reporting requirements and benefits? Are there certain thresholds where these requirements change?

- What does it cost to set up the legal structure? What are the ongoing costs?

- What types of funding does it allow you to access? What types of funding does it mean you won't have access to? Include all types of funding in your thinking: grants, donations, loans, capital for equity, work (sweat) for equity

- How do you manage risk exposure and liability? What insurances are required, and what do they cost? Are there thresholds where these requirements change?

- What jurisdiction does it allow you to operate in? Are there jurisdictions it prevents you from operating in?

- What ownership models are permitted (if any)? Can you be staff or community owned?

- Is there any financial reward for the startup risk you take and the money you invest?

- Are there restrictions on the salary you can pay yourself or other team members? Is it legal to use unpaid volunteers?

- Is it possible to change your legal structure in the future? If yes, what is involved, and how much would it cost? Would it have tax implications?

- Can and should you operate a multiple-entity or hybrid legal structure? Can you merge or spin-off an entity in the future?

Bonus question for established organisations: what are the benefits, risks, and constraints between running your social enterprise offering/brand as part of the existing legal entity vs spinning it off as its own legal entity?

Mission Lock

Mission lock is a term that means that the mission of your organisation is protected and not easily changed. In our context, we're specifically talking about your social and/or environmental purpose.

The mechanics to achieve this will vary depending on the legal structure you choose, and some might automatically provide this. The thing in common for the different legal structures is that your purpose needs to be clearly articulated in your organisation's governing documents.

There may be some other clauses to include – and this is where reliable legal advice for your context is really important.

Your Team Legals

Your team legals cover a broad range of things. This includes what's expected of each team member, what they can expect from the organisation – and to some degree what team members can expect of each other.

These are legal decisions that often happen by default without much thought given to the relative benefits and trade-offs of the different options. From my experience, a lot of this happens organically, and everyone is caught up in the excitement of the possible. The set of legal decisions you can make for the team is also heavily dependent on the legal structure of the organisation.

The approach I recommend here is to use this to first personally reflect on what you are hoping for, are able to invest, and need from the organisation. This is a good time to refer to the work you did on your team, strengths and assets, and personal sustainability in Chapter 1... and also your purpose, vision, and theory of change in Chapter 4.

If you have a founding team or are part of an existing organisation, discussing these expectations early and openly to understand everyone's perspective is really important. Noam Wasserman from the Harvard Business School studied 10,000 founders, and his research showed that 65% of startups fail because of co-founder conflict.

Some of these points might be confronting to think about and hard to talk about, but the objective of this conversation is to get things in the open, so you can address them before things go wrong. You might not agree on some of these points, but it's better to find that out early and reach an agreed position, rather than avoiding them. Hard conversations don't get easier when they're delayed.

Some key questions to discuss and scenarios to explore:

- What are the goals and expectations you have for the organisation?

- What are the goals you have for yourself?

- How are accountable people appointed? How do voting and control work? What are the thresholds for different types of decisions?

- How do you want to spend your time (specific work and activities)?

- How much time and money can you invest? How long can you invest time without being paid and still be personally sustainable?

- Longer-term, do you want this to be your paid job or a side project? What role do you want in the organisation?

- What is your risk exposure? What level of risk and liability is acceptable? What insurances do you need to protect yourselves?

- Who will pay for what expenses? Are expenses shared, or is one person providing the funds? Is this a loan to the organisation, a donation, or for a share of ownership?

- When there are sufficient funds, who gets paid first and why?

- What happens if someone wants to stop contributing to the organisation?

- What happens if someone can't continue to contribute because of sickness, disability, or death?

- Do you want external funding? Are there organisations or people you won't accept funding from? Do you have an agreed ethical/sustainability filter?

- Who has rights to the intellectual property (IP) that's created? What are those rights?

- Is it ok to launch or work on another startup organisation? Are there any conflicts of interest that need to be managed – now or in the future?

- How will disputes be resolved?

For organisations with an ownership model, you also need to agree:

- Who gets what percentage of ownership/shares and why? Is there a vesting cliff, and what is the vesting schedule?

- How do voting and control work? (Ownership and control are often conflated, but they are two distinct things.)

- What happens if someone wants to sell the organisation, raise capital for equity, or stop contributing to the organisation? Who makes these decisions? How will the company be valued? What happens to equity shares?

- Will you offer ownership/shares to employees and advisers in exchange for unpaid or partially paid work (sweat equity) or as part of employee remuneration and reward? (Also relevant for employee ownership models.)

- Will you offer ownership/shares to customers or a specific community? (Relevant for co-ops and community ownership models.)

This isn't an exhaustive set of questions, but should help draw out expectations on scenarios that commonly result in mismatched expectations and disputes. It's important to document each point as you reach an agreement. This documentation will make it a lot easier and cheaper to put together a document to make this a legal agreement. This may be a shareholder agreement, co-founder agreement, or employment contract – depending on your organisation and team structure.

An important note is many of these decisions can have both legal and tax implications. It's worth getting good advice specific to your situation, so you don't end up with any nasty surprises.

Sharing Ownership, Revenue & Profit

I know the idea of ownership is going to have very mixed perspectives. Thankfully, social enterprise exists independent of different philosophies on ownership. Again, the key thing is you have shared expectations and an agreement with your founding team and key stakeholders.

Ownership can take many shapes, including an individual, a group of shareholders, a collective, employees, a community, members, or a structure where there isn't any real ownership. Something to remember is ownership comes with legal obligations and liability. Some of these models have very well-established legal structures. Others are more emergent. The more emergent or complex the structure, the more you need legal advice.

There are a lot of terms and concepts that are important to understand when it comes to ownership shares – or equity. A couple I just mentioned are vesting cliffs and vesting schedules. I'm not going to go into detail here, but visit dynamic4.com/sptm for links to some good resources.

There are also ways to share revenue or profit without sharing ownership. This might be an appropriate model in certain contexts.

Slicing Pie

The Slicing Pie model is focused on creating a "perfectly fair equity split" in an early-stage, bootstrapped startup company. *Slicing Pie* is a great book by Mike Moyer. I recommend it. Mike teaches entrepreneurship at Northwestern University and the University of Chicago Booth School of Business. He also published *Will Work for Pie* in 2021.

I'm a big fan of the Slicing Pie model, and have been using it on early-stage social enterprise ideas since 2014. It's primarily focused on tracking equity shares, but I've found it works just as well for fairly and transparently tracking revenue and profit share agreements too.

Certifications, Licenses, Permits & Insurances

To be able to legally operate in certain industries and locations, you may be required to have a specific certification, license, or permit. Some of these might require you to have a specific qualification too. It's critical to know what these requirements are and if they apply to your idea. In some cases, these requirements can be prohibitively expensive and/or take a long time. You really need to know this early to include it in your planning and financial model. Sometimes it might even mean refining your idea, so that they aren't required.

Insurances are another thing to check. These can be required by a government or even a customer as part of the contract. Common insurances include protection against these types of risks:

- You or your product accidentally causes someone's injury, death, or property damage

- Someone claims you provided inadequate advice or services that caused them to lose money

- One of your employees is injured at work

- Legal action is taken against the accountable person or people for their management of the organisation

- Your business property or assets are lost or damaged by something like theft, fire, flood, or accident

These are the sort of things that a lot of people don't realise or include in their planning – and can result in some very nasty surprises if you don't research them early.

There are some other certifications specific to purpose-driven organisations. Having these certifications isn't required to legally operate, but does help you establish credibility – and some customers will preference suppliers with these certifications in their supply chain.

Social Enterprise Certification

Currently, there isn't an international social enterprise certification – but some countries have an organisation which does. In Australia, we have Social Traders (socialtraders.com.au).

There are also social enterprise peak bodies and communities. Generally, these organisations don't provide certification, but being a member can give a level of credibility. In Australia, state and territory bodies represent local social enterprises. We also have the Alliance of Social Enterprise Networks Australia (ASENA) to bring together national-level collaboration.

I have the privilege of being a founding board member and the treasurer of the Social Enterprise Council of NSW & ACT (SECNA) in Australia. We're focused on helping raise awareness of social enterprise, building a connected ecosystem, and advocating to governments. I recommend connecting with your local social enterprise community.

B Corporations

B Corps are a global movement that use the power of business to create a positive impact. In 2021, there are more than 4,000 B Corps in 153 industries and 77 countries. The B Corp website defines them as "businesses that meet the highest standards of verified social and environmental performance, public transparency, and legal accountability to balance profit and purpose. B Corps are accelerating a global culture shift to redefine success in business and build a more inclusive and sustainable economy".

I'm proud that my company Dynamic4 has been a certified B Corp since early 2016, and I love being part of the B Corp community.

Fairtrade

Fairtrade is a global movement that's been around since 1997. The Fairtrade website outlines their purpose as making trade fair "through better prices, decent working conditions and a fairer deal for farmers and workers in developing countries". There are over 1.8 million farmers and workers involved in Fairtrade, and the Fairtrade mark appears on more than 30,000 products.

Employees

Employment agreements are pretty standard, so I won't go into detail here. It's common for most of the terms and minimum pay ranges to be determined by the employment law of your country.

It can seem like unnecessary paperwork to have an employment agreement when you're a small organisation, but the same principle of shared expectations applies. It's also just basic governance – and there's a good chance it's actually a legal requirement.

Volunteers

There are legal and ethical considerations when it comes to hiring unpaid volunteers. It's important to know what the law is in your situation. Even if it's legal, I think it's worth thinking about what's really fair too. I encourage you to think about it as a value exchange. The value volunteers provide to an organisation is usually pretty clear. What value do you as an organisation provide to the volunteer?

Some questions to think through:

- Do the organisation and the volunteer have shared expectations?

- Does the volunteer know they're an unpaid volunteer donating their time and skills and not expecting payment or a financial return in the future?

- What is the agreed amount of time they're donating? What is the work they've agreed to do?

- What is the risk to the organisation of having unpaid volunteers?

- What insurances are required or recommended to cover volunteers?

It's good practice to have a volunteer agreement in place. If you have insurance cover for volunteers, they will likely require this documentation and a register of volunteers.

Advisers

Advisers often fall into a grey area. Some are happy to volunteer some of their time (up to a point), others might expect to be paid, and some might want a share of ownership.

The theme of this chapter applies here too… don't make assumptions. Have the conversation to make sure you have shared expectations – and document it.

Partnerships & Collaborations

Partnerships and collaborations are really common in the social enterprise ecosystem. There's often more desire to collaborate than there are meaningful opportunities to do so, but it's exciting when the opportunity happens. In all the excitement, it's common to just get into working on something together without making sure there's agreement on how the collaboration will actually work.

Some of the questions to think through and discuss are very similar to the ones you have with your founding team:

- Are there organisations or people you won't collaborate with? Do you have an agreed values and ethical/sustainability standards filter?

- What is each organisation's share of the revenue or profit/surplus?

- Who will pay for what expenses? Are expenses shared (equally or on a different basis), or is one organisation providing the funds?

- What are the agreed expenses? Fully loaded team costs, direct/cost of sale only?

- Who is taking the most risk (financial, reputational, operational)? It's very unlikely to be equal. Is there any financial reward for taking the risk?

- How will the accounting be tracked and transparent?

- What happens if there's a loss/deficit – not a profit/surplus?

- What happens if one of the partners wants to stop contributing to the collaboration?

- What happens if one of the partners can't continue to contribute because of sickness, disability, or death?

- What happens if one of the partners fails to deliver or meet their agreed obligations?

- If one of the partners stops contributing or fails to deliver, can it go ahead with the remaining partner? Does the partner who stopped still have rights to a share of revenue or profit/surplus? Is there a penalty?

- Who has rights to the IP that's created? Is ownership shared by both organisations? Can the IP be used independently, or can it only be used by both together?

This isn't an exhaustive set of questions, but should help draw out expectations on scenarios that commonly result in mismatched expectations and disputes. It's important to document each point as you reach an agreement. This documentation will make it a lot easier and cheaper to put together the document to make it a legal agreement – which might be a partnership agreement or collaboration agreement.

This chapter probably sounds like a lot of paperwork and maybe quite bureaucratic. It doesn't have to be. The most important things are the thinking and conversations. When you have that agreed, the paperwork is normally very easy. If you find yourself pulling out a contract and referring to clauses, things have probably already gone wrong, and it's usually an expensive nightmare to enforce. In most cases, you hope to never look at those contracts again, and they've served their purpose of achieving shared expectations.

The scenarios we've covered come up more often than you might think – and the conversations get a lot harder as soon as money is involved. Do the thinking and have the conversations now, before you face the issue.

During Part 3: Solution & Business Model, you've explored possible solutions and business models with your prototypes and experiments. This has included working out the right pricing, and what it means for your financials and legals. This approach has been helping you learn and refine your ideas rapidly – and find your early customers – before you build.

I hope you've been able to iterate to find a business model and solution that aligns with your purpose and theory of change – while creating real value that people want, is financially sustainable, and that you can make happen. A solution that solves a problem that really matters.

In Part 4: Sustain Momentum, we'll do some deeper reflection on the journey so far, and help you find your sustainable pace – so you can keep moving forward with confidence.

Sustain Momentum

Part 4

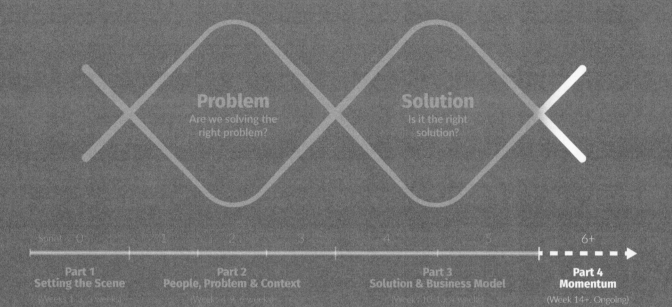

Weeks 14+. Sprint 6+

This is the ongoing part of making your social enterprise idea real. You'll design, build, and launch aspects of your idea during the Solution & Business Model phase, but you'll need to continue refining your idea as you continue to respond to what you're learning.

We focus on sustaining momentum and getting support.

Part 4 Chapters

16. Share Your Story

17. Get Support

Part 4: Sustain Momentum

The focus here is to continue the sustainable rhythm and momentum you've been building to move forward with confidence past the 90 days of the standard program. You'll continue designing, building, and launching refinements to your solution based on insights from real use.

The Big Questions

The big questions we focus on in Part 4 are, how do I/we:

- Communicate our purpose, theory of change, and the social/environmental value we'll create?

- Identify our customers, understand what they really care about, and know if they'll buy and use our solution?

- Design, build, and launch our solution as an end-to-end experience, and test what our customers will pay for it?

- Build our team to make it happen?

- Plan our approach to get into a good rhythm to build momentum and get traction?

- Share our story to attract the support we need?

- Stay healthy and positive on this journey without getting overwhelmed and burnt out?

From this point, you'll continue through cycles of doing more research to understand the People, Problem & Context – and experimenting with refinements to your Solution & Business Model. This is the continual nature of taking a human-centred approach to design, build, and launch your social enterprise idea – to solve problems that matter.

Chapter 14

Bring It All Together

Well done! You've reached the end of the 90-day program, and you're now into the ongoing part of making your social enterprise idea real.

I'm sure the past 90 days have been full of twists and turns. Moments of absolute joy and excitement… but also some challenging times, where what you were learning was very confronting. You might even have thought about giving up – but decided to persevere.

I hope you've been looking after your personal sustainability.

In the next chapter, we'll pause and reflect on what's happened over the past 90 days – what you've learnt, how you're feeling about things, and most importantly, how you'll build your sustainable pace.

Before we do that, I'll briefly cover a couple of topics that are beyond the scope of this book, but are part of bringing together all of the pieces you've been working on.

Brand Design

Brand design is one of those things that, in practice, comes up a lot earlier than it ideally would. In reality, the moment you come up with a name for the organisation and write it down, you've already started creating some key aspects of your brand. How people feel when interacting with you is also part of your brand experience.

It's outside the scope of this book to cover brand design in any real detail, but I'll briefly talk about some basics. The good news is that you've already done a lot of the foundational work needed to design a meaningful brand.

What is brand? A brand is a lot more than a logo. Even a logo is only one part of your visual identity. A brand is the collection of elements that come together to make an impression on people – how you and your organisation are perceived. Brand recognition involves some facts, a lot of emotion, and usually some misconceptions too.

To follow on from the circles of influence we covered in Chapter 4, we "design for" great experiences, but we can't actually make someone else have the experience we want or design someone else's behaviour. We can choose to positively influence others though.

As I mentioned, by taking a human-centred approach to designing, building, and launching your social enterprise idea, you've already done the thinking and testing for a lot of the questions I'm about to ask. Here's the brand design framework I've created over many years of designing brands.

Who is the Brand?

Brands effectively have personalities. What do you want your brand's personality to be?

- Who is the brand for? Who should the brand appeal to?

- What does the brand stand for? What is its purpose, and what are its values?

- What does the brand want to be known for? What's its reputation? (This tends to work well as contrasting adjectives like "positive, not pessimistic")

- What other brands need to be considered in the architecture? What are the roles, entities, and brands that need to be considered – and what is the relationship?

How Does the Brand Feel?

People have an emotional response when interacting with brands. How would you like your brand to feel for people?

- What mood should the brand create?

- What relationship should the brand set up with the people interacting with it?

- How should the brand sound? (Tone of voice)

In an ideal world, you'd have clarity on the brand personality and how you want the brand to feel before you even choose a name. In my experience, that's rarely the case, and for one reason or another, you've already had to name the organisation – and sometimes even the solution.

You've possibly already registered the organisation name, bought a domain name, and you might've already designed a logo.

Understanding this reality, I recommend not holding on to the brand too tightly in the early stages, and actively testing how your ideal customers respond to it. In some cases, this might even mean changing the name.

How Does the Brand Look?

Brands usually have a visual identity. This tends to be what most people think of when talking about branding. It becomes a lot easier to make decisions about the visual brand when you've worked through the other aspects of the brand design, so please resist the temptation to skip those steps and jump straight into designing a logo.

- How will you write and stylise your organisation name? Logo has a specific technical meaning, but in general use, it includes wordmarks, graphic marks or symbols, and use of colour

- What colour palette helps create the right perception of the brand?

- What typography will you use in communications?

- What type and style of imagery fit the brand personality?

The Sponge is a B Corp based in Australia, and an organisation I love collaborating with. Their purpose is to "help all brands be good for the world". Luke Faccini is the founder and CEO, and the author of *Impact Brand Storytelling* which is worth checking out. Brand design and marketing are now very much about sharing meaningful stories with purpose and personality.

Visit dynamic4.com/sptm for an example of Dynamic4's brand design and links to other resources.

Marketing Plan

While we haven't focused on marketing in this book, you've taken a human-centred approach to understand who your ideal customers, early adopters, and segments are – and tested your value proposition and messaging with them. This is the foundation for effective marketing.

A lot of marketing is about sharing a clear and compelling story. You started crafting your story in Chapter 3, and you've iterated it as you progressed. We'll check in on that again briefly in Chapter 16.

I recommend *The 1-Page Marketing Plan* by Allan Dib as a great guide to help you create your marketing plan. The 1-Page Marketing Plan Canvas takes a lifecycle and journey approach, and is a simple tool that builds on what you've already done to reach and engage more of your ideal customers.

Visit dynamic4.com/sptm for the link.

> "Marketing is no longer about the stuff that you make, but about the stories you tell."
>
> **Seth Godin**

Chapter 15

Momentum

A core focus of this book is to help you get into a rhythm to build sustainable momentum.

I've used the word momentum dozens of times in this book. It's extremely valuable. It can be hard to build and easy to lose, but when you keep it going, everything flows with much less effort.

Let's talk briefly about some of the key elements that will help you maintain momentum as you move forward with confidence past the 90 days of the standard program.

Your Sustainable Pace

When people are in the early stages of exploring their social enterprise idea, there tends to be a lot of excitement. This often leads to people working at a pace that isn't sustainable over the long term.

This happens even more when people do incubator and accelerator programs. Unfortunately, it's common for them to reach the end of a program and fall over in a heap. Often, the intent is to take a week or two off to get their breath back and maybe catch up on all of the things they'd deferred. This turns into three weeks or more, and some never really manage to get back into it.

That's not the outcome we want here.

It's really important that you adjusted the standard 90-day plan to your own situation in Chapter 3 – in a way that maintains your personal sustainability. You might be reading this at the end of the 90 days or maybe even later. However long it's taken to get here, it's ok. It's probably taken longer than you hoped or planned. That's ok too.

It doesn't help you or anyone else to beat yourself up about delays or missed targets. What does help is our reflective practice and making improvements.

Your Quarterly Planning Cycle (Every 90 Days)

It's now time to reflect on what's been working for you. And what's not. Then the really important thing is to understand why. Reflect on the sprint rhythm we covered in the Agile Ways of Working section of Chapter 2, and the planning we did for it in Chapter 3: Make It Happen.

As you review the first 90-day cycle and plan the next 90-day cycle, what improvements will you make to your workflow? Are two-week sprints working for you, or should they be a bit longer? Or maybe shorter? How have your showcases, retros, and sprint planning sessions been going? Is the way you're documenting, prioritising, and tracking your sprint plan working? How are you going with your happiness habits?

I apply the same Sprint Review & Plan approach and format on a quarterly basis. Just as I use sprints as a two-week cycle of sustained focus, I use quarterly planning to focus on key themes aligned with my OKRs. At the end of each cycle, I pause, take a breath, reflect on how it went, and plan for the next cycle.

Grading your OKRs is also an important part of quarterly planning. Remember, we set OKRs that are ambitious and slightly out of reach. When we grade OKRs to see how we've progressed and performed, the sweet spot is getting to 60-70% achieved.

This is going to mean some things that were only partially achieved. As you set the OKRs for the next quarter, you need to decide if the things that weren't 100% met are high enough priority to roll over into the next 90 days, or have you actually achieved what really matters for the objective?

By the end of the quarterly planning session, everyone involved needs to be clear – and for it to be captured – on what you plan to do, by when, and how progress will be tracked and communicated – internally as a team and with other key stakeholders. Or even just for yourself.

To keep things simple and to build a natural rhythm, I treat this process basically the same as the two-week sprint planning process but for a longer time horizon.

What do your next 90 days look like?

Your Yearly Planning Cycle

I apply the same approach and format on an annual basis, but there's a big difference in planning the next two weeks or quarter and planning the next year or three years.

In my experience, the longer the time horizon and the more complexity and uncertainty I'm working in, the more the planning needs to focus on intent and direction – and less on detailed plans full of untested assumptions, tasks, and dates.

It can be easy to give up on planning when you feel uncertain, but I think it's a time when doing some planning focused on intent and direction is even more important. It can help give hope and a future to work toward. It's also important to not let the things we can't do stop us from doing what we can do.

There's a lot we don't know, but reflecting on our individual and organisational purpose, the direction we want to go, and how we want to spend our time – both now and in the coming years, is a helpful way to stay in a positive headspace.

It's funny how things start coming together as we get more clarity on our intent and direction. With a clear sense of direction, we can plan the shorter time horizons of sprints and quarters with more certainty – and that allows us to refine our plans as we

learn. As we do this, we need to keep a strong connection between longer-term planning focused on intent and direction with short-term planning.

We used OKRs for the one-year time horizon as well as 90 days. Generally, OKRs are used for 90-day periods with other frameworks for longer periods. To avoid that complexity, we used OKRs for both.

It's also the time to grade your OKRs for the year. When using OKRs on an annual basis, it's especially important to view them as a way to track how we've progressed and performed, and remember a great result is getting to 60-70% achieved. Over time you might want to experiment with other frameworks for longer-term planning.

It's now time to set your OKRs for the next year – which flow through to your quarterly OKRs. What are your objectives for the next 12 months? What key results will help you know how you've progressed? Be ambitious!

The critical thing from this planning is to find your sustainable pace... but keep moving and maintain your momentum. Even if that means moving a bit slower.

Repeatable Sales

The concept of repeatable sales flows directly on from the mantra to sell before you build and is another key part of Ash Maurya's *Customer Factory Manifesto*. Achieving repeatable sales is also key to building and sustaining momentum.

The idea is simple. The execution is much harder. One thing I do know is that when we solve problems that matter to the people experiencing them, and we have a business model and solution that achieves results for our ideal customers, it creates happy customers, and as Ash Maurya says, "happy customers get you paid".

Repeatable customer acquisition is generally the first constraint to solve to achieve repeatable sales. It's more important to focus on this than designing and building the first working version of your solution.

I recommend reading Ash Maurya's *Customer Factory Manifesto*, where he outlines his "systematic approach to building a repeatable and scalable business model". You can find it on his blog (blog.leanstack.com) or visit dynamic4.com/sptm for the link.

Build Your Team

Building and sustaining momentum is a team effort. Now is a good time to reflect on the Your Team action you did in Chapter 1. Still using the broad definition of "team" – including your personal support network – how is your team looking right now? How have you engaged them and kept them in the loop over the past 90 days?

As you move forward, you'll need to build your team. As you do this, remember to set things up with clear and shared expectations. Refer to the Team Legals section of Chapter 13 to help with these conversations.

Your team doesn't necessarily need to be the traditional model of people working for you. I prefer to think of it as people you work with. It's a collaboration to pursue a shared purpose and goals. With this mindset, your team doesn't even need everyone to be from the same organisation.

Think beyond traditional command and control organisational structures. I recommend exploring models like holacracy, collectives, collaborations, and strategic partnerships. How might you bring together a team where all team members have the freedom and flexibility to work in ways that suit their workstyle preferences and availability?

Design, Build & Launch Your Solution

You're probably not going to design, build, and launch a completely new working solution in four weeks (two sprints). You may have already had a solution in the market before starting this 90-day program – a lot of people I work with do.

As I mentioned in Chapter 10, there's often a rush to design and build the first working version of the solution – and there are usually very high expectations about how perfect and polished it will be too. I also wrote about what it means to launch your solution – it's an ongoing process rather than a single event.

This is an area where it can be easy to confuse activity with meaningful progress and momentum.

For the past 90 days, you've been designing, building, and launching your solution. That process has only just begun. Innovation never stops. How will you approach this moving forward? I hope you'll continue with the human-centred approach we've been following in this book… and just keep iterating through the cycles.

In most cases, the recommendation to sell before you build is the best approach. Keep testing your riskiest assumptions and doing safe to fail experiments. At this point in the journey, there's still the very real risk of overinvesting in a solution that no one wants, will use, or will pay for.

What am I saying? Don't rush into designing and building the working version of your new solution, and if you already have a solution in market, here's what I recommend. Take a breath.

Don't skip the step of selling before you build. This applies equally to solutions in new organisations, to solutions already in market that don't yet have repeatable sales, and if you're designing and building a new solution within an already successful organisation.

Have you found a way to achieve repeatable sales? This is the evidence you need to know that you're solving a problem that really matters to your ideal customers, that it's a priority for them, and that they're willing to pay to do something about it. Now.

Keep learning as quickly and cheaply as possible.

This is how you'll build and sustain momentum.

Chapter 16

Share Your Story

Share Your Story

339

Sustain Momentum

Sharing your story is an important part of the journey. A good story is authentic and believable. It will resonate with your audience, engage their curiosity, and generate conversation.

In the Share Your Story section of Chapter 3, we talked about how to craft your story in detail. I recommend reviewing that section and taking a moment to reflect on how your story has iterated and evolved over the past few months.

As you move forward, wherever possible prepare your story for a specific purpose and audience, to be shared at specific times, through specific channels, and be mindful of the feedback loop and how the conversation can continue.

These are the basic building blocks, and are relevant no matter what stage you're at or the mix of channels you're using. Experimentation and practice are the keys to getting better at sharing your story.

A clear and compelling story will help attract customers, team members, and supporters.

Gaddie Pitch

You crafted your first Gaddie Pitch in Chapter 3, and I hope you've tested and refined it as you've progressed over the past 90 days.

What have you found resonates? What makes people glaze over and lose interest, or feel confused? How has your call to action changed as you've progressed?

Now is a good time to iterate your Gaddie Pitch again, so you can concisely share your story and where you're currently at.

Pitch Deck

You drafted your pitch deck in Chapter 3, and I've recommended adding specific content as we've progressed.

Have you used it to share your story? What questions does it raise for people? What part of the pitch deck do they tend to zoom in on? How has it evolved as you've progressed?

Now is a good time to refine your pitch deck. Does it communicate a relevant and compelling story for your target audience?

Simple Profile

I have a simple profile document that provides a useful summary of the social enterprise idea and the current status. It's an overview of the key facts about the organisation, a bullet point summary of some of the content included in the pitch deck, and more detail about the vision and goals.

This profile helps a coach or adviser get a clear snapshot of where things are at and how they can help.

Visit dynamic4.com/sptm to download the simple profile template.

The Story Canvas

Digital Storytellers are a social enterprise and B Corp based in Sydney, and an organisation I love collaborating with. They craft impactful stories by creating "a more inclusive narrative by helping to tell stories that matter, and sharing their knowledge and resources to empower a wider community of storytellers".

They created the Story Canvas as a simple tool to develop and iterate your story ideas. I recommend downloading the canvas from digitalstorytellers.com.au/the-story-canvas or visit dynamic4.com/sptm for a link.

Websites & Digital Solutions

In most contexts, designing and building at least a simple website is needed relatively early in the journey. Digital might even play a key role in your solution – leveraging the power of tech to deliver and scale your impact.

I've been designing and building websites, online shops and marketplaces, and other digital solutions since the 1990s – with a strong focus on mobile. Things have changed a lot since the early days, and it's now relatively easy to create great solutions with technology that has been simplified a lot – you can even build sophisticated solutions without code. But it can still seem a complex process and a bit daunting.

As I mentioned in the intro, it's beyond the scope of this book to focus on tech/digital products or do a UX/UI deep dive. I spend a lot of time working with clients as a tech adviser and also as their virtual chief technology officer (CTO) and chief product officer (CPO), so I'll briefly share some key points.

The most important thing with websites and digital solutions is to view the tech as an enabler. It has a lot of power, but there's no such thing as a digital-only experience.

Firstly, there are people involved. This includes how they think, feel, behave, what they expect, what motivates them, their ergonomics and how they interact with devices, and in what contexts. Designing for inclusion and accessibility is important, and results in better solutions for everyone – the power of universal design.

From your channels and touchpoints, I'm sure you've identified a range of other non-digital ways that your ideal customers find out about and interact with you. There's also a market full of existing alternatives and competitors.

I recommend starting simple and building from there. Don't try to do it all at once. This advice is just as relevant to getting started with a new website as when making updates and improvements to an existing site. It's very easy to overinvest. Getting your digital solution live is the start of your investment – not the end.

Designing and building a good website means focusing on how it will help you achieve your organisation's goals, and how it will deliver a great experience for your visitors and customers. You've already done this thinking as you've worked through this book

A key question to consider is: what role does your website play in the end-to-end journey? Mapping this out on your desired state Experience Blueprint will give you clarity on your requirements without getting lost in features.

Here are four simple points to help get you started.

People

- Who's it for? Who's your target audience?
- Why would they visit your site?
- What do they want to achieve when they visit?

Purpose & Goals

- What do you want to achieve when people visit your site?
- What do you hope people will do on the site?
- What do you hope they'll do next?

Message & Content

- What do you want to communicate?
- What content (text, graphics, images, video) do you need to achieve this?
- What are your calls to action?

Journey & Features

- What would you like people to do when they visit your site?

- What experience do you want to design for?

- How does the website fit with the other channels and touchpoints on the customer journey?

- What are the core features needed?

When you have clarity on these points, you can focus on what's important and use digital as a powerful tool that enables your organisation to deliver on your purpose and theory of change.

There are plenty of great digital design tools and frameworks and a growing number of no/low code platforms. New and better options are coming out all the time, so anything I mention here will probably be out of date by the time you read this.

Visit dynamic4.com/sptm to download the Dynamic4 Website Brief template, and for links to great tools, frameworks, and platforms.

Your story will continue to evolve. You'll speak with a variety of audiences, have different messages to communicate, and use all sorts of channels.

As things get more sophisticated, my advice is to stay focused on the basics – and always start with who.

"The only way to make sense out of change is to plunge into it, move with it, and join the dance."

Alan Watts

Chapter 17

Get Support

Congratulations!

We've covered a lot of ground together. As you've worked through this book, I hope you've felt like I'm with you and working alongside you. Cheering you on, but also helping to challenge you, to test and refine your thinking, and iterate – so you can succeed sooner.

With this book, there are four goals I aimed to help you with:

- Take a human-centred design approach to innovation to really understand your customers, what's important to them, and help solve problems that matter

- Design a sustainable business model that has purpose and impact embedded in the way you do things while also being financially successful

- Look after your personal wellbeing while making a positive impact

- Have a practical guide and method to follow so you can build momentum and get the support you need

How have we done? Let's take a moment to reflect on the journey so far… and think about what comes next.

The Journey So Far

We started with a strong focus on mindset, personal sustainability, and happiness habits – to help you look after your personal wellbeing while making a positive impact.

This flowed into the core theory with the concepts, terms, and ways of thinking and working that we used in the book – to get into a rhythm to build sustainable momentum. You articulated your vision and the problem you're working on.

And that was just Part 1: Setting the Scene.

During Part 2: People, Problem & Context, you increased your understanding of the systems involved, and you spent time with the people you want to help – and who you hope will use and pay for your solution. This helped you build more empathy and gave you a clearer picture of how they experience the problem and the market.

You tested your riskiest assumptions, refined your thinking, and got sharp clarity on the problem that matters – based on evidence, insight, and meaningful empathy.

Building on that sharp clarity, you explored possible solutions and business models. You prototyped and tested them while experimenting with your pricing and financial model.

From this process in Part 3: Solution & Business Model, I hope you've made good progress toward finding a solution that people want, that's financially sustainable, and that you can make happen.

While this sounds like a sequential linear journey, you've hopefully found that it's circular and iterative. Even when you're primarily focused on your solution and business model, you never want to stop talking with your customers or refining your understanding of the system and how it works. The ways of thinking and working that you started putting into practice from Part 1 will continue to refine and mature.

Part 4: Sustain Momentum focused on bringing all of the pieces together and continuing the sustainable rhythm and momentum you've been building over the past 90 days. During this time, the goal has been to improve focus, get clarity, and develop meaningful relationships – so you can keep moving forward with confidence.

This is the beginning, not the end of the journey. The journey is long, and it's important to keep getting support.

Coaching & Advice

As you know, designing, building, and launching your social enterprise idea can be a very rewarding experience… but there are also plenty of challenges. You don't need to do it alone. Getting coaching and advice from experienced people who've been on the journey – and ideally still are – will help you ask good questions and keep perspective.

A good coach is a valuable trusted partner, guide, and sounding board who'll make things feel easier – but also challenge you. They help you think things through by asking insightful questions and by freely sharing their experience. They approach the conversation with humility and empathy – knowing no two situations or relationships are the same – and that you need to make your own decisions.

It's also important to find the right coach for you. There generally needs to be a certain chemistry and mutual respect for the coaching relationship to work well. Shared expectations are key. Every coach will approach things a bit differently and have their own style based on who they are, their experience, and training. What works for you?

Don't forget your virtual mentors too. There are plenty of great books, blogs, video content, and more that provide valuable lessons. I've referenced many in this book.

To balance this recommendation out, be mindful of the risk of spending too much time looking to others for what they think you should do. And remember, there will always be conflicting advice. Testing your thinking with your ideal customers is the most reliable way of learning. Einstein had some thoughts on this... (I made a minor update to remove the gendered language).

"Reading, after a certain age, diverts the mind too much from its creative pursuits. Anyone who reads too much and uses their own brain too little falls into lazy habits of thinking."

Albert Einstein

Find Your Community

We don't need heropreneurs. We need connected and collaborative ecosystems. Daniela Papi-Thornton talked about this in her *Tackling Heropreneurship* article in the *Stanford Social Innovation Review* – and makes many good points.

This can be a long and lonely journey, so it's really important to find a community of people who are values aligned and on a similar path to share stories and collaborate with. It's great to have a local community, but there are plenty of global communities to be a part of too.

In my acknowledgements, I mentioned a few communities that I really value being a part of. Come and join us! If the community you're looking for doesn't already exist, why not spend some time bringing people together.

What Next?

From here, you'll continue designing, building, and launching refinements to your solution and business model based on insights from real use.

The purpose of this book is to help more people globally take a human-centred design approach to solving problems that matter. Success will only be realised by working together – and we've got a lot of work to do.

I hope this book has played a helpful role in your social enterprise journey. We're not done though. We can continue working together.

My vision is a world where organisations and leaders solve problems that matter in more empathic and innovative ways – and measure success in outcomes for people, our planet, and prosperity... so people and communities have increasing quality of life, are happier, and live on a planet that is cleaner and healthier.

All the work I do is aligned with my purpose and theory of change – focused on helping create the conditions for people and communities to be more empowered and inclusive, and live in more sustainable ways.

What's next for this book? As I mentioned, continual iteration is how I work and experience the world... this means I'm always learning, and my thinking evolves. Very few things are static. Contexts change, trends and patterns emerge, new technologies come to market.

A book is a snapshot at a point in time, but I think of this one as a product rather than a traditional book. Here are a couple of ways I've created space so Solve Problems That Matter can keep evolving and not be completely trapped in time:

- Visit dynamic4.com/sptm for free downloadable worksheets – as well as links to websites, articles, books, and events. There's also a consolidated list of the resources I've mentioned in this book

- I intend to refine the digital versions of the book (PDF and ebook) based on feedback and as I learn new things. When you buy the book in these digital formats, you'll get the refined editions for free

Please join the Dynamic4 and Solve Problems That Matter community to get these resources – and stay in touch.

Have fun!

The social enterprise journey is a rollercoaster. Even though we're often working on very serious things, it doesn't mean we need to be very serious. At least not always. It's important to create and keep space for fun and things that bring us joy. We need unstructured time for play and to experiment. We need to live our lives in sustainable ways.

Keep practicing your happiness habits. They feel good – and remember, we're 30% more effective and productive when we're positive. It's important to me that you enjoy this journey and stay healthy and well... ideally feeling even happier as you do work that gives you meaning and fulfilment.

I hope Solve Problems That Matter is helping you take a human-centred approach to design, build, and launch your social enterprise idea – and build momentum. I'd love to hear about your experiences.

Good luck on your social enterprise journey... and **have fun while you solve problems that matter!**

Want some extra support on your social enterprise journey?

Some ways Ben Pecotich and Dynamic4 can help:

- Coaching and advice for individuals and teams
- Dynamic4 Jetpack incubator and coaching program for early-stage social enterprise ideas
- Workshops, masterclasses, and speaking
- Project-based experiential learning programs
- Discount pricing available on 10+ copies

To find out more or for media enquiries, please email hello@dynamic4.com or visit dynamic4.com.

Lightning Source UK Ltd.
Milton Keynes UK
UKHW050334310123
416191UK00010B/207